# THE BOOK OF PROFESSIONAL STANDARDS FOR HIGHER EDUCATION 1997

**Theodore K. Miller**

The University of Georgia

Editor

**Council For The Advancement Of Standards In Higher Education**

**Washington, DC**

# *The CAS Book of Professional Standards for Higher Education*

**Library of Congress Cataloging-in-Publication Data**

Miller, Theodore K., 1932–
    The CAS Book of Professional Standards in Higher Education
    Includes bibliographic references.

    ISBN 0-9659337-0-9
    1. Student Affairs. 2. Student Services. 3. Professional Standards
    4. Advising, 5. Counseling, 6. Student Personnel

Copy Editor:  Pat Farrant, ACT, Iowa City, IA
Interior Design: Ann McCollum, HBP, Hagerstown, MD
Cover Design: Vickie Humphries, HBP, Hagerstown, MD
Printing and Binding: HBP, Printing, Graphics & Information Services, Hagerstown, MD

This book represents a major revision of *CAS Standards and Guidelines for Student Services/Student Development Programs* published by the American College Testing Program in 1986.

# Council for the Advancement of Standards in Higher Education

## *The Book Of Professional Standards For Higher Education 1997*

## Contents

## Appendices

# COUNCIL for the ADVANCEMENT
# of STANDARDS in HIGHER EDUCATION
## CAS President's Letter to the Profession

It has been my professional opportunity to have been involved with the Council for the Advancement of Standards in Higher Education from the beginning. It has been my professional honor to serve as the CAS President since 1989. The head and heart of CAS grow each year as the representatives of its member associations realize the necessity of promoting educationally purposeful, high-quality programs and services for students.

The CAS member associations and their representatives have worked toward the common good by providing vision, direction, and strategies for professional practice in higher education programs and services. This has happened as the associations and CAS directors have shared responsibility, authority, and accountability for achieving results, especially the CAS Standards and Guidelines. Now the CAS community must set priorities for future action.

The education and development of each and every college student matter and make a difference as we seek to facilitate a meaningful balance between each student's personal development and academic achievement. The CAS Standards promote connections between the life of the mind and the life of the student, especially as the content and format of these standards support the responsibility leaders in higher education have as advocates for educating the whole student.

As we review the history and heritage of the student affairs profession, it is important to realize and recognize the value the CAS Standards have for practitioners and their institutions. Today, higher education claims to provide meaningful learning environments that challenge students and support them in intellectual, personal, and social development. The CAS Standards form the base for rigorous planning and creative action. The Standards are solid and clear; they provide:

- Measures of program and service effectiveness
- Designs for program and service development and assessment
- Criteria for institutional self-studies and preparation for accreditation
- Opportunities for staff development
- Directions for student learning and development
- Frameworks for accountability

The CAS Standards clearly challenge practitioners and provide support for their efforts both to enhance institutional missions and to serve students by providing systematic opportunities for growth that require creative and critical thinking, along with smart working, and yield slow, steady, and stable progress.

The CAS Standards and Guidelines have served us well and will continue to be a significant resource for quality assurance designed and managed to emphasize top-quality programs and services for students.

Phyllis Mable
Vice President for Student Affairs
Longwood College
Farmville, Virginia
May 1997

# Prologue

The Council for the Advancement of Standards in Higher Education (CAS) was established nearly two decades ago to develop and promulgate standards of professional practice to guide practitioners and their institutions, especially in their work with college students. Currently, the Council's Board of Directors is composed of representatives from 29 professional associations [see Appendix A]. These international, national, and regional entities reflect the length and breadth of the field of student affairs and related programs and services for student development and educational support common to most institutions of higher learning today. To date, CAS has developed and adopted 23 sets of functional area standards and guidelines and one set of master's-level standards for academic preparation programs. This publication presents these 24 CAS professional standards and guidelines and describes the contexts in which they are intended to be used.

The CAS Standards and Guidelines are viewed as living documents that are constantly evolving and developing. Over time, institutions of higher education and individual practitioners face new challenges that require new responses, often leading to institutional change. When this occurs, the institution demands concurrent change in the ways faculty and staff members implement their educational responsibilities, including the structures used to design and manage the processes involved. What worked well yesterday may need to be amended if it is to be effective tomorrow. The developmental needs that students bring to campus may become manifest in different ways as time passes, requiring new and different strategies to provide the support services necessary to meet them effectively. Consequently, as institutions and their clienteles change over time, so must the vehicles that exist to guide practice within the ever-changing context of higher education. As new developments produce previously unrecognized or newly identified student needs, institutions and their student support programs and services must change accordingly. In light of these facts, users of the CAS Standards and Guidelines must anticipate that they, too, will evolve as change occurs and demands shift over time.

The Council for the Advancement of Standards in Higher Education (CAS), a name adopted in 1992 to reflect the council's expanded context, was established in 1979 as a not-for-profit corporation called the Council for the Advancement of Standards for Student Services/Development Programs. The impetus for CAS's existence came about because of a movement among certain counseling associations to develop professional standards to guide and accredit *academic programs* that prepare counselors and counselor educators. This movement, which culminated with the establishment of the Council for the Accreditation of Counseling and Related Educational Programs (CACREP) in 1980, provided the American College Personnel Association (ACPA) with the impetus to create a set of standards for master's-level preparation programs. Rather than promulgating these standards as its own, ACPA sought to identify other interested professional associations. The National Association of Student Personnel Administrators (NASPA) indicated an interest in the project and the two associations jointly called a meeting of interested professional associations in June 1979. Seven professional student affairs associations sent representatives to the exploratory meeting; it was decided that an interassociation consortium should be established to develop and promulgate professional *standards of practice* as well as standards for preparation programs. All professional associations who might be interested in the interassociation consortium project were then invited to send representatives to an organizational meeting. CAS was officially incorporated in September 1979, with 11 member associations [see Appendix A].

After 18 years of continuous work and a name change reflecting its expanded interests, the Council currently is composed of 29 member associations [see Appendix A], and has generated 23 sets of functional area standards and guidelines and one set of standards for master's-level preparation for student affairs administration.

## CAS Mission

The Council for the Advancement of Standards in Higher Education was established with the intent of accomplishing several purposes from a profession-wide perspective. The following six statements reflect the mission that has guided CAS initiatives from the beginning.

1. To establish, adopt, and disseminate unified and timely professional standards for student services, student development programs, academic support

services, and related higher education programs and services.

2. To promote the assessment and improvement of higher education services and programs through self-study, evaluation, and the use of CAS standards.

3. To establish, adopt, and disseminate unified and timely professional preparation standards for the education of student affairs practitioners.

4. To promote the assessment and improvement of professional preparation programs for student affairs practitioners through self-study, evaluation, and the use of CAS standards.

5. To advance the use and importance of standards among professional practitioners and educators in higher education.

6. To promote inter-association efforts to address the issues of quality assurance, student learning, and professional integrity in higher education.

As the mission statements indicate, CAS was established to accomplish several complementary tasks. Its first important task was to establish a broadly representative profession-wide entity that would embrace the full range of student affairs, student development, and student support services and programs in higher education today. This entity, CAS, aimed to provide to organizations concerned with the development and promulgation of professional standards in higher education a single voice that would speak for the profession as a whole. To bridge divisions caused by the numerous specialty areas now so prevalent in higher education, a consortial approach was used. Viable linkages were built between and among the many professional associations, most of which spoke individually for the interests of highly specialized programs and services. Through this collaboration, professional standards of practice and preparation that represent a profession-wide perspective could be developed and promulgated collectively rather than individually. It was believed that a single voice would have greater impact on the evaluation and improvement of student support services and programs than would many voices speaking for special interests. Likewise, the collective voice would influence and enhance the use of professional standards and guidelines by individual student support service practitioners.

## *CAS Rationale*

CAS was clearly an outgrowth of the need for the profession to establish standards for both its practice

and the preparation of those who seek to enter the profession. Though not a new idea, the desire to establish a profession-wide entity that could speak as one voice was an aspiration of many experienced practitioners that had not previously been fully accomplished. Before CAS, the most comparable consortial group of student affairs associations was the Council of Student Personnel Associations in Higher Education (COSPA). This relatively short-lived council, which functioned as a consortium of some 10 professional associations during the late 1960s and early 1970s is best known for the *COSPA Statement* (1983), "Student Development Services in Post-Secondary Education."

CAS was established on a consortial basis comparable to that of COSPA, for an equally important although less ambitious purpose. Whereas COSPA was intended to represent a group of professional associations and to deal with a full range of professional issues and concerns, CAS was established to focus on the development and promulgation of professional standards and on informing practitioners about the role and function of such standards in higher education. The Council prides itself on its lack of politicization and on being driven by values rather than special interests. Without a CAS-like group, the creation and dissemination of standards of good practice for the profession as a whole would not have been accomplished.

Some may ask, "Does CAS truly need to exist?" The answer is a resounding "yes." Without CAS, which involves and speaks collectively for all concerned practitioners and their functional specialties, it is unlikely that a profession-wide threshold of good practice could be crossed. Others may ask, "Who should be represented by CAS?" The answer is, "Every general educator and functional area specialist who deems the education and personal development of college and university students of all ages and heritages to be important."

Although individual professional associations, and in some instances, small interassociational task forces, may seek to establish standards of good practice, they are unlikely to succeed and become part of the culture of higher education unless or until they are viewed by a majority of practitioners as representing both the interests of the students with whom they work and their own personal and professional interests. Further, it is easier to establish credibility in the whole of higher education through collective action than through the narrowly defined interests of separate professional associations. To be viable and effective, professional standards for student affairs, student development, and student support services and programs must reflect the interests and values of each participating professional organization and its functional areas of responsibility. This does not mean that CAS is a panacea for the profession in the area of standards and guidelines. The simple fact is that at this point in the evolution of student support services, there is no other single body that speaks effectively for this group of higher education student support functions and their advocates.

## Foundations For Standards and Guidelines

The *CAS Standards and Guidelines* (CAS, 1986) were written on the premise that practitioners concerned with high quality professional practice need access to a comprehensive set of criteria upon which they can rely as they judge how well they are fulfilling their responsibilities. Further, these standards should represent best practices that are reasonably achievable by *any and all programs* of quality within all institutions of higher learning.

Most functional specialty areas have some characteristics in common with other administrative or program counterparts. For example, although considerably different in purpose, an admission program, a campus activities program, and a career planning and placement program will each benefit from establishing a mission statement that is compatible with the mission of their institution. Although the mission and purpose of each functional area program will vary from both comparable and dissimilar programs within and among institutions, a clearly defined mission that articulates the program's primary and secondary purposes and objectives is essential for program effectiveness. This is also true for such areas as human, fiscal, and physical resources; legal responsibilities; campus and community relations; professional ethics; and evaluation efforts. Consequently, the CAS Standards and Guidelines incorporate a number of *general standards* that are relevant and essential for all functional areas, no matter what their focus and reason for being. These standards statements use the auxiliary verbs "**must**" and "**shall**" and appear in **bold** print throughout the text so that users can quickly identify *standards* and distinguish them from *guidelines*. In addition to the general standards, all functional areas have *specialty standards* that are both essential to accomplishing the program's purpose, and unique to a particular specialty. These specialty standards, which also appear in **bold** print, are not usually found in other functional area standards.

The CAS Standards were constructed to represent the minimum criteria that every institution and its programs should, with the application of adequate effort, be expected to meet over time. To clarify these standard statements, to assure they are being properly interpreted, and to enhance or strengthen programs, and because effective practice occurs and can be viewed as a continuum, there is need to provide users with additional criteria that *may* be used as circumstances warrant. Consequently, in addition to the standards, CAS has established guideline statements designed to clarify and amplify the standards and to guide enhanced practice beyond the essential levels of the various standards. That is, when a program has achieved effectiveness, according to the standards, opportunity to achieve enhanced effectiveness has been built into the statements and is referred to as *guidelines*. Guidelines use the auxiliary verbs "*should*" and "*may*" and are presented in small regular print to distinguish them from standards.

In summary, CAS functional area standards and guidelines are basic statements that should be achievable by any program in any institution when adequate and appropriate effort, energy, and resources are applied. Further, *standards* reflect a level of good program practice generally agreed upon by the profession at large. In addition to the standards, *guidelines* have been included for each functional area to amplify and explain the standards and to guide enhanced practice. This two-tiered presentation is most helpful because functional area programs in both early and advanced stages of development can use CAS Standards and Guidelines to good purpose. Most important, however, these standards and guidelines have been conceived and developed via a profession-wide process that assures continuity and consistency of practice among programs throughout higher education.

## CAS Applications

The *CAS Standards and Guidelines* were established for institutions and their student support services programs to use for program development, program self-study, and staff development purposes. Although the standards and guidelines have utility for institutional and program accreditation purposes, CAS has not been inclined to establish an accreditation body for student affairs programs and services, but rather takes the position that *self-regulation* is the preferred route to enhanced program quality and effectiveness. Institutions and programs can use the CAS Standards and Guidelines for self-assessment, to promote program development and program effectiveness. Although CAS is not in the accreditation business and promulgates its professional standards for self-regulation, there is little doubt that CAS standards can be used to frame self-studies for regional or specialty accreditation. At this time, as a profession-wide entity, CAS considers its role to be developing and promulgating professional standards to guide practice, not to accredit, certify, or otherwise sanction professional student support service practices or programs.

## CAS Role in Professional Practice

The professional role of the Council for the Advancement of Standards in Higher Education has become increasingly important over the past two decades. The first order of business was to develop and promulgate professional standards of practice and preparation for student affairs, student development, and student support programs and services. Today, CAS is also considered by many in the profession to be an important resource for educational and professional development.

*Survey Results.* In a survey of users of CAS Standards and Guidelines, respondents identified how CAS had influenced their professional work. Following is a summary of responses with emphasis upon the professional value of CAS.

• One comment that reflects the value of the CAS effort for beginning professionals is most telling. "I can easily imagine that the standards would provide indispensable guidance for some of our younger or less-experienced colleagues in graduate education. It must be like having a consultant's report at your fingertips that attests, 'Do at least this much well, and you will find success in your program'." This comment suggests that the CAS Standards and Guidelines are very useful for providing a foundation of practice to which all college student service providers can aspire. It also suggests that academic preparation programs and staff development programs can be enhanced by incorporating the CAS Standards in their curricula.

• The CAS project has led to a number of offshoots; some professional groups have expanded on the Standards to meet sometimes highly specific professional needs. For example, in the area of learning assistance, as one respondent noted, "No sooner than the first Learning Assistance Program Standards were

published, we were already talking about how to build upon that work. Whereas the CAS Standards addressed broad basic elements that are essential to a comprehensive learning assistance program, practitioners in the field expressed interest in obtaining similar statements that addressed pedagogical components as well." Consequently, the National Association for Developmental Education (NADE) responded to the challenge by creating "NADE Guides." These documents emulated the CAS Standards assessment model and addressed the specific functions of tutoring services, adjunct instructional programs, developmental coursework, and the teaching/learning process. This developmental activity led to interassociation cooperation among learning assistance and developmental education organizations and paved a path for communication and collaboration in the current revision of the CAS Learning Assistance Program Standards, which follow in this volume. As the respondent noted, "I can think of no other project that has generated, nurtured, and advanced such interassociation collaboration. I see the CAS Standards as being a major force in consolidating a diverse profession."

• A related comment was made by a close observer of CAS activities during the past two decades. "I have two general observations. First, CAS has filled a void that no other organization could accomplish. A network has been established to mutually equip the student affairs profession with standards of performance. Second, the CAS effort has attracted increased attention and offered increased value over the years. A genuine service has been provided to the academy by helping and guiding all students toward achieving holistic development."

• Another respondent noted the value and utility of the CAS Standards to a specific functional area in a mid-sized public institution. "The CAS Standards were an excellent guide to use in assessing and improving the progress and success of our career center. They outlined expectations and served as a model in striving to achieve high quality services for the college community."

• Some practitioners view the CAS Standards and Guidelines as one of their most important professional documents because they speak to issues common to campuses everywhere, as practitioners have struggled to meet the needs of student bodies changing not only in numbers but also in age, gender, race, ethnicity, ability, and long term goals. One respondent shared the perspective that, "As each campus has examined its own situation, and looked to its peers for ideas, the CAS Standards have guided not only implementation but review and evaluation. Most of this work was done in expansionary times. Now as we regroup, downsize, retrench, whatever institutions name it, we need to have some means by which to measure what we do. The CAS Standards, in all of the functional areas, serve as an excellent tool to begin that process. They are flexible without being vague, broad without being limitless, and ideal for what we constantly face in higher education, change."

There can be little doubt that the CAS initiative has been most fruitful during its short existence. Although much remains to be done, especially in the standards education arena, the Council for the Advancement of Standards in Higher Education has made a professional difference and stands ready to continue its important efforts toward the professionalization of the fields of student affairs and student services.

## *Revised Edition*

This book is a major revision of the first edition of the 1986 *CAS Standards and Guidelines for Student Services/Development Programs,* commonly referred to as the "CAS Blue Book." Not only have the previous functional area standards and guidelines been revised and updated, but seven new standards not included in the initial publication have been developed [see Appendix B]. This edition has been designed as both an educational tool and a resource. Material about the history, role, and function of CAS for those who would use the CAS Standards and Guidelines in their professional work has also been included. This edition will also be a useful tool for students enrolled in master's and doctoral programs alike.

Many individuals have been involved in the development of the CAS Standards and Guidelines over the years and in the preparation of this book—far too many to acknowledge individually. Each and every member of the CAS Board of Directors has contributed to both the new and revised functional area standards over the past decade. A list of CAS Board of Director members and the associations they represent appear in Appendix C. CAS officers, Executive Committee members, and Public Representatives are included in that appendix as well.

A major feature of this revision is the addition of a "Functional Area Contextual Statement" that introduces the nature and context of each new and revised functional area standard and guideline. These contextual statements were crafted by both CAS Board members and other representatives of the various member associations. Included with these statements are recommended readings and resources for more information about the functional areas. Readers who are relatively unfamiliar with one or more of the functional area standards and guidelines will find the contextual statements valuable because each provides a short history of the function and a summary of its primary contributions to higher education. The names of individuals who wrote, co-wrote, or critiqued these contextual statements are listed in Appendix D.

In many ways, this volume is the result of a great deal of professional dedication by all involved. All royalties from its publication will be used to provide the Council for the Advancement of Standards in Higher Education with funds to continue its important work. The Department of Counseling and Human Development Services in the College of Education at the University of Georgia provided much of the human and technical support for generating the initial drafts of the functional area standards and guidelines and related material; CAS provided the services of a graduate assistant to aid in the process.

If you know of a professional association that is not currently represented on the CAS Board of Directors but should be, please contact the CAS President for information and application materials. CAS is a consortium of professional higher education associations concerned with the development and promulgation of professional standards in support of students' learning and personal development. CAS seeks to be all inclusive and welcomes the interest and involvement of all professional organizations in higher education that aspire to similar goals and purposes.

Ted K. Miller
The University of Georgia
Athens, Georgia
May 1997

# Part 1
# CAS Standards: The Context

A set of standards to guide practice in nearly any human endeavor is one of the more salient characteristics associated with the establishment of a profession. At some point in the maturation of a profession, a relevant set of standards and guidelines will be developed and promulgated by those who work in that area. For those employed in student affairs, student development, and student support services in higher education, the Council for the Advancement of Standards in Higher Education (CAS) was founded as a profession-wide entity to establish standards to guide professional practice. With a current membership of 29 professional associations in higher education, CAS represents over 80,000 individual and institutional educational service providers and student development educators who work with college and university students. This book has been prepared to share with the profession at large the 23 current CAS functional area standards and guidelines. The standards herein presented are the second major iteration, the first having been published in 1986 as *CAS Standards and Guidelines for Student Services/Development Programs.*

Over the years, higher education student services and student development programs have evolved from the employment of faculty members assigned on part-time bases to attend to students' needs beyond the classroom to the establishment of institutional divisions of student affairs, student development, and student services designed to complement divisions of academic affairs. It is clear that the complexity of the enterprise of student support services has increased as organizational structures have expanded. It is largely in response to this increased complexity of role, function, and purpose that the CAS standards were developed. As the field has grown and the responsibilities of its practitioners have expanded, a complementary need for increased accountability has resulted. It is no longer feasible, let alone desirable, for practitioners to be guided by best guesses or intuition when it comes to the task of creating environments conducive to student development. Likewise, practitioners have demanded that standards be developed to guide the quality of practice. The CAS functional area standards and guidelines are now in place to meet this important professional need.

The Council for the Advancement of Standards in Higher Education was designed as an eclectic entity that deliberately seeks to function as a bellwether for the profession at large. To assure cross-fertilization of theories, research, and application strategies from the field as a whole, representatives from the many member professional associations strive to bring to the table the most current thinking in the functional areas they represent. This commitment to collaboration among functional area specialties assures that no single component will dominate the thinking that underlies the generation, revision, and presentation of CAS standards. Although the standards reflect a broad range of interests, they are clearly value driven. Underlying them is a set of basic principles upon which CAS was founded and by which it is guided.

Following is a series of fundamental principles, categorically organized, underlying the work of CAS. They were derived from the theories and conceptual models in human development, learning, and administration that inform the work of student affairs administrators, student development educators, and student support service providers.

## Students and Their Institutions

1.  The individual student must be considered as a whole person.
2.  Institutions of higher learning are purposeful in nature and function as social and cultural resources, which students can use to learn and develop in holistic ways.
3.  Each student is a unique person and must be treated as such.
4.  Students seek higher education in responsible ways as they strive to enhance their academic learning and personal development for purposes of becoming mature, well-educated leaders and contributors to the world in which they live.
5.  The student's total environment is educational and must be used to achieve full individual development.
6.  Institutions of higher learning reflect the diversity of the societies and cultures in which they exist; they are intended to guide, instruct, and educate today's youth to be tomorrow's leaders and to provide opportunities for life long learning to all.

7. The major responsibility for personal and social development rests with the student and his or her personal resources.
8. Institutions of higher education are responsible for creating learning environments designed to provide students with a choice of educational opportunities and to challenge students to learn and develop while providing support to nurture their development.
9. The CAS Standards presuppose that students will search out relevant educational resources if they are provided, if students know they are available, if students are encouraged to access them, and if they are truly relevant to the student's educational and developmental needs.

The first four odd-numbered principles presented above were derived from the 1938 and 1949 editions of the *Student Personnel Point of View* (Miller & Prince, 1976, p. 4) and reflect fundamental "truths" upon which the *CAS Standards and Guidelines* were based. The even-numbered principles reflect institutional perspectives that complement the student-focused viewpoint. When combined, these principles represent the presuppositions upon which student support programs and services are founded. Each of the CAS functional area standards and guidelines is designed to inform practitioners about the criteria that represent the *minimal* level of programmatic and organizational application all institutions and their programs must meet if they are to be viable facilitators of student growth and development.

In effect, when an institution of higher education provides its students with programs and services that meet or exceed the CAS criteria, the institution can be considered to have implemented an environment conducive to the education and personal development of its students, both individually and collectively. The CAS Standards and Guidelines do not dictate that each and every student conform to a prescribed standard of involvement or behavior, but rather require that the institution's student affairs, student development, and student support programs and services meet a standard of programmatic and organizational efficiency and effectiveness sufficient to assure students ample opportunity to grow, develop, and achieve individual potentials. The institution and its educational programs are viewed as social resources that provide citizens with opportunities for expanding educational and personal horizons. The CAS Standards and Guidelines have been developed and promulgated from a profession-wide point of view to provide institu-

tions with a relevant, reasonable, and achievable set of voluntary professional standards. Although the standards were designed for institutional use to guide practice, no professional organizations or agencies are known to purport to use the CAS Standards to evaluate, accredit, or otherwise approve or endorse practice.

## *Diversity and Multiculturalism*

10. Recognizing the nature of racial and ethnic diversity on campuses, student support programs and services are committed to eliminating barriers that impede student learning and development, paying special attention to establishing and maintaining diverse human relationships essential to survival in today's global society.
11. Justice and respect for differences bond individuals to community; and thus education for multicultural and interracial awareness is essential to the development and maintenance of a health-engendering society.

Although issues of diversity and affirmative action in institutions of higher education are often fraught with dissension and discord, the CAS Standards and Guidelines affirm the importance of considering them in the process of creating and implementing educational and developmental initiatives. In an increasingly complex world, it is essential that the students of today, the leaders of tomorrow, learn to function effectively when faced with diverse ideas, values, and cultures. To do otherwise would be to perpetuate a world in which contention and strife predominate, to the detriment of all.

The CAS Standards and Guidelines consistently call for institutions of higher learning and their student support programs and services to recognize both the increasing diversity in society and the importance to future generations of establishing effective means of accommodating to today's diversity so as to function effectively tomorrow. Individuals and institutions may not necessarily take pleasure from the demands imposed by diverse viewpoints and cultures, but they must learn to acknowledge diversity and appreciate its potential for enhancing the importance and viability of higher education. The spirit of affirmative action is inherent in the delivery of student support services; discrimination against any student population or employment category is inimical to belief in the dignity of the individual. This proposition is fundamental to student development theory and its applications to practice. The CAS Standards and Guidelines stand firmly on the ground that those responsible for creating environments for learning in higher education need to be open to and accepting of differences, and to recognize their role in enhancing the quality of education provided and learning achieved. Further, the Standards consistently call for a staff whose ethnic and racial characteristics reflect those of the institution's constituencies. In addition, all students must have access to the educational and cocurricular resources available to the academic community at large; no student, for any reason, should be denied access to them.

## Organization, Leadership, and Human Resources

12. Capable, credible, and knowledgeable leadership is essential for institutional success; organizational units are most successful when their missions and outcome expectations are effectively documented and understood by all relevant constituents.

13. Effective programs and services require well-qualified staff members who understand and support the student learning and development outcomes the programs are intended to provide.

14. Enhanced student learning and personal development will occur when staff members at all levels of responsibility possess appropriate, relevant, and adequate educational preparation and practical experience.

The CAS Standards and Guidelines were founded on the belief that because *form follows function,* the structure of an organization should reflect the purpose for which it was established. Consequently, it is essential that institutions, programs, and services be based on a mutually determined, clearly stated, and well-understood purpose. Without a mission, institutions and their programs will be virtually rudderless and will founder. Lines of authority must also be drawn, job responsibilities described in some detail, and policies and procedures established to guide the desired processes. Student affairs leaders must remember that since theory without practice is empty, and practice without theory is blind, it is essential that our theory be connected to our purposes in the pursuit of quality practice.

CAS Standards are not intended to prescribe the organizational or administrative structures to which institutions and programs are expected to adhere, for every institution is unique and must establish the frame of administrative reference most appropriate to

its particular mission. Rather, the Standards provide fundamental criteria that practitioners can use to judge the effectiveness of their structures. For example, certain crucial elements clearly are essential to functional success including employing leaders who possess viable visions of how and what is to be achieved and are suitably positioned for access to the highest administrative levels. Leaders and staff alike must possess effective managerial skills, be properly titled, and be well qualified by both education and experience. This latter is essential for maintaining quality programs and services that will effectively accomplish the program's stated objectives. Under educated and under experienced staff members, good intentions notwithstanding, will invariably fail in the long term.

## Health Engendering Environments

15. Student development and student affairs programs and services prosper in benevolent, attractive environments that provide students with appropriate levels of challenge and support.

The purpose of education is to promote change in those it serves. Student affairs programs and services, as well as student development schemes, are first and foremost educational enterprises. Clearly, the Student Learning Imperative (ACPA, 1996) prevails throughout the CAS functional area standards because an important purpose of the standards is to provide criteria that can be used to judge a program's worth. Establishment of educational environments conducive to student learning and development is essential if an institution of higher learning is to achieve its educational purposes.

Institutional environments of quality combine credible educational philosophies and values, physical facilities, human resources, and fiscal support to have positive input on the education and development of students. Seeking to reflect this important integration of components, CAS Standards and Guidelines provide both criteria against which programs and services can be tested and guidelines to explain and amplify the standards for effective application.

## Ethical Considerations

16. Because special mentoring relationships develop between students and the educators who facilitate their learning and development, educators must exemplify impeccable ethical behavior and practice.

A major section in each CAS functional area standard incorporates the fundamental ethical standards to which student affairs administrators, student development educators, and student support service providers must adhere to assure fair and equitable practice. Just as a mission statement is essential to provide programs and services with direction, ethical standards are essential to provide these programs with integrity. As it emerges, every profession establishes the ethical standards that guide the behavior of its members. Although CAS Ethical Standards are minimalist, they provide the essential base upon which to found humane, ethical practice. Without a clearly defined code of ethics, professional student affairs, student development, and student service practitioners would have little or no guidance for establishing and maintaining a reasonable level of effective moral and ethical behavior. The best of intentions are insufficient if they are not founded on a solid ethical base that can be understood and acknowledged by all concerned.

## *Putting CAS Standards To Work*

The CAS Standards and Guidelines were designed to be highly utilitarian in nature. Their purpose is to provide higher education with a set of criteria that every program of quality should meet in order to provide an effective level of student support. The Standards provide a set of criterion measures against which programs and services can assess themselves. Using the CAS Standards and Guidelines as a framework for self-study, practitioners can evaluate how well their programs and services measure up both to standards in specific functional areas and to standards within a comprehensive, overall perspective. Practitioners can determine how their programs compare with a nationally established set of criterion measures that reflect the basic expectations of quality and effectiveness for every comparable program in higher education.

At least eight steps can be implemented for purposes of self-study (Yerian & Miller, 1989).

1. Staff members must determine the type of self-study and who will be involved. It is usually effective to involve all professional staff members actively in self-assessment; involving classified and technical staff members and knowledgeable students also has utility. In this way, everyone has a voice and can share ownership of the evaluation. Each staff member might first review statements and judge how well the existing program meets the criteria. Then the full staff can col-lectively review and discuss the standards and their assessments of how well the program is achieving them. This approach not only provides opportunity to evaluate the program, but also permits the staff to interpret the standards and explore together how well the program is accomplishing its stated purpose.

2. Staff members need to determine if any of the guidelines will be used to function as standards for the self-study. Many mature programs aspire to levels of quality and effectiveness that exceed the minimal standards, and will wish to treat selected guidelines as if they were standards. For example, a functional area guideline might include a statement such as, "facilities should include a private office where individual consultations can be held." Staff may decide that this statement should become a standard for purposes of their self-study. If so, it would be treated as if it were a standard when it comes to testing the program against the criteria.

3. Carefully examine the standards collectively before making individual or group judgments. Have the full staff discuss each standard to determine the level of consensus about its meaning. Discrepancies should be examined and agreement reached as to how the standard will be interpreted for purposes of the self-study.

4. Identify and summarize evaluative evidence. Judging the program against the standard is not an end-point of the self-study process; rather, the process requires documentation of the evidence that supports a judgment. Such documentation can be both quantitative and qualitative. For example, quantitative measures might include the staff-to-student ratio for a given activity or an analysis of the cost effectiveness of a given activity. Qualitative documentation might include notes taken on the process used to develop the program's mission or outcome objectives. Essential documentation includes relevant publications [e.g., student and staff handbooks), program descriptions (e.g., career decision-making workshop outlines), program evaluation data (e.g., survey results), institutional data (e.g., student profiles), and self-study initiated research (e.g., student survey results). No self-study should be considered complete without relevant data and related documentation to support and validate the judgment of the staff and others.

5. Describe discrepancies between assessment criteria and program practice. Staff members should compare their interpretations of program accomplishment against the standard and its various criteria. Only if the program can define its operational problems clearly can it hope to find viable solutions. For exam-

ple, the standards call for a mission statement consistent with the nature and goals of the institution. If the program has no written mission statement or an outdated one, then the discrepancy between the standard and actual program practice clearly calls for the establishment of a current, relevant program mission statement that is consistent with the institution's mission.

6. <u>Delineate required corrective action.</u> Describe in some detail the adjustments required to achieve the quality and effectiveness to which the program aspires. For example, using the mission situation previously noted, the action required would be for the staff to draft a statement of the goals they believe have already been agreed upon, circulate them for review and comment, and then prepare and disseminate a final program mission statement. The key point here is that it is important to subdivide the overall task into manageable parts that can be accomplished in a step-by-step fashion.

7. <u>Recommend special actions for program enhancement.</u> Even excellent programs can be further refined to provide more desirable and effective outcomes. This step is particularly relevant for programs that have identified selected guidelines that call for enhanced operations. Unless staff members are satisfied with meeting minimal standards only, usually additional work can be done to enhance program quality and effectiveness.

8. <u>Prepare a statement of overall action.</u> The staff identifies and places priority on desired future directions, comparing past performance with desired outcomes. This step is best accomplished following a careful review of the first seven steps to assure that all the bases have been touched. The action plan should acknowledge the program's strengths and its shortcomings and establish a strategic approach for correcting deficiencies and making enhancements. The primary goal of this final step is to identify and set priorities for future directions, after comparing past performance with the outcomes to which the program aspires.

The standards are also useful for staff development. Staff can study the various criteria to determine how well, individually and collectively, they are implementing the standards in their daily work with students. A comprehensive staff development process, using one of the functional area standards and guidelines as its framework for training, might include from six to twelve hours of meetings, during which members share responsibility for presenting and leading discussions about the 13 components of the CAS Standards and Guidelines. This approach would be particularly valuable if a program self-study were to be implemented in the near future. Staff members would not only learn about the CAS Standards and how they can guide and influence good practice but also be prepared to implement a program self-study. Training staff before conducting a self-study typically produces a more comprehensive and valuable program evaluation process and outcome.

## *Credibility*

All professions and practitioners require credibility in order to perform their service functions. Individuals and agencies lacking user confidence will be unutilized and will ultimately vanish. Credibility is essential to the life of all service agencies, including higher education. Through publication of and adherence to standards, institutions seek to assure potential users and the general public of their competence and credibility.

Both the public and professionals alike impute credibility to programs, professions, and institutions that meet stringent standards; compliance with such standards demonstrates that quality is present.

Several means have been established to provide quality assurance. Institutional and academic program credibility is typically established through *accreditation* a process by which voluntary organizations of institutions and agencies encourage and assist institutions and their specialized subunits (e.g., colleges, schools, departments, and programs) to evaluate and improve their programs and services. The names of institutions and programs that voluntarily meet or exceed acceptable standards of quality and effectiveness are then made known by the accrediting body. It is not uncommon for unaccredited institutions to be denied federal aid and other resources available to accredited institutions. Accreditation is intended to assure the public that institutions and programs are providing quality education to their constituents.

But the general public cannot be assured that individuals who have diplomas, certificates, or degrees from accredited institutions and programs are, in fact, effective practitioners of what was taught. Consequently, various structures have been established by professional oversight agencies and state governments to judge the professional qualifications of service providers in education, health, and social service areas.

Three primary methods enable individuals to document their professional qualifications: *registry, certification,* and *licensure.* CAS has focused little attention on these credentialing options, although some in higher education would like the Council to expand its focus into registry and certification, which are often initiated by non-governmental professional bodies. Licensure, on the other hand, is the province of governments. For instance, licenses based on generally comparable criteria are required of physicians, psychologists, and lawyers in all states; counselors, morticians, and engineers, on the other hand, require licenses in only some states and are judged by diverse criteria from state to state. A recent trend in some states has been to require persons who perform duties of counselors and psychologists to be licensed in order to be eligible for employment in such traditional student affairs areas as counseling and career centers. Although yet to be fully tested in the courts, such initiatives will likely increase during the coming decade.

As demand for accountability in higher education increases, so too will demand for practitioner accountability. There may come a day when higher education will need to establish professional eligibility criteria for its staff or face the prospect of having external agencies, such as state or federal government set the criteria. CAS and other professional groups may be called on to join the discussion. CAS currently endorses self-regulation as the most viable approach to program accountability and credentialing, calling for each institution to initiate a program of self-assessment for its student support services and programs. Whether student service departments are administratively assigned to student affairs, academic affairs, business affairs, or elsewhere in the organizational hierarchy, they should be reviewed and evaluated on a continuing basis, using the *CAS Standards and Guidelines*. From this perspective, self-regulation would become the preferred strategy to establish credibility. When deemed appropriate and desirable, the various functional areas could invite representatives from peer institutions to review their self-assessment reports as part of the validation process. Self-regulation requires institutions and their leaders to establish their own policies and procedures for institutional assessment and evaluation and to follow them as they evaluate quality and effectiveness. Thus, through continuing assessment, institutions could, over time, compile the internal documentation required by regional accrediting bodies. Self-regulation would provide institutions and their student support services and programs with the tools for achieving minimum quality assurance. The key message is that if institutions do not accept responsibility for meaningful, seriously considered assessment, sooner or later external

agencies will, a change that would not bode well for the future of higher education.

## CAS Initiatives

The Council for the Advancement of Standards in Higher Education was established as a profession-wide collaborative agency to develop and promulgate professional standards and to inform those responsible for providing higher education with information about how the standards can be used productively. The 23 CAS functional area standards and guidelines presented in the following section are viewed as living, evolving documents. The Council has established a five year review program to assure that each set of functional area standards and guidelines undergoes regular review and updating. Protocols to guide development of new standards and review and revision of existing functional area standards and guidelines have been established [see Appendix E]. These protocols identify the processes and procedures that CAS uses to create and review its standards and guidelines and the participants involved. Completion of a typical standard review takes approximately one year from initiation to Board adoption. It takes CAS approximately the same length of time to develop a new standard, once the initial draft is in place. This drafting process usually involves a professional association or an interested group of professionals and may take considerably longer to complete. Because of the serious and often laborious nature of standards development, the process can be time consuming. Nevertheless, by the time a functional area standard has undergone this long, arduous process of development and review, the CAS Board of Directors has nearly always been unanimous in its decision to adopt a new or revised standard.

## Applying CAS Standards and Guidelines

In addition to its primary purposes of standards development and promulgation, CAS takes seriously its responsibility to inform and educate higher education practitioners and the public about the role and function of professional standards and their use for institutional and program self-assessment purposes. An important long range CAS goal is to sponsor an invitational colloquium on professional standards involving higher education leaders, faculty members, and student affairs and student support services personnel as well as representatives from government and business. The colloquium will engage leaders in higher education, business, and government in conversation about the accountability of higher education to its constituent populations and its ability to foster education through quality learning environments. This conversation will examine the relationship between the maintenance of quality standards to guide educational practice and the nature and expectations of the outcomes of higher education. Issues concerning quality assurance would be both the head and heart of the colloquium.

Many student service practitioners and faculty members have used the CAS Standards to enhance institutional program development and/or as instructional tools to inform staff members and graduate students about the nature and characteristics of the various student affairs functional areas.

*Example Applications.* Following are description of how the Standards have been applied in practice and for purposes of professional development to edify readers as to various approaches practitioners have used over the years.

• From an institutional perspective, the CAS standards are, according to Professor Don G. Creamer at Virginia Polytechnic Institute and State University, viewed as a staple for conducting comprehensive program reviews in the student affairs division. Although there is no requirement that the CAS Standards be used, established policy requires that some standard external to the institution be chosen for the basis of these comprehensive reviews. CAS Standards are readily available and easily understood and used and thus are often chosen by administrative units planning reviews. The fact that operational versions of the Standards in the form of CAS Self-Assessment Guides are also available has increased both the availability and ease with which the Standards can be used for program review purposes. In addition, the very presence of the CAS Standards and Guidelines seems to raise awareness among of practitioners that professional practice in the field is neither ad hoc nor layman's work; rather, it consists of the application of the collective wisdom of the profession and is subject to assessment and regulation.

• From a programmatic perspective, the CAS Standards have special utility, especially for emerging student support programs and services. Perhaps because it is a relatively "young" function in education, those responsible for guiding programs of learning assistance and developmental education have shown strong commitment to promoting the use of professional standards in their ranks. Many leaders in this arena

literally "invented" their programs and learned from each other what worked best to produce quality outcomes. The CAS Learning Assistance Programs Standards and Guidelines became a shared document during the past decade, one to which everyone could contribute and build a collective declaration of quality programs, practices, values, and philosophy. Spearheaded by ACPA's Commission XVI, learning assistance program leaders drew people together from across many professional organizations to focus on the commonalties of learning assistance programming and to join forces in assuring that the standards, as written, were truly representative of a diverse group of specialties composing this professional responsibility. These initiatives resulted in a newly revised set of CAS Standards and Guidelines for this particular functional area that are made public for the first time in this volume.

• From another program-specific perspective, there are two primary uses of the Standards in addition to the very obvious self-assessment function. One is for use as a guide for initiating new programs and the other is for advocacy. Barely does a week go by that Barbara Jacoby, Director of the National Clearinghouse for Commuter Programs (NCCP) at the University of Maryland at College Park, does not receive a request from an institution desiring to create a commuter program. What most practitioners interested in such initiatives do not know is the scope of the functions that are required for a comprehensive program. Often, the initiator is interested in establishing a particular type of program (e.g., peer mentoring, orientation for commuters) or service (e.g., off-campus housing referral, commuter newsletter). When such requests are made, the CAS Commuter Student Programs Standards and Guidelines are readily available as a nationally sanctioned document that provides guidance to those interested in campus commuter populations.

• The second noted use of the standards—advocacy—is often helpful when consulting with higher education institutions about commuter student programs. In this context, the CAS Standards and Guidelines are vital to making a case for broadening administrators' understanding of what is required to meet bare minimums. All too often, campus administrators tend to limit their initial thinking about commuter programs to issues such as parking and transportation, and not to think in terms such as programs to integrate commuters into the life of the campus. The CAS Standards have great utility in opening institutional leaders' eyes to the importance of comprehensive programming in this arena.

• When the South Dakota School of Mines and Technology was preparing for a North Central accreditation visit in 1996, Dean of Students Douglas K. Lange and the Division of Student Affairs he directs used the CAS Standards and Guidelines to prepare portions of the university self-study report. Lange noted that over 50 faculty, staff, students, alumni, and community leaders were involved in the various task forces that reviewed each of the functional areas. The year-long self-study established a division-wide vision and stimulated considerable creativity to assist and facilitate student learning. Mission statements developed for departments evidenced a genuine concern for each and every student. As a result of this process, the student affairs division continues to move toward promoting a university environment in which academic and student affairs are blended to maximize student learning, thereby blurring the lines of distinction between the two.

• From a national professional association perspective, Greg Singleton, President of the Association of Fraternity Advisors [AFA] found the standards to be extremely beneficial in relating the purpose of his association to the mission of higher education and those of various institutions. He noted that if colleagues would utilize the CAS Standards in establishing or reorganizing various programs and services that are offered to students, the very existence of those programs would not be questioned because of the credibility the CAS Standards and Guidelines provide.

• From the perspective of graduate education, many master's preparation and doctoral programs have integrated the CAS Standards into their curricula. The concept of quality assurance is vague to most graduate students, especially at the master's level, but the concept of applying standards to practice is more concrete and they can quickly come to understand the role, function, and utility of professional standards. Thus, even beginning students can undertake the process of engaging in the professional interests of self-regulation and improvement. The College

Student Affairs academic program at the University of Georgia, for instance, has incorporated the CAS Standards into its various student affairs practicum and internship components. Students complete a "mini-self-study" of the functional areas to which they are assigned as part of their practical field-work experiences. This not only assures that future practitioners know about the existence of the Standards, but also provides them with direct experience that enhances their ability to put the Standards into practice as part of their daily work.

The CAS Standards have gone a long way to express to students, faculty, and administrators the complex and vital nature of student affairs work and its relationship to student development. There are ample indications within higher education that there exists a lack of understanding about student affairs work and related student support services in higher education. Over the years, the field of student affairs has often been viewed as secondary, supportive, or supplemental to the academic mission, rather than integral to it. The establishment of clearly articulated professional standards has gone far to deepen the understanding of faculty and administrative colleagues and their confidence in the valuable educational and developmental role that student affairs provides on behalf of students. There is little doubt that the CAS Standards have had and will continue to have a major impact on higher education well into the next century. In addition to the functional area standard and guideline statements, which follow in Part 2, CAS publishes a three-ring bound set of 24 operational standards entitled *CAS Self-Assessment Guides* (SAG). The SAGs are designed for practitioners to use for program evaluation purposes, including self-studies. Each CAS Standard is presented in a format that lists individual criterion measures designed to be rated and used to determine the extent to which a program is in compliance with the CAS Standards. Each functional area standard has a complementary self-assessment guide for practitioners to use for assessment and evaluation purposes.

### Special Note:

In the 24 CAS Standards and Guidelines that follow in Part 2, the **Standards are presented in bold print** and use the auxiliary verbs "must" and "shall" whereas the Guidelines are presented in regular, smaller font size print and use the auxiliary verbs

"should" and "may". The Standards reflect essential criteria for quality programs while the Guidelines represent either additional desirable characteristics or seek to clarify or amplify the Standards in some fashion.

# Part 2
# CAS Functional Area Standards and Guidelines

## Preamble

*Let us raise a standard to which the wise and honest can repair.*
—George Washington, 1787

### The CAS Purpose

The Council for the Advancement of Standards in Higher Education (CAS) develops and promulgates standards that enhance the quality of a student's total learning experience in higher education. CAS is a consortium of associations in higher education whose representatives achieve consensus on the nature and application of standards that guide the work of practitioners. CAS derives its authority from the prestige and traditional influence of its member associations and from the consensus of those members in establishing requirements for high-quality practice.

The CAS philosophy is grounded in beliefs about excellence in higher education, collaboration between teacher and learner, ethics in educational practice, student development as a major goal of higher education, and student responsibility for learning.

- The beliefs about excellence require that all programs and services in institutions of higher education function at optimum levels.
- The beliefs about collaboration require that learning be accomplished in concert by students and educators.
- The beliefs about ethics require that all programs and services be carried out in an environment of integrity and high ideals.
- The beliefs about student development require that the student be considered as a whole person in the context of a diverse population and a diversity of institutions, that outcomes of education be comprehensive, and that the total environment be structured to create opportunities for student involvement and learning.
- The beliefs about responsibility require that the institution recognize the rights and responsibilities of students as its citizens and that it provide an array of resources and learning opportunities that enable students to exercise their responsibility to take full advantage of them.

Taken together, these beliefs about practice shape the vision for all CAS endeavors.

CAS collectively develops, examines, and endorses standards and guidelines for program and service areas in higher education. The CAS approach to quality educational experiences anchors itself in the assumption that standards and guidelines can be used in a variety of ways to enhance institutional quality. They can, for example, be used for design of programs and services, for determination of the efficacy of programs, for staff development designed to enhance the skills of those providing professional services, for programmatic self-assessment to assure institutional effectiveness, and for self-regulation purposes.

### Background

The Council for the Advancement of Standards in Higher Education was established in 1979 as the Council for the Advancement of Standards for Student Services/Development Programs, a consortium of professional associations representing student affairs practitioners committed to assuring quality programs and services for students. Members of nearly 30 established professional associations have directed their interests, talents, and resources to develop and promulgate professional standards and guidelines based on state-of-the-art thinking about educational programs and services. From the beginning, the Council has employed an open process of consensus-building among the representatives of member associations as the primary tool for producing its standards and guidelines.

The Council published the original set of 16 functional area standards and the academic preparation standards in 1986, with a grant from American College Testing (ACT). In 1988, CAS developed a Self-Assessment Guide (SAG) for each set of functional area standards (Miller, Thomas, Looney, & Yerian, 1988) to facilitate program assessment and evaluation. Each SAG is an operational version of a functional area standard designed to provide practitioners with a detailed instrument for self-assessment.

The Council's current name and expanded mission were adopted in 1992, to be inclusive of all programs for students in higher education, including those serving undergraduate, graduate, traditional, and nontraditional students. CAS now oversees the development of standards for new service areas and the systematic review and periodic revision of existing standards and guidelines.

## *The CAS Approach to Self-Regulation and Self-Assessment*

Self-regulation is an internally motivated and directed institutional process devoted to the creation, maintenance, and enhancement of high-quality programs and services. CAS believes this approach is preferable to externally motivated regulation, because those within an institution generally have the clearest perceptions of its mission, goals, resources, and capabilities. The essential elements of self-regulation include:

- Institutional culture that values involvement of all its members in decision-making
- Quality indicators that are determined by the institution
- Use of standards and guidelines in quality assurance
- Collection and analysis of data on institutional performance
- Commitment to continuing improvement that presupposes freedom to explore and develop alternative directions for the future.

The success of self-regulation depends on mutual respect between an institution and its members. Within the self-regulated institution, individual accomplishments are valued, goals are based on shared vision, systems are open and interactive, processes are carried out in a climate of mutual trust and caring, conflicts are mediated in the best interests of the entire community, and achievements are recognized and rewarded. Such an environment stimulates individual and group initiatives and fosters self-determination of goals.

In a self-regulating environment, members identify quality indicators in consultation with a variety of internal and external constituencies and stakeholders, including professional associations. These indicators may include professionally derived standards, such as those of CAS, which comprise the views of many professional practitioners and professional associations.

Self-regulation relies on the willingness and capacity of the organization to examine itself meticulously, faithfully, and reliably, and then to assemble the pertinent results of that examination into coherent reports that constituents can comprehend and use. Such reports are essential for recording the evidence assembled in self-study, for displaying synthesis and analysis of information, for fostering the broad participation of members in the self-regulation process, and for registering benchmark results and conclusions for future reference.

Finally, the self-regulation process relies on the institution's capacity to modify its own practices as needed. A culture that supports self-regulation must operate in a climate that permits members to make independent choices among reasonable alternatives. These choices constitute a commitment to constant improvement of educational practices and of the health of the organization.

Approved by CAS Board Of Directors
November 18, 1994
Washington, DC

# References

American College Personnel Association (ACPA). (March/April 1996). Special issue: The student learning Imperative. *Journal of College Student Development* 37(2), whole issue.

Council for the Advancement of Standards in Higher Education (CAS). (1986). *CAS standards and guidelines for student services/development programs.* Iowa City: American College Testing Program.

Council of Student Personnel Associations in Higher Education (COSPA). (1983). Student development services in post-secondary education. In: G. L. Saddlemire & A. L. Rentz.(Eds.) *Student affairs—A profession's heritage: Significant articles, authors, issues and documents,* Media Publication No. 35, pp. 384-395. Carbondale, IL: American College Personnel Association.

Miller, T. K., & Prince, J. S. (1976). *The future of student affairs: A guide to student development for tomorrow's higher education.* San Francisco: Jossey-Bass.

Miller, T. K., Thomas, W. L., Looney, S. C., & Yerian, J. M. (1988). *CAS self assessment guides.* Iowa City: American College Testing Program.

Yerian, J. M., & Miller, T. K. (1989). *Putting the CAS standards to work.* College Park, MD: Council for the Advancement of Standards for Student Services/Development Programs.

# THE ROLE of ACADEMIC ADVISING
## CAS Standards Contextual Statement

Academic advising is an essential element of a student's collegiate experience. It evolves from the institution's culture, values, and practices and is delivered in accordance with these factors. Academic advising is one of the few endeavors universal to all college and university students and plays a significant role in their education.

Academic advising, long a purview of faculty who accepted the responsibility in earnest with the advent of electives into the curriculum, is also now delivered by professional, full-time staff members outside the tenure track structure and by graduate and undergraduate students. Today's academic advising is well assisted by rapidly growing technologies in registration activities and information dissemination.

Academic advising is one of the very few institutional activities that connect all students to the institution. As the curricula of higher education becomes increasingly complex and as educational options expand, the pressure to make the educational experience as meaningful as possible for students has increased as well. Higher education, in turn, has responded with renewed attention to the need for quality academic advising. With the establishment of the National Academic Advising Association (NACADA), recognition has been accorded to those in higher education who saw their work in academic advising as purposeful and unique. To enable all academic advisers to examine their behaviors within a professional framework, NACADA developed a *Statement of Core Values,* a document that was written in response to a growing need for ethical principles to guide those who advise and delineates the core values of the profession.

Publications on academic advising increased during the 1980s and 1990s; see Gordon's chapter in *Teaching through Academic Advising: A Faculty Perspective* (Reinarz & White, 1995). Additional resources, including annotated bibliographies, are available from the Clearinghouse on Academic Advising. NACADA publishes a monograph series that examines various aspects of advising; the first monograph, *Reaffirming the Role of Faculty in Academic Advising,* advances the premise that the faculty-student interaction in an advising context is one of the most prevalent advising models in use today.

Academic advising has been described as a crucial component of all students' experiences in higher education. Within this context, students can find meaning in their lives, make significant decisions about the future, be encouraged to rise to their highest levels of potential, and access all that higher education has to offer. When practiced with competence and dedication, academic advising can increase retention rates. In an age increasingly characterized by impersonality and detachment, academic advising provides a human contact students so often need and ask for.

## References, Readings and Resources

Cramer, G. L., & Childs, M. W. (eds.) (1996). *Transforming academic advising through the use of information technology.* (Monograph No. 4). Manhattan, KS: National Academic Advising Association.

Frost, S .H. *Academic advising for student success: A system of shared responsibility.* ASHE-ERIC Higher Education Report no. 3. Washington, DC: The George Washington University.

Glenner, R. E., & Vowell, F. N. (eds.). (1995). *Academic advising as a comprehensive campus process* (Monograph No. 2). Manhattan, KS: National Academic Advising Association.

Gordon, V. N. *Academic advising: An annotated bibliography.* Westport, CT: Greenwood Press, 1994.

Reinarz, A. G., & White, E. R. (eds.) (1995). *Teaching through academic advising: A faculty perspective.* San Francisco: Jossey-Bass.

Upcraft, M. L., & Cramer, G. L. (eds.) (1995). *First-year academic advising: Patterns in the present pathways to the future* (Monograph No. 18). Columbia, SC: National Resource Center for the Freshman Year Experience and Students in Transition.

Winston, R. B. Jr., Ender, S. C., & Miller, T. K. (eds.) (1982). *Developmental approaches to academic advising.* New Directions for Student Services, No. 17. San Francisco: Jossey-Bass.

Winston, R. B. Jr., Miller, T .K., Ender, S. C., Grites, T. J., & Associates (1984). *Developmental academic advising: Addressing students' educational, career, and personal needs.* San Francisco: Jossey-Bass.

Clearinghouse on Academic Advising, 110 Enarson Hall, The Ohio State University, Columbus, OH 43210.

*NACADA Journal.* National Academic Advising Association, 2323 Anderson Avenue, Manhattan, KS 66502.

# ACADEMIC ADVISING
## CAS STANDARDS and GUIDELINES

## Part 1. MISSION

The academic advising program must develop, record, disseminate, implement and regularly review its mission and goals. Mission statements must be consistent with the mission and goals of the institution and with the standards in this document.

The primary purpose of the academic advising program is to assist students in the development of meaningful educational plans that are compatible with their life goals.

The institution must have a clearly written statement of philosophy pertaining to academic advising which must include program goals and expectations of advisors and advisees.

> The ultimate responsibility for making decisions about educational plans and life goals rests with the individual student. The academic advisor should assist by helping to identify and assess alternatives and the consequences of decisions.
>
> Institutional goals for academic advising should include:
>
> - development of suitable educational plans;
> - clarification of career and life goals;
> - selection of appropriate courses and other educational experiences;
> - interpretation of institutional requirements;
> - enhancement of student awareness about educational resources available (e.g., internship, study abroad, honors, and learning assistance programs);
> - evaluation of student progress toward established goals;
> - development of decision-making skills;
> - reinforcement of student self-direction;
> - referral to and use of institutional and community support services; and
> - collection and distribution of data regarding student needs, preferences, and performance for use in making institutional decisions and policy.

## Part 2. PROGRAM

The formal education of students is purposeful, holistic, and consists of the curriculum and the co-curriculum.

The academic advising program must be (a) intentional, (b) coherent, (c) based on theories and knowledge of teaching, learning and human development, (d) reflective of developmental and demographic profiles of the student population, and (e) responsive to the special needs of individuals.

The academic advising program must promote learning and development in students by encouraging experiences which lead to intellectual growth, ability to communicate effectively, realistic self-appraisal, enhanced self-esteem, clarification of values, appropriate career choices, leadership development, physical fitness, meaningful interpersonal relations, ability to work independently and collaboratively, social responsibility, satisfying and productive lifestyles, appreciation of aesthetic and cultural diversity, and achievement of personal goals.

The academic advising program must assist students in overcoming educational and personal problems and skill deficiencies.

The academic advising program must identify environmental conditions that may negatively influence student academic achievement and propose interventions that may neutralize such conditions.

The academic advisor must review and use available data about students' academic and educational needs, performance, aspirations, and problems.

The academic advising program must assure that academic advisors collaborate in the collection of relevant data about students for use in individual academic advising conferences.

Individual academic advising conferences must be available to students each academic term.

> Through private, individual conferences with students, the academic advisors should provide assistance in refining goals and objectives, understanding available choices, and assessing the consequences of alternative courses of action. Course selection, understanding and meeting institutional requirements, and providing clear and accurate information regarding institutional policies, procedures, resources, and programs may be carried out individually or in groups.
>
> The academic status of the student being advised should be taken into consideration when determining caseloads. For example, first year, undecided, under prepared, and honors students may require more advising time than upper division students who have declared their majors.

Academic advising caseloads must be consistent with the time required for the effective performance of this activity.

> When determining workloads it should be recognized that advisors may work with students not officially assigned to them and that contacts regarding advising may extend beyond direct contact with the student.

The academic advising program must provide current and accurate advising information to academic advisors.

Supplemental systems for the delivery of advising information, such as on-line computer programs, may be employed.

Referrals to appropriate institutional or community support services should be made as needed.

The academic advising program should make available to academic advisors all pertinent research (e.g., about students, the academic advising program, and perceptions of the institution).

# Part 3. LEADERSHIP

The institution must appoint, position, and empower the leader of the academic advising program to accomplish stated missions. Leaders at various levels must be selected on the basis of formal education and training, relevant work experience, personal attributes, and other professional credentials. Expectations of accountability must be defined for academic advising program leaders, and their performance fairly assessed.

Leaders of academic advising programs must exercise authority over those resources for which they are responsible to achieve their respective missions. Leaders must articulate a vision for their organization; set goals and objectives; prescribe and practice ethical behavior; recruit, select, supervise and develop others in the organization; manage, plan, budget, and evaluate; communicate effectively; and marshal cooperative action from colleagues, employees, other institutional constituencies, and persons outside the organization. Leaders must address individual, organizational, or environmental conditions that inhibit the achievement of goals. Leaders must improve programs and services continuously in response to changing needs of students and institutional priorities.

# Part 4. ORGANIZATION and MANAGEMENT

The academic advising program must be structured purposefully and managed effectively to achieve its stated goals. Evidence of an appropriate structure must include current and accessible policies and procedures, written expectations for performance of all employees, and organizational charts. Effective management practices must be evident, including clear sources and channels of authority, effective communication, procedures to make decisions and resolve conflicts, responsiveness to changing conditions, accountability systems, and recognition and reward processes.

The academic advising program must provide channels within its organization for regular review of administrative policies and procedures.

The design of the academic advising program must be compatible with the institution's organizational structure and its students' needs. Specific advisor responsibilities must be clearly delineated, published, and disseminated to both advisors and advisees.

In some institutions, academic advising is a centralized function, while in others, it is decentralized, with a variety of people throughout the institution assuming responsibilities. Whatever system is used, students, faculty advisors, and professional staff should be informed of their respective advising responsibilities.

# Part 5. HUMAN RESOURCES

The academic advising program must be staffed adequately by individuals qualified to accomplish its mission and goals. The academic advising program must establish procedures for selection, training, and evaluation of advisors, set expectations for supervision, and provide appropriate professional development opportunities.

An academic advisor must hold an earned graduate degree or must possess an appropriate combination of education and experience.

Graduate students, interns, others in training, student employees, peer advisors, and volunteers must be carefully selected and adequately trained, supervised, and evaluated. When their knowledge and skills are not adequate for particular situations, they must refer students or others in need of assistance to a qualified professional staff member.

The academic advising program must have sufficient support personnel to accomplish its mission. Such staff must be technologically proficient and qualified to perform activities including reception duties, office equipment operation, records maintenance, and mail handling.

Appropriate salary levels and fringe benefits for academic advising program personnel must be commensurate with those for comparable positions within the institution, in similar institutions, and in the relevant geographic area.

The academic advising program must intentionally employ advisors who reflect the diversity of the institution's student population, to ensure the existence of readily identifiable role models for students, and/or to enrich the campus community.

Affirmative action must occur in hiring and promotion practices to ensure diverse staffing profiles as required by institutional policy and local, state/provincial, and federal law.

The institution must designate a specific individual to direct the academic advising program.

The director of an academic advising program must possess either an earned graduate degree or equivalent combination of academic and educational experience, previous experience as an academic advisor, and knowledge of the literature of academic advising. The director must be skilled in fiscal management, personnel selection and training, conceptualization, planning and evaluation tasks.

Academic advisors should have an understanding of student development; a comprehensive knowledge of the institution's programs, academic requirements, majors, minors, and support services; a demonstrated interest in working with and assisting students; a willingness to participate in pre-service and in-service workshops and other professional activities; and demonstrated interpersonal skills.

Sufficient personnel should be available to meet students' advising needs without unreasonable delay. Advisors should allow an appropriate amount of time for students to discuss plans, programs, courses, academic progress, and other subjects related to their educational programs.

Academic advising personnel may be organized in various ways. They may be full-time or part-time professionals who have advising as their primary function or may be faculty whose responsibilities include academic advising. Paraprofessionals (e.g., graduate students in practice, interns, or assistants) or peer advisors may also assist advisors.

Support personnel should maintain student records, organize resource materials, receive students, make appointments, and handle correspondence and other operational needs. Technical staff may be used in research, data collection, systems development, and special projects.

Technical and support personnel should be carefully selected and adequately trained, supervised, and evaluated.

## Part 6. FINANCIAL RESOURCES

The academic advising program must have adequate funding to accomplish its mission and goals. Priorities, whether set periodically or as a result of extraordinary conditions, must be determined within the context of the stated mission, goals, and resources.

Special consideration should be given to providing funding for training and development of advisors, particularly those for whom the advisory function is part-time and/or secondary assignment.

Financial resources should be sufficient to provide high quality print and non-print information for students and training materials for advisors. Also, there should be sufficient resources to promote the academic advising program.

## Part 7. FACILITIES, TECHNOLOGY, and EQUIPMENT

The academic advising program must have adequate and suitably located facilities, technology, and equipment to support its mission and goals. Facilities, technology, and equipment must be in compliance with relevant federal, state/provincial, and local requirements to provide for access, health and safety.

The academic advising program must assure that technology-assisted advising includes appropriate approvals, consultations, and referrals.

Computing equipment and access to local networks, student data bases, and the Internet should be available to academic advisors.

Privacy and freedom from visual and auditory distractions should be considerations in designing appropriate facilities.

## Part 8. LEGAL RESPONSIBILITIES

Academic advisors must be knowledgeable about and responsive to law and regulations that relate to the academic advising program. Sources for legal obligations and limitations include constitutional, statutory, regulatory, and case law; mandatory laws and orders emanating from federal, state/provincial and local governments; and the institution through its policies.

Academic advisors must use reasonable and informed practices to limit the liability exposure of the institution, its officers, employees, and agents. Academic advisors must be informed about institutional policies regarding personal liability and related insurance coverage options.

The institution must provide access to legal advice for academic advisors as needed to carry out assigned responsibilities.

The institution must inform academic advisors and students, in a timely and systematic fashion, about extraordinary or changing legal obligations and potential liabilities.

## Part 9. EQUAL OPPORTUNITY, ACCESS, and AFFIRMATIVE ACTION

The academic advising program must ensure that services are provided on a fair and equitable basis and are accessible to all students. Hours of operation must be responsive to the needs of all students. The academic advising program must adhere to the spirit and intent of equal opportunity laws.

The academic advising program must not be discriminatory on the basis of age, color, disability, gender, national origin, race, religious creed, sexual orientation, and/or veteran status. Exceptions are appropriate only where provided by relevant law and institutional policy.

Consistent with the mission and goals, the academic advising program must take affirmative action to remedy significant imbalances in student participation and staffing patterns.

## PART 10. CAMPUS and COMMUNITY RELATIONS

The academic advising program must establish, maintain, and promote effective relations with relevant campus offices and external agencies.

Academic advising is integral to the educational process and depends upon close working relationships with other institutional agencies and the administration. The academic advising program should be fully integrated into other processes of the institution.

For referral purposes, the academic advising program should provide academic advisors a comprehensive list of relevant external agencies, campus offices, and opportunities.

## Part 11. DIVERSITY

Within the context of the institution's unique mission, multi-dimensional diversity enriches the community and enhances the collegiate experience for all; therefore, the academic advising program must nurture environments where similarities and differences among people are recognized and honored.

The academic advising program must promote cultural educational experiences that are characterized by open and continuous communication, that deepen understanding of one's own culture and heritage, and that respect and educate about similarities, differences and histories of cultures.

The academic advising program must address the characteristics and needs of a diverse population when establishing and implementing policies and procedures.

## Part 12. ETHICS

All persons involved in the delivery of the academic advising program must adhere to the highest of principles of ethical behavior. The academic advising program must implement statements of ethical practice. The academic advising program must publish these statements and insure their periodic review by all concerned.

> Ethical standards or other statements from relevant professional associations should be considered.

The academic advising programs must ensure that confidentiality is maintained for all records and communications (i.e., paper and electronic), unless exempted by law.

Information disclosed in individual academic advising sessions must remain confidential, unless written permission to divulge the information is given by the student. However, all academic advising personnel must disclose to appropriate authorities information judged to be of an emergency nature, especially when the health and safety of the individual or others are involved. Information in students' educational records must not be disclosed to non-institutional third-parties without appropriate consent, unless classified as "Directory" information or when the information is subpoenaed by law. The academic advising program must

apply a similar dedication to privacy and confidentiality to research data concerning individuals.

All academic advising personnel must be aware of and comply with the provisions contained in the institution's human subjects research policy and in other relevant institutional policies addressing ethical practices.

All academic advising personnel must recognize and avoid personal conflict of interest or appearance thereof in their transactions with students and others. All academic advising personnel must strive to ensure the fair, objective, and impartial treatment of all persons with whom they interact.

When handling institutional funds, all academic advising personnel must ensure that such funds are managed in accordance with established and responsible accounting procedures.

All academic advising personnel must maintain the highest principles of ethical behavior in the use of technology.

All academic advising personnel must not participate in any form of harassment that demeans persons or creates an intimidating, hostile, or offensive campus environment.

All academic advising personnel must perform their duties within the limits of their training, expertise, and competence. When these limits are exceeded, individuals in need of further assistance must be referred to persons possessing appropriate qualifications.

All academic advising personnel must use suitable means to confront unethical behavior exhibited within the educational community.

## Part 13. ASSESSMENT and EVALUATION

The academic advising program must regularly conduct systematic qualitative and quantitative evaluations of program quality to determine the extent to which stated mission and goals are being met. Although methods of assessment may vary, the academic advising program must employ a sufficient range of measures to insure objectivity and comprehensiveness. Data collected must include responses from students and other affected constituencies. Results of these evaluations must be used in revising and improving the academic advising program and in assessing the performance of personnel.

# THE ROLE of COLLEGE ADMISSION PROGRAMS
## CAS Standards Contextual Statement

"When any scholar is able to read Tully or such like classical Latin author *ex tempore,* and make and speak true Latin in verse and prose *suo (ut aiunt) Marte,* and decline perfectly the paradigms of nouns and verbs in the Greek tongue, then may he be admitted into College, nor shall any claim admission before such qualifications." Statues of Harvard, 1646

(Goodchild & Wechsler, 1989)

This statement describes the first criteria for admission established by the founders of the first educational institution in the New World. When America's first colonial colleges were founded, their primary mission was similar to the English tradition of providing liberal education and professional study for young men of intellectual and financial ability. Admission focused on identifying and admitting young men for the ministry. However, as other colleges were subsequently founded, chartered, and funded, their missions changed to address changes in student needs, ages, religions, social class, and proximity to campus.

Against the backdrop of American higher education's 350 year history, the role of admission professionals and the process of admission today might best be understood by considering two competing forces: service to the institution and service to prospective students. In general, the job of admission professionals is to help students understand the process of transition to college, admission criteria, and the competitiveness of their credentials. These tasks are typically accomplished through personal interactions, group presentations, publications, and other recruitment and counseling strategies.

The admission professional must also have a firm understanding of the institution's mission, enrollment goals, fiscal priorities, and student and departmental needs. When performing well, the successful admission professional serves a vital role establishing good matches between students and institutions. Just as changes in demographics, finances, laws, and shifts in the competitiveness of their credentials have affected prospective college students, the role of the admission officer has also changed over time, from the functions suggested by titles such as registrar, counselor, dean and director, marketer, and recruiter to that of enrollment manager.

In general, admission professionals:
- Provide information and assistance to prospective students, families, and secondary school counselors on the academic, financial, and co-curricular offerings of their institutions
- Evaluate the academic and personal qualifications of applicants
- Develop, implement, and coordinate the institution's strategic marketing or recruitment plans
- Work with the college faculty and administration to develop, implement, and evaluate enrollment policies and goals for the institution
- Establish cooperative relationships with secondary school counselors and other relevant constituencies
- Work in concert with other campus offices to ensure that students are not only recruited but retained and eventually graduate.

The admission professional today is faced with many challenges: diverse students and student needs, high college costs, limited financial aid, and intense competition for students. They must also apply new technologies to deliver messages about the institution. The more than 3,000 postsecondary institutions in the US have admission policies ranging from "open-admission" to highly competitive and selective. Similarly, the hundreds of thousands of applicants present varying ability levels, financial concerns, personal challenges, and academic interests, and admission officers must be prepared to serve them all. Admission offices must have appropriate and adequate staff, policies, and skills in human relations to manage their important roles.

As the new century approaches, admission professionals recognize the benefits of cooperating with other student affairs professionals to enhance students' educational experiences. During the past decade, enrollment management models have been developed to bring greater sophistication to efforts to recruit, retain, educate, and graduate students. On today's campuses, models for admission offices may include such areas as admissions, recruitment or outreach, financial assistance, orientation, housing, and academic advising—all reporting to a central administrator. Enrollment management assumes the establishment of activities based on understanding of market research, student impact research, and organizational theory. Enrollment management paradigms are viewed as on-going processes that can enable college and university administrators to exert greater influence over factors that shape their enrollments. Clearly, today's admission professionals must continue to respect students and their need for quality counseling and support throughout the whole admission process, while they also address institutional expectations. The Admission Program Standards and Guidelines that follow have been designed to facilitate the admission professional's response to these increasingly complex demands.

## References, Readings and Resources

Goodchild, L. F., & Wechsler, H. W. (eds.) (1989). The Statues of Harvard, 1646. *ASHE Reader on The History of Higher Education.* pp. 89-90. Needham Heights, MA: Ginn Press.

American Association of Collegiate Registrars and Admissions Officers. (1997). *The college admission handbook.* Washington, DC: Author.

American Association of Collegiate Registrars and Admissions Officers (AACRAO), The College Entrance Examination Board (CEEB), The Educational Testing Services (ETS), and the National Association of College Admission Counselors (NACAC). (1995). *Challenges in college Admissions: A report of a survey of undergraduate admissions policies, practices, and procedures.* Washington, DC: Authors.

Fetter, J. (1995) *Questions and admissions: Reflections on 100,000 admissions decisions at Stanford.* Stanford, CA: Stanford University Press.

Hossler, E. & Litten, L. (1993). *Mapping the higher education landscape.* New York: The College Entrance Examination Board.

Loeb, J. (1992). *Academic standards in higher education.* New York: The College Entrance Examination Board.

National Association for College Admission Counseling. (1993). *Achieving diversity: Strategies for the recruitment and retention of traditionally underrepresented students.* Alexandria, VA: Author.

American Association of Collegiate Registrars and Admission Officers (AACRAO)
One Dupont Circle, NW, Suite 330, Washington, DC 20036-1171
202-293-9161; 202-872-8857 (fax); http://www.reg.uci.edu/aacrao
Publisher of the journal *College and University*

The College Board
45 Columbus Avenue, New York, NY 10023
212-713-8000; http://www.collegeboard.org
Publisher of *The College Review*

The National Association for College Admission Counseling (NACAC)
1631 Prince Street, Alexandria, Virginia 22314-2818
703-836-2222; 703-836-8015 (fax); http://www.na cac.com
Publisher of the *Journal of College Admission*

The National Association of Graduate Admissions Professionals (NAGAP)
Donald Resnick, President
Office of Graduate Admission
Hofstra University, 100 Hofstra University
Hempstead, New York 11550
516-463-6319

# ADMISSION PROGRAMS
## CAS STANDARDS and GUIDELINES

## Part 1. MISSION

The institution's admission program must develop, record, disseminate, implement and regularly review its mission and goals. Mission statements must be consistent with the mission and goals of the institution and with the standards in this document.

College and university admission programs must:

- address the abilities needs and expectations of prospective students as they move from secondary to postsecondary education, from one postsecondary institution to another, or as they return from a period of non-enrollment to formal learning;
- establish, promulgate, and implement admission criteria that accurately represent the mission, goals, and purposes of the institution, and that accommodate the abilities, needs, and interests of potential students;
- reflect the mission, goals, policies, procedures, facilities, and characteristics of the parent institution, and must be compatible with the ability of the institution to bring adequate resources to bear upon the relevant needs and aspirations of all students accepted for enrollment;
- develop and regularly review institutional goals for admission with appropriate individuals within the institution; such goals must be consistent with good admission practices and with the nature and mission of the institution.

Generally, in higher education, the terms "admission," "admission program," and "admission counselor" refer respectively to the processes, the agencies, and the institutional agents involved in the many activities that are related to the formal entry of students into postsecondary institutions. These generally include recruitment, counseling, selection, enrollment, orientation, advisement, and retention of students. In practice, institutions may establish separate agencies to provide these programs and services.

Admission programs should provide or ensure personalized counseling that is responsive to the needs and expectations of each prospective student and his or her family, with particular attention given to the transition process.

Admission criteria should also reflect a variable approach which includes the student's academic record (e.g., grade point average, test scores, class rank), personal characteristics, and extracurricular involvement.

## Part 2. PROGRAM

The formal education of students is purposeful, holistic, and consists of the curriculum and the co-curriculum.

Admission programs and services must be (a) intentional, (b) coherent, (c) based on theories and knowledge of learning and human development, (d) reflective of developmental and demographic profiles of the student population, and (e) responsive to special needs of individuals.

Admission programs must promote learning and development in students by encouraging outcomes such as intellectual growth, ability to communicate effectively, realistic self-appraisal, enhanced self-esteem, clarification of values, appropriate career choices, leadership development, physical fitness, meaningful interpersonal relations, ability to work independently and collaboratively, social responsibility, satisfying and productive lifestyles, appreciation of aesthetic and cultural diversity, and achievement of personal goals.

Admission programs must:

- provide programs and services designed to establish, meet, and maintain desired enrollment;
- promote and maintain integrity, timeliness and accuracy in program delivery;
- promote deliberate educational planning opportunities for all relevant constituencies;
- provide oral and written information for all relevant constituencies;
- promote and provide equal access to all eligible prospective students interested in and capable of pursuing an education at the institution.

Admission priorities, preferences, and objectives must be stated clearly in the formal admission policies and procedures of the institution. This statement must be easily obtainable by individuals seeking admission.

Not every student is suited for a particular postsecondary institution. Proper student-institutional matches are a major factor in the persistence of students toward graduation.

The distribution of current and complete information is an important priority for admission offices. Students and parents require comprehensive information on admission policies, requirements and procedures, as well as on institutional program offerings, selection criteria, acceptance decisions and financial aid opportunities. All admission personnel should be well informed and able to share such information in a variety of contexts in the interest of deliberate planning.

All admission professional staff members should be expected to perform the admission counseling function.

This includes the following activities and interventions:

- assistance and direction of students engaged in the admission process to encourage an appropriate match between student interests and available postsecondary opportunities;

- acquisition and dissemination of timely, accurate and relevant information regarding postsecondary opportunities, curriculum choices, and future educational plans;
- promotion and development of individual problem-solving practices by students;
- referral of students to appropriate institutional or other resources in response to particular needs;
- encouragement of students toward deliberate choices and realistic expectations regarding institutional and personal standards of performance;
- effective work with students of different levels of ability;
- acknowledgment and positive use of proper interest in the student on the part of high school counselors, faculty, administrators, and students' families;
- facilitation of proper exchange of non-restricted information among high schools, postsecondary institutions, families, students, and others involved in the admission process;
- encouragement of students to engage in effective life planning;
- provision of opportunities for a personal interview to students who are being considered for enrollment where appropriate;
- making available to prospective students information regarding financial aid opportunities and deadlines; standard financial aid forms should be available through the admission office as well as through any financial aid office;
- providing to students who are offered admission information about academic advising and counseling, and student orientation programs and activities. Any other information regarding student services which may enhance success at the institution should be provided.

The admission program may be accomplished through practices which may include but are not limited to:

- recruitment, marketing and public relations activities (e.g., high school visits, college fairs, direct mail campaigns, publications, alumni relations and assistance, dissemination of admission and financial aid information);
- admission counseling (e.g., evaluation of student credentials, selection, and notification);
- pre-enrollment counseling (e.g., academic advisement and orientation);
- establishment of institutional policies regarding advanced placement, prior college level credit, or credit for equivalent experience.

## Part 3. LEADERSHIP

**Effective and ethical leadership is essential to the success of all organizations. Institutions must appoint, position and empower leaders within the administrative structure to accomplish stated missions. Leaders at various levels must be selected on the basis of formal education and training, relevant work experience, personal attributes, and other professional credentials. Institutions must determine expectations of accountability for leaders and fairly assess their performance.**

**Leaders of admission programs and services must exercise authority over resources for which they are responsible to achieve their respective missions. Leaders must articulate a vision for their organization; set goals and objectives; prescribe and practice ethical behavior; recruit, select, supervise, and develop others in the organization; manage, plan, budget, and evaluate; communicate effectively; and marshal cooperative action from colleagues, employees, other institutional constituencies, and persons outside the organization. Leaders must address individual, organizational, or environmental conditions that inhibit goal achievement. Leaders must improve the admission programs and services continuously in response to changing needs of students and institutional priorities.**

## Part 4. ORGANIZATION and MANAGEMENT

**Admission programs and services must be structured purposefully and managed effectively to achieve stated goals. Evidence of appropriate structure must include current and accessible policies and procedures, written performance expectations for all employees' functional work flow graphics or organizational charts, and service delivery expectations. Evidence of effective management must include clear sources and channels of authority, effective communication practices, decision-making and conflict resolution procedures, responsiveness to changing conditions, accountability systems, and recognition and reward processes.**

**The admission program must provide channels within the organization for regular review of administrative policies and procedures.**

**The institution must appoint or designate a chief admission officer. This officer must be positioned in the institutional organization so that the needs of students and the operations of admission are both well-represented and advocated at the highest levels of administration.**

The specific title and lines of accountability may vary among institutions in light of particular settings and institutional needs. Selection of the chief admission officer should be based on personal characteristics as well as formal training.

The chief admission officer should be able to develop advocate, and implement a statement of the mission goals and objectives for the admission program on campus.

The chief admission officer should create an effective system to manage the programs, services, and personnel of the admission office. He or she should plan, organize, staff, lead, and regularly assess programs. The leader should also be able to coordinate the admission program with other institutional services and with institutional development activities.

The chief admission officer should attract and select qualified staff members who are capable of making informed decisions about policies, procedures, personnel, budgets, facilities and equipment. He or she should assume responsibility for program and staff development, assessment, and improvement.

Administrative policies and organization structures should be written, properly disseminated and posted, and modified when necessary.

Admission programs, policies, and procedures should minimally include:

- an organizational chart which depicts areas of accountability and reporting relationships for units and personnel as appropriate
- job descriptions that accurately reflect the duties and responsibilities for all admission program personnel;
- clearly stated criteria used in the decision making process for admission to the institution and the source of authority for the criteria employed;
- steps for appealing, evaluating, or revising policies and procedures.

# Part 5. HUMAN RESOURCES

The admission program must be staffed adequately by individuals qualified to accomplish its mission and goals. Admission programs and services must establish procedures for staff selection, training, and evaluation; set expectations for supervision, and provide appropriate professional development opportunities.

Professional admission staff members must hold an earned graduate degree in a field relevant to the position description or must possess an appropriate combination of education and experience.

Degree or credential seeking interns and others in training must be qualified by enrollment in an appropriate field of study and relevant experience. These individuals must be trained and supervised adequately by professional staff members.

Student employees and volunteers must be carefully selected, trained, supervised, and evaluated. When their knowledge and skills are not adequate for particular situations, they must refer students or others in need of assistance to qualified professional staff.

Each admission unit must have secretarial and technical staff adequate to accomplish its mission. Such staff must be technologically proficient and qualified to perform activities including reception duties, office equipment operation, records maintenance, and mail handling.

Appropriate salary levels and fringe benefits for all staff members must be commensurate with those for comparable positions within the institution, in similar institutions, and in the relevant geographic area.

Admission programs and services must intentionally employ a diverse staff to reflect the diversity of the institution's student population, to ensure the existence of readily identifiable role models for students and to enrich the campus community.

Affirmative action must occur in hiring and promotion practices to ensure diverse staffing profiles as required by institutional policies and local, state/provincial, and federal law.

Admission programs and services must have a regular system of staff selection and evaluation, and must provide continuing professional development opportunities for staff including inservice training programs, participation in professional conferences, workshops, and other continuing education activities.

The admission office must be provided with or have designated adequate and qualified professional staff to fulfill the mission of the agency and to implement all aspects of the program.

PROFESSIONAL STAFF

The chief admission officer should be an experienced and effective manager and have substantial work experience in admission-related employment.

Professional staff members should be competent to provide assistance to the prospective student and to work effectively to assist each student with his or her educational goals. This assistance may include, but should not be limited to, the following:

- ethical and objective presentation of the institution's programs and opportunities; careful and concerned analysis of each student's goals;
- establishment of a clear understanding of likely student-institution compatibility;
- responsible decision-making in the selection of an institution;
- knowledgeable guidance and counseling on all admission issues and concerns; interpretation of tasks and statistical data;
- explanation of and placing in a proper context any relevant governmental policy or practice on education.

The professional staff should be knowledgeable in the areas of marketing, financial aid, and testing, and should demonstrate knowledge and sensitivity to the needs of traditionally under-represented students and students with a special talent. Activities in these special areas of concern should contribute positively to the reputation of the institution and its position in the higher education marketplace.

Each admission staff member should be specifically trained to articulate the institution's unique and essential aspects. This training should be supplemental to formal outside training. While no specific timeline is prescribed, a minimum of two weeks' specialized training is recommended. Included in this training should be:

- a thorough tour of the campus;
- familiarization with the college catalog, all academic programs, freshman and transfer admission policies, and all service and social aspects of the institution;
- systematic orientation to relevant other facets of the institution; and
- familiarization with clerical and financial aid operations.

Institutions should provide ongoing opportunities for career-related information and professional growth to the entire admission staff. This process will promote effective admission services and encourage the continued involvement of admission personnel in the field. Numerous avenues promote professional growth. These include inservice workshops, membership and participation in professional organizations, and the development of an admission library. A library should include current scholarly literature, research findings, trade journals, and newspapers.

Continuing education is essential for all admission officers. It is important to be alert to changes within the field and to be able to integrate changes into daily practice when appropriate. Every admission officer should be:

- willing to seek out and implement new ideas;
- able to translate new ideas into practical methods for improving the overall operation of the admission function;
- willing to seek out and use new conceptual frameworks and equipment that bring information to students more clearly and effectively; and
- aware of relevant developments in the broad context of formal education and able to incorporate these developments in his or her work.

For formal training in preparation for professional admission work, suggested areas for graduate work include student services administration and higher education management. Additional course work may include computer literacy, research and statistical methods, counseling, enrollment management, legal issues relating to admission and higher education, leadership skills, transcript evaluation and public relations.

### CLERICAL AND SUPPORT STAFF

Support staff members such as administrative assistants, transcript evaluators, and office assistants, should possess the academic background, experience, personal interest, and competence necessary for effective performance of their responsibilities. Support staff should be skilled in interpersonal communications, public relations, referral techniques, and dissemination of information.

Training in procedures, policies, and good office practices should be included in the employment orientation for clerical and support staff. Such training will promote a consistent presentation of the institution and dependable performance of staff.

An annual admission staff workshop to plan and review admission programs is recommended. Topics and components of the workshop may include current issues in college admission, team development, marketing, computer operations, and financial aid issues and status.

## Part 6. FINANCIAL RESOURCES

**The admission program must have adequate funding to accomplish its mission and goals. Priorities, whether set periodically or as a result of extraordinary conditions, must be determined within the context of the stated mission, goals, and resources.**

**The admission program budget must be properly prepared, clearly detailed and defined, continually monitored and adequately funded for full program support.**

**The institution must prescribe policies governing:**

- **in-kind consideration in lieu of cash payment, reimbursement, or remuneration for approved admission related activity or participation,**
- **any necessary external contractual agreements (e.g., professional consultation fees, special mailings);**
- **travel, accommodations, and all expenditures authorized for recruitment purposes; reimbursements for out-of-pocket expenses.**

Institutions should provide support for an admission program that offers prospective students ample opportunities to:

- inquire about the entrance requirements and nature of the institution;
- inquire about and receive counseling regarding the institution's admission process; apply for admission; and, where appropriate;
- receive financial aid information and forms;
- be interviewed as applicants for admission;
- receive assistance in orientation and academic advisement.

Institutional admission offices should be able to respond in a timely manner to requests for information, literature, programs and services upon the request of prospective students.

## Part 7. FACILITIES, TECHNOLOGY, and EQUIPMENT

**The admission program and must have adequate, suitably located facilities and equipment to support its mission and goals. Facilities, technology, and equipment must be in compliance with relevant federal, state, provincial, and local requirements to provide for access, health and safety.**

Sufficient office space should be allocated for confidential interviews and counseling, processing of all relevant documents, files, and staff supervision.

Office space should be adequate and properly equipped for the secure and confidential storage of student records as appropriate.

Security measures, facilities, and equipment appropriate for handling cash or negotiable paper should be provided when necessary.

The admission office should be readily accessible to prospective students, parents and others who have need for admission services or personnel.

Special concern for providing readily accessible and nearby parking, or the availability of convenient public transportation is strongly recommended.

Campus maps and highly visible signage that will assist visitors and prospective students to locate the admission office are strongly recommended.

# Part 8. LEGAL RESPONSIBILITIES

Admission program staff members must be knowledgeable about and responsive to law and regulations that relate to their respective program or service. Sources for legal obligations and limitations include constitutional, statutory, regulatory, and case law; mandatory laws and orders emanating from federal, state, provincial and local governments; and the institution through its policies.

Staff members must use reasonable and informed practices to limit the liability exposure of the institution, its officers, employees, and agents. Staff members must be informed about institutional policies regarding personal liability and related insurance coverage options.

The institution must provide access to legal advice for admission program staff members as needed to carry out assigned responsibilities.

The institution must inform staff and students, in a timely and systematic fashion, about extraordinary or changing legal obligations and potential liabilities.

Admission counselors must be aware of the legal and ethical limits and standards relevant to their professional roles, and perform any counseling or guidance functions accordingly.

# Part 9. EQUAL OPPORTUNITY, ACCESS, and AFFIRMATIVE ACTION

Admission program staff members must ensure that services and programs are provided on a fair and equitable basis. Each program and service must be accessible. Hours of operation must be responsive to the needs of all students. Each program and service must adhere to the spirit and intent of equal opportunity laws.

Admission programs and services must not be discriminatory on the basis of age, color, disability, gender, national origin, race, religious creed, sexual orientation, and/or veteran status. Exceptions are appropriate only where provided by relevant law and institutional policy.

Consistent with their mission and goals, admission programs must take affirmative action to remedy significant imbalances in student participation and staffing patterns.

All admission publications and forms must clearly state students' rights and responsibilities in the admission process. Admission practices must be congruent with the institution's policies on Equal Opportunity, Access, and Affirmative Action. Admission publications must reflect relevant institutional policies.

# Part 10. CAMPUS and COMMUNITY RELATIONS

Admission programs and services must establish, maintain, and promote effective relations with relevant campus offices and external agencies.

Admission documents used by academic advising and counseling, orientation, housing, counseling, testing, the office of records and international student services must be accurate and handled with confidentiality.

Institutional organizational functions and constituencies linked to admission typically include financial aid, student development, student activities, athletics, student accounts, academic support, counseling, career planning and placement, the registrar, records, the faculty, the alumni, and institutional advancement. Residents of the larger community in which the institution is located may also have special interests regarding institutional admission practices.

Students with special needs should be identified and referral made to the appropriate office. Special needs may include those with learning disabilities, physical handicaps, deficiencies in certain academic skills, and those who come from educationally disadvantaged backgrounds. Financial aid and admission decisions should be made independently. However, the financial aid office should have access to appropriate information in the student's admission file. After financial aid has been allocated, the admission office should have access to information regarding the amount and characteristics of the financial aid award. Admission decisions should be based on the establishment or a match between the student's needs and the characteristics of the institution. A student's apparent ability to pay for the services of the institution should not affect the admission decision.

# Part 11. DIVERSITY

Within the context of each institution's unique mission, multi-dimensional diversity enriches the community and enhances the collegiate experience for all; therefore, admission programs and services must nurture environments where similarities and differences among people are recognized and honored.

Admission programs must promote cultural educational experiences that are characterized by open and continuous communication, that deepen understanding of one's own culture and heritage, and that respect and educate about similarities, differences and histories of cultures.

Admission programs must address the characteristics and needs of a diverse population when establishing and implementing policies and procedures.

# Part 12. ETHICS

All persons involved in the delivery of admission programs and services must adhere to the highest principles of ethical behavior. Admission programs must develop or adopt and implement statements of ethical practice addressing the issues unique to each program and service. Programs and services must publish these statements and insure their periodic review by all concerned.

Admission staff members must ensure that confidentiality is maintained with respect to all communications and records considered confidential unless exempted by law.

Information disclosed in individual counseling sessions must remain confidential, unless written permission to divulge the information is given by the student. However, all staff members must disclose to appropriate authorities information judged to be of an emergency nature, especially when the safety of the individual or others is involved. Information contained in students' educational records must not be disclosed to non-institutional third parties without appropriate consent, unless classified as "Directory" information or when the information is subpoenaed by law. Programs and services must apply a similar dedication to privacy and confidentiality to research data concerning individuals. All staff members must be aware of and comply with the provisions contained in the institution's human subjects research policy and in other relevant institutional policies addressing ethical practices.

Admission staff members must recognize and avoid personal conflict of interest or appearance thereof in their transactions with students and others. Staff members must strive to insure the fair, objective, and impartial treatment of all persons with whom they deal.

When handling institutional funds, admission staff members must ensure that such funds are managed in accordance with established and responsible accounting procedures.

Staff members must not participate in any form of harassment that demeans persons or creates an intimidating, hostile, or offensive campus environment.

Admission staff members must perform their duties within the limits of their training, expertise, and competence. When these limits are exceeded, individuals in need of further assistance must be referred to persons possessing appropriate qualifications.

Staff members must use suitable means to confront and otherwise hold accountable other staff members who exhibit unethical behavior.

Staff members must maintain the highest principles of ethical behavior in the use of technology.

All printed material including application forms, financial aid information, and promotional literature must accurately represent the institution's goals, services, programs, and policies.

As professional members of the institution's staff, admission personnel must receive compensation in the form of a fixed salary, rather than commissions or bonuses on the number of students recruited or enrolled.

Admission officers must insure timely and fair administration of policies regarding: admission decisions; proper notification; wait-listing; evaluating student competencies, credentials, and prior credits and confidentiality in keeping with federal and state laws.

Promotional publications, written communications, and presentations must:

- state entrance requirements clearly and precisely;
- include a current and accurate admission calendar;
- provide precise information on opportunities for financial aid;
- offer accurate and detailed information regarding special programs; and
- include realistic descriptions, illustrations, and photographs of the campus and community.

Development of admission criteria must be centered around the probability of academic success. When evaluating applicants, particularly those with special talents, admission officers must be guided by their best judgment and should make exception to established admission policies only after a thorough and prudent evaluation of all relevant circumstances including where appropriate, consultation with relevant other agencies.

> In some cases applicants may possess outstanding talent in drama, music, athletics, art, or other areas. These students might not meet all established criteria for academic success. However, in some cases a special talent can motivate a student to perform well in a secondary school program. Where this is possible, admission officers are encouraged to acknowledge the special talent when evaluating the applicant.

> In some cases, the applicants may possess special needs. For instance, students with learning disabilities or those from academically disadvantaged backgrounds might be admitted. Ethical practices would insist that the appropriate support services be available for these students if they are admitted.

Any comparisons made between or among institutions must be based on accurate and appropriate data. General comments of a disparaging nature about other institutions must be avoided.

# Part 13. ASSESSMENT and EVALUATION

Admission programs must regularly conduct systematic qualitative and quantitative evaluations of program quality to determine whether and to what degree the stated mission and goals are being met. Although methods of assessment vary, programs and services must employ a sufficient range of measures to insure objectivity and comprehensiveness. Data collected must include responses from students and other affected constituencies. Results of these evaluations must be used in revising and improving programs and services and in recognizing staff performance.

Each institution should require that its admission offices, programs, and staff be evaluated regularly. This evaluation should determine the effectiveness of services to students and their families, achievement of departmental and institutional goals and direction toward more efficient cost-effective operations. The periodic study of needs, interests, and expectations of prospective and current students and others served by the program may be conducted in conjunction with these evaluations. Data collected from the study should be used to determine the effectiveness of institutional admission policies and programs. Marketing and recruitment techniques used by the admission officer should be regularly reviewed.

# THE ROLE of ALCOHOL and OTHER DRUG PROGRAMS
## CAS Standards Contextual Statement

While abuse of alcohol and other drugs has historically been a major concern for institutions of higher education, only recently have programs been developed for education and prevention on campus. During the past decade, many colleges and universities have employed professional staff members to administer campus based alcohol and other drug programs. Most of these programs were initially established to respond to student needs, but increasingly are being developed to serve the entire campus, including faculty, staff and their families. Campus administrators are now recognizing that the behaviors of all community members affect the nature of the problem and that efforts at education and prevention must be addressed to the whole college community.

Major factors that helped focus attention on the problems of alcohol and other drug abuse include:

- *1981* creation of the Inter-Association Task Force on Alcohol and Other Substance Issues, a consortium of professional associations
- *1984* creation of National Collegiate Alcohol Awareness Week
- *1985* promulgation of Guidelines for Beverage Alcohol Marketing on College and University Campuses
- *1986* passage by Congress of the Drug Free School and Communities Act
- *1987* establishment by the US Department of Education of a network of higher education institutions committed to the elimination of substance abuse on their campuses
- 1990 development of Standards and Guidelines for Alcohol and Drug Programs by the Council for the Advancement of Standards in Higher Education

Alcohol and Other Drug Programs (AODP) plays an important role in challenging individual behaviors detrimental to the maintenance of civility in an increasingly complex microcosm of society, the college campus. AODP staff members serve as counselors, advisers, educational programmers, change agents, and collaborators for many campus constituencies exploring appropriate venues to discuss, formulate, and educate campus groups about program mission and philosophy; policy enforcement; intervention strategies; treatment, referral, and support groups; healthy alternative activities; resource needs; target population needs; and appropriate assessment, evaluation, and research efforts. The professional staff member who is primarily responsible for the AODP program generally serves as its campus spokesperson and must also handle public relations issues.

An effective, comprehensive campus AODP must be supported by the institution's chief administrative office and all other campus leaders. Those who voice support for these programs must view the problems as solvable and believe that confronting the problems created by alcohol and other drug abuse is a major responsibility facing educational institutions. Any effective strategy to combat these issues must emphasize the necessity for individual action, choice, and assumption of responsibility.

# References, Readings and Resources

Anderson, D. S., & Milgram, G. G. (1996). *Promising Practices: Campus Alcohol Strategies.* George Mason University, VA. (Presents 10 distinct topic areas that comprise a comprehensive campus effort comprises policies and implementation, assessment and evaluation, training, peer-based initiatives, environmental and targeted strategies, enforcement, curriculum, awareness and information, support and intervention services, and staffing and resources.).

Coombs, R. H., & Ziedonis, D. (1995). *Handbook on drug abuse prevention: A Comprehensive strategy to prevent the abuse of alcohol and other drugs.* Boston: Allyn & Bacon.

Wechsler, H., Dowdall, G., Davenport, A., & Castillo, S. (July, 1995). Correlates of college student binge drinking. *American Journal of Public Health,* 85, No. 7.

*Journal of Drug Education:* Baywood Publishing Co., Inc., P.O. Box 337, Amityville, NY 11701

# ALCOHOL and OTHER DRUG PROGRAM
## STANDARDS and GUIDELINES

## Part 1. MISSION

The alcohol and other drugs program (AODP) must develop, record, disseminate, implement and regularly review its mission and goals. Mission statements must be consistent with the mission and goals of the institution and with the standards in this document.

The goals of AODP must address institutional needs to

- develop, disseminate, interpret, and enforce campus regulations that are consistent with institutional policies and local, state/provincial, and federal law;
- promote healthy choices concerning the use of alcohol and other drugs, emphasizing the elimination of illegal use and the elimination or reduction of high-risk and harmful use;
- promote a climate in which abstention from the use of alcohol and other drugs is acceptable and promote a climate in which those who choose to drink alcohol learn to do so in a manner that minimizes risks of negative consequences to themselves or to others;
- define AODP prevention, education, intervention, and treatment policies and practices; and
- protect relevant legal rights of students.

## Part 2. PROGRAM

The formal education of students is purposeful, holistic, and consists of the curriculum and the co-curriculum.

The alcohol and other drugs program must be (a) intentional, (b) coherent, (c) based on theories and knowledge of learning and human development, (d) reflective of developmental and demographic profiles of the student population, and (e) responsive to special needs of individuals.

The AODP must promote learning and development in students by encouraging outcomes such as intellectual growth, ability to communicate effectively, realistic self-appraisal, enhanced self-esteem, clarification of values, appropriate career choices, leadership development, physical fitness, meaningful interpersonal relations, ability to work independently and collaboratively, social responsibility, satisfying and productive lifestyles, appreciation of aesthetic and cultural diversity, and achievement of personal goals.

At minimum, the AODP must include the components of (a) policy, (b) assessment, (c) information, (d) education and training, and (e) student assistance.

Policies must be developed to

- maintain consistency with federal, state/provincial, and local laws;
- promote an educational environment free from the abuse of alcohol and use of illegal drugs;
- define geographic jurisdictions and demographic characteristics of populations that are to be governed;
- define individual behavior and group activity that are prohibited both on campus property and at off-campus events controlled by the institution;
- specify the potential consequences for using or possessing different amounts and/or categories of alcohol and other drugs;
- establish protocols and procedures for the involvement of campus law enforcement and other campus entities;
- establish protocols and procedures for referring individuals with alcohol or other drug problems to appropriate sources of assistance;
- define campus guidelines on the general marketing of alcoholic beverages; and
- define appropriate guidelines for any sanctioned use of alcohol.

Institutional alcohol and other drugs programs should also be established for faculty and staff members whose behaviors often serve as models for students.

The AODP must assess systematically the following campus factors:

- attitudes, beliefs, and behaviors regarding alcohol and other drug use, abuse, and dependency; and
- consequences of alcohol or other drug use or abuse on academic, work, or social performance; property damage; health, counseling, and disciplinary caseloads; and other indicators of problems.

The AODP and other campus entities must exchange general and nonconfidential assessment results of mutual application and benefit.

The AODP should assess the norms, behaviors, and behavioral consequences of specific target groups identified as appropriate for campus programs.

The AODP must gather and disseminate information to students on alcohol and other drug problems, resources and related topics.

The AODP must develop and/or provide education and training programs for students.

Educational topics should include the legal, physiological, psychological, and social aspects and effects of alcohol and other drug use, abuse, and dependency; high-risk uses of alcohol; federal, state/provincial, local, and campus regulations; techniques and protocols for identifying and referring students with problems to appropriate campus entities; risk factors for at-risk students and groups, including adult children of alcoholics, recovering alcoholics, women, and victims of alcohol or other drug related sexual assaults; and the impact of alcohol and other drug use related to physiological and behavioral differences linked with gender.

The AODP should develop, provide, and/or advocate activities that model practical applications of prevention theories and research results, including such activities as alcohol-free tailgate events, comedy and night club events, theatrical presentations, and outdoor events.

The AODP should provide training for faculty and staff in identifying, counseling, and referring students with alcohol and other drug problems.

The AODP should use such strategies as peer education, co-sponsorships, competitions for alcohol-free programming, alcohol and other drug awareness weeks, and health fairs to broaden student participation and involvement of other members of the campus community in education and training efforts.

The AODP should advocate incorporating alcohol and other drug information within relevant courses and curricula, and expanding campus library holdings.

**The AODP must provide remedial support services for students with alcohol or drug related behavior problems.**

Student involvement in an assistance program may be voluntary, upon self-initiation or referral, or mandatory, upon referral by judicial authorities or other entities.

Student assistance services should provide opportunities for students to explore the general risks of using and abusing alcohol and other drugs; to assess, in individual sessions, their personal attitudes, behaviors, and risks in using or abusing alcohol or other drugs; and to make decisions based on their individual situations.

Student assistance services should identify and maintain contacts with campus or community entities which offer effective treatment, education, and support to students, family members, and friends. Such services may include structured education and counseling sessions for individuals and groups; community service work; self-help groups such as Alcoholics Anonymous, Narcotics Anonymous, Alanon and adult children of alcoholics support groups; and detoxification and inpatient therapy.

Student assistance services should utilize resources from the campus and community to assist students by answering questions, sharing experiences, or accompanying them to self-help groups.

## Part 3. LEADERSHIP

**Effective and ethical leadership is essential to the success of all organizations. Institutions must appoint, position and empower leaders within the administrative structure to accomplish stated missions. Leaders at**

**various levels must be selected on the basis of formal education and training, relevant work experience, personal attributes, and other professional credentials. Institutions must determine expectations of accountability for leaders and fairly assess their performance.**

**Leaders of the alcohol and other drugs program must exercise authority over resources for which they are responsible to achieve their respective missions. Leaders must articulate a vision for their organization; set goals and objectives; prescribe and practice ethical behavior; recruit, select, supervise, and develop others in the organization; manage, plan, budget, and evaluate; communicate effectively; and marshal cooperative action from colleagues, employees, other institutional constituencies, and persons outside the organization. AODP leaders must address individual, organizational, or environmental conditions that inhibit goal achievement. Leaders must improve programs and services continuously in response to changing needs of students and institutional priorities.**

## Part 4. ORGANIZATION and MANAGEMENT

**The AODP must be structured purposefully and managed effectively to achieve stated goals. Evidence of appropriate structure must include current and accessible policies and procedures, written performance expectations for all employees, functional work flow graphics or organizational charts, and service delivery expectations. Evidence of effective management must include clear sources and channels of authority, effective communication practices, decision-making and conflict resolution procedures, responsiveness to changing conditions, accountability systems, and recognition and reward processes.**

**The AODP must provide channels within the organization for regular review of administrative policies and procedures.**

**The AODP director or coordinator must be placed within the institution's organizational structures so as to be able to promote cooperative interaction with appropriate campus and community entities and to develop the support of high-level administrators.**

The scope and structure of the AODP should be defined by the size, nature, complexity, and philosophy of the institution and by the services offered.

The alcohol and other drugs program should maintain an advisory board, comprised of knowledgeable members of the campus and community, for advice and support on polices and programs.

## Part 5. HUMAN RESOURCES

**The alcohol and other drugs program must be staffed adequately by individuals qualified to accomplish its**

mission and goals. The AODP must establish procedures for staff selection, training, and evaluation; set expectations for supervision; and provide appropriate professional development opportunities.

Professional staff members must hold an earned graduate degree in a field relevant to the position description or must possess an appropriate combination of education and experience.

Degree or credential seeking interns or others in training must be qualified by enrollment in an appropriate field of study and relevant experience. These individuals must be trained and supervised adequately by professional staff members.

Student employees and volunteers must be carefully selected, trained, supervised, and evaluated. When their knowledge and skills are not adequate for particular situations, they must refer students or others in need of assistance to qualified professionals.

The AODP must have secretarial and technical staff adequate to accomplish its mission. Such staff members must be technologically proficient and qualified to perform activities including reception duties, office equipment operation, records maintenance, and mail handling.

Appropriate salary levels and fringe benefits for all staff members must be commensurate with those for comparable positions within the institution, in similar institutions, and in the relevant geographic area.

The AODP must intentionally employ a diverse staff to reflect the diversity of the institution's student population to ensure the existence of readily identifiable role models for students and to enrich the campus community.

Affirmative action must occur in hiring and promotion practices to ensure diverse staffing profiles as required by institutional policies and local, state/provincial, and federal law.

The AODP must have regular systems of staff selection and evaluation, and must provide continuing professional development opportunities for staff including in-service training programs and participation in professional conferences, workshops, and other continuing education activities.

The AODP should provide for training, including recognition and referral procedures, for faculty, professional, pre-professional, and paraprofessional staff members.

The AODP should be supervised by professional staff members who have earned a master's degree from an accredited institution in fields of study such as student services/development programs, psychology, social work, counseling, education, public health, or other appropriate health-related area,

and who have relevant training and experience. Such training and experience should include primary prevention and intervention, treatment issues and strategies, and supervised work with older adolescents and adults of all ages.

## Part 6. FINANCIAL RESOURCES

The alcohol and other drugs program must have adequate funding to accomplish its mission and goals. Priorities, whether set periodically or as a result of extraordinary conditions, must be determined within the context of the stated mission, goals, and resources.

The institution should provide sufficient funding for the AODP so that staff members may spend the majority of their time on planning, programming, providing services, and evaluation rather than on seeking new or continuing funding sources.

## Part 7. FACILITIES, TECHNOLOGY, and EQUIPMENT

The AODP must have adequate, suitably located facilities and equipment to support its mission and goals. Facilities, technology, and equipment must be in compliance with relevant federal, state/provincial, and local requirements to provide for access, health, and safety.

Facilities for the AODP should support a range of activities, including prevention, education, intervention, programming, and information.

Office space should be physically separate from campus law enforcement and judicial units.

Facilities and furnishings should accommodate securing confidential files.

The AODP should be provided facilities that include a private waiting area and a location in which students, faculty, and staff might access and read information on alcohol and other drugs.

The AODP should possess, or have access to, equipment and services such as audio-visual equipment and services, printing services, campus and community media resources, and computers.

## Part 8. LEGAL RESPONSIBILITIES

AODP staff members must be knowledgeable about and responsive to law and regulations that relate to their respective program or service. Sources for legal obligations and limitations include constitutional, statutory, regulatory, and case law; mandatory laws and orders emanating from federal, state, provincial, and local governments; and the institution through its policies.

Staff members must use reasonable and informed practices to limit the liability exposure of the institution, its officers, employees, and agents. AODP staff members must be informed about institutional policies regarding personal liability and related insurance coverage options.

The institution must provide access to legal advice for AODP staff members as needed to carry out assigned responsibilities.

The institution must inform staff and students, in a timely and systematic fashion, about extraordinary or changing legal obligations and potential liabilities.

## Part 9. EQUAL OPPORTUNITY, ACCESS, and AFFIRMATIVE ACTION

AODP staff members must ensure that services and programs are provided on a fair and equitable basis. The program must be accessible. Hours of operation must be responsive to the needs of all students. The AODP must adhere to the spirit and intent of equal opportunity laws.

The AODP must not be discriminatory on the basis of age, color, disability, gender, national origin, race, religious creed, sexual orientation, and/or veteran status. Exceptions are appropriate only where provided by relevant law and institutional policy.

Consistent with its mission and goals, the AODP program must take affirmative action to remedy significant imbalances in student participation and staffing patterns.

Personnel policies shall not discriminate on the basis of race, sex, color, religion, age, national origin, and/or disability. In hiring and promotion policies, student services professionals must take affirmative action that strives to remedy significant staffing imbalance, particularly when resulting from past discriminatory practices. The AODP must seek to identify, prevent, and/or remedy other discriminatory practices.

## Part 10. CAMPUS and COMMUNITY RELATIONS

The alcohol and other drugs program must establish, maintain, and promote effective relations with relevant campus offices and external agencies.

The AODP, in order to promote a healthy environment in which the use or abuse of alcohol and other drugs does not interfere with the learning, performance, or social aspects of college life, should maintain good relations with various campus offices and community agencies. Campus offices include, where applicable, student affairs; student health services; counseling; law enforcement, safety, and judicial offices; residential life; athletics; student and other campus media; student activities offices and student organizations; academic departments; and personnel services. Community agencies include area treatment facilities; support groups; and relevant local, state/provincial, and federal agencies and authorities.

## Part 11. DIVERSITY

Within the context of the institution's unique mission, multi-dimensional diversity enriches the community and enhances the collegiate experience for all; therefore, the AODP must nurture environments where similarities and differences among people are recognized and honored.

The AODP must promote cultural educational experiences that are characterized by open and continuous communication, that deepen understanding of one's own culture and heritage, and that respect and educate about similarities, differences, and histories of cultures.

The AODP must address the characteristics and needs of a diverse population when establishing and implementing policies and procedures.

## Part 12. ETHICS

All persons involved in the delivery of alcohol and other drugs programs and services must adhere to the highest principles of ethical behavior. The AODP must develop or adopt and implement statements of ethical practice addressing the issues unique to each program and service. The programs must publish these statements and insure their periodic review by all concerned.

AODP staff members must ensure that confidentiality is maintained with respect to all communications and records considered confidential unless exempted by law. Information disclosed in individual counseling sessions must remain confidential, unless written permission to divulge the information is given by the student. However, all staff members must disclose to appropriate authorities information judged to be of an emergency nature, especially when the safety of the individual or others is involved. Information contained in students' educational records must not be disclosed to non-institutional third parties without appropriate consent, unless classified as "Directory" information or when the information is subpoenaed by law. Programs and services must apply a similar dedication to privacy and confidentiality to research data concerning individuals. All staff members must be aware of and comply with the provisions contained in the institution's human subjects research policy and in other relevant institutional policies addressing ethical practices.

Staff members must recognize and avoid personal conflict of interest or appearance thereof in their transactions with students and others. Staff members must strive to insure the fair, objective, and impartial treatment of all persons with whom they deal.

When handling institutional funds, AODP staff members must ensure that such funds are managed in accordance with established and responsible accounting procedures.

Staff members must not participate in any form of harassment that demeans persons or creates an intimidating, hostile, or offensive campus environment.

Staff members must perform their duties within the limits of their training, expertise, and competence. When these limits are exceeded, individuals in need of further assistance must be referred to persons possessing appropriate qualifications.

Staff members must use suitable means to confront and otherwise hold accountable other staff members who exhibit unethical behavior.

Staff members must maintain the highest principles of ethical behavior in the use of technology.

## Part 13. ASSESSMENT and EVALUATION

The alcohol and other drugs program must regularly conduct systematic qualitative and quantitative evaluations of program quality to determine whether and to what degree the stated mission and goals are being met. Although methods of assessment vary, the AODP must employ a sufficient range of measures to insure objectivity and comprehensiveness. Data collected must include responses from students and other affected constituencies. Results of these evaluations must be used in revising and improving programs and services and in recognizing staff performance.

# THE ROLE of CAMPUS ACTIVITIES
## CAS Standards Contextual Statement

One of the first noted formal campus organizations established for the purpose of bringing students together (primarily for debating important issues of the day) was the Oxford Union founded in 1823. The Union's clubs also provided educational opportunities beyond the classroom, through such group activities as discussions of literature and poetry and involvement in hobbies and recreational activities. Today, numerous clubs and organizations (hundreds on some campuses) offer students opportunities to become involved in campus life. There is little debate now that the collegiate experience involves what occurs outside the classroom and that a college education includes more than what goes on in the classroom.

Campus activities is the combined efforts of clubs and organizations established for and/or by students, including, but not limited to, governance, leadership, cultural, social, diversity, recreational, artistic, political and religious activities. Many of these efforts focus on programs that serve to educate, develop, or entertain club, organization, or group members, their guests, and the campus community.

Theory of involvement contends that the amount of energy—both physical and psychological—that students expend at their institution positively affects their development during college. Students who are involved in campus life also devote considerable energy to their academic programs, spend considerable time on campus, participate actively in student organizations, and interact frequently with other students. Campus activities is one of the vehicles for involving students with the institution.

Though students' efforts are the backbone of campus activities, campus activity advisors serve as the catalysts for these efforts. They plan and implement training for student leaders and group members to assist them in attaining their goals, primarily regarding working with others; provide continuity for student clubs and organizations from year to year; educate students about institution policy, related legal matters, and fiscal responsibility; mediate conflicts between individuals and groups; encourage innovation and responsibility in program implementation; provide opportunities to practice leadership and organizational skills; integrate knowledge gained in the classroom with actual practice; and instruct about ethics, diversity, and other important and timely issues.

The role of campus activity advisors is certainly linked to the quality of a student's involvement experience and thus a student's development. The CAS Standards and Guidelines that follow offer direction for campus activity advisors to create quality campus activity programs that are engaging, developmental, and experiential.

## References, Readings and Resources

Boatman, S. (1997). Leadership programs in campus activities. *The management of campus activities.* Columbia, SC: National Association of Campus Activities Education Foundation.

Cuyjet, M. J. (1996). Program development and group advising. In S. R. Komives & D. B. Woodward, Jr. (Eds.), *Student services: A handbook for the profession* (3rd ed., pp. 397-414). San Francisco: Jossey-Bass.

Julian, F. (in press). Legal issues in campus activities. *The management of campus activities.* Columbia, SC: National Association of Campus Activities Education Foundation.

Meabon, D., Krehbiel, L., & Suddick, D. (1996). Financing campus activities. *The management of campus activities.* Columbia, SC: National Association of Campus Activities Education Foundation.

Metz, N. D. (1996). Student development in college unions and student activities. Bloomington: Association of College Unions-International.

American College Personnel Association (ACPA), Commission IV. Students, Their Activities and Their Community, One Dupont Circle, N.W., Suite 300, Washington, DC 20036-1110 (202) 835-2272.

Association of College Unions International (ACUI), One City Center, 120 W. Seventh Street, Suite 200, Bloomington, IN 47404-3925

National Association for College Activities (NACA), 13 Harbison Way, Columbia, SC 29212-3401 (803) 732-6222.

# CAMPUS ACTIVITIES
## CAS STANDARDS and GUIDELINES

## Part 1. MISSION

The campus activities program must develop, record, disseminate, implement and regularly review its mission and goals. Mission statements must be consistent with the mission and goals of the institution and with the standards in this document.

The campus activities program must complement the institution's academic programs. The purposes must enhance the overall educational experiences of students through development of, exposure to, and participation in social, cultural, multicultural, intellectual, recreational, community service, and campus governance programs.

Campus activities programs should provide environments in which students and student organizations are afforded opportunities and are offered assistance to:

- participate in co-curricular activities; participate in campus governance;
- develop leadership abilities;
- develop healthy interpersonal relationships; use leisure time productively;
- explore activities in individual and group settings for self-understanding and growth;
- learn about varied cultures and experiences, ideas and issues, art and musical forms, and styles of life;
- design and implement programs to enhance social, cultural, multi-cultural, intellectual, recreational, community service, and campus governance involvement; comprehend institutional policies and procedures and their relationship to individual and group interests and activities; and learn of and use campus facilities and other resources.

Campus activities programs should be planned and implemented collaboratively by students, professional staff, and faculty. Such programs should reflect the institution's ideals and should serve to achieve its goals. These programs especially serve to enhance the appropriate recruitment and retention of students, to strengthen campus and community relations, and to reinforce accurate images of the institution.

Campus activities programs should be comprehensive. They should reflect and promote the diversity of student interests and needs, allowing especially for the achievement by students of a sense of self-worth and pride.

## Part 2. PROGRAM

The formal education of students is purposeful, holistic, and consists of the curriculum and the co-curriculum.

The campus activities program must be (a) intentional, (b) coherent, (c) based on theories and knowledge of learning and human development, (d) reflective of developmental and demographic profiles of the student population, and (e) responsive to special needs of individuals.

Campus activities must promote learning and development in students by encouraging outcomes such as intellectual growth, ability to communicate effectively, realistic self-appraisal, enhanced self-esteem, clarification of values, appropriate career choices, leadership development, physical fitness, meaningful interpersonal relations, ability to work independently and collaboratively, social responsibility, satisfying and productive lifestyles, appreciation of aesthetic and cultural diversity, and achievement of personal goals.

Campus activities must include social, cultural, multicultural, intellectual, recreational, governance, leadership, group development, campus and community service, and entertainment programs. Effective administrative support and individual and group advising must be provided.

Campus activities programs should be based on valid indicators of student needs and interests, such as results of needs assessment surveys, research findings, professional literature, and judgments of professionals.

Campus activities programs should be of broad scope, inclusive of all educational domains for student learning and development. Representative programming includes activities that:

- reinforce classroom instruction and complement academic learning; offer instruction and experience in social skills and social interactions; provide opportunities for individual participation in group membership and leadership;
- develop citizenship through participation in campus and community affairs; foster campus and community intergroup participation in common concerns and interests;
- promote physical and psychosocial well-being; stimulate the cultural, intellectual, and social life of the campus community; promote understanding of people of varied cultures and ethnic backgrounds;
- raise an awareness about and address the needs of women, persons with disabilities and other special populations; and
- develop and disseminate activities calendars, organizational directories, student handbooks, and other materials on public events; and foster meaningful interactions between students and members of the faculty, administration, and staff.

Campus activities programs should be promoted and produced according to professional practices and protocols. They should blend into the fabric of the institution, adding richness and texture to on-going and integral functions.

Campus activities programs may evolve from student self-governing bodies which may conduct a wide variety of activities and services, including executive, judicial, legislative, business functions, and educational programs consistent with institutional values and mission.

A constituency-based advisory system should be in place for activities planning, execution, and evaluation.

Campus activities programs may involve recruiting, negotiating, and contracting with performers by students. Entertainment should reflect the values stated in the campus activities mission statement. Admission fees for activities should be maintained at levels that encourage wide-spread student attendance at events. Policies should discourage hospitality requirements allowing for the provision of alcohol for entertainers.

# Part 3. LEADERSHIP

Effective and ethical leadership is essential to the success of all organizations. Institutions must appoint, position and empower leaders within the administrative structure to accomplish stated missions. Leaders at various levels must be selected on the basis of formal education and training, relevant work experience, personal attributes, and other professional credentials. Institutions must determine expectations of accountability for leaders and fairly assess their performance.

Leaders of campus activities programs must exercise authority over resources for which they are responsible to achieve their respective missions. Leaders must articulate a vision for their organization; set goals and objectives; prescribe and practice ethical behavior; recruit, select, supervise, and develop others in the organization; manage, plan, budget, and evaluate; communicate effectively; and marshal cooperative action from colleagues, employees, other institutional constituencies, and persons outside the organization. Campus activities leaders must address individual, organizational, or environmental conditions that inhibit goal achievement. Leaders must improve campus activities programs continuously in response to changing needs of students and institutional priorities.

# Part 4. ORGANIZATION and MANAGEMENT

The campus activities program must be structured purposefully and managed effectively to achieve stated goals. Evidence of appropriate structure must include current and accessible policies and procedures, written performance expectations for all employees, functional work flow graphics or organizational charts, and service delivery expectations. Evidence of effective management must include clear sources and channels of authority, effective communication practices, decision-making and conflict resolution procedures, responsive-

ness to changing conditions, accountability systems, and recognition and reward processes.

The campus activities program must provide channels within the organization for regular review of administrative policies and procedures.

The administrative leader of campus activities programs normally is responsible to the chief student affairs officer.

# Part 5. HUMAN RESOURCES

The campus activities program must be staffed adequately by individuals qualified to accomplish its mission and goals. Programs and services must establish procedures for staff selection, training, and evaluation; set expectations for supervision, and provide appropriate professional development opportunities.

Professional staff members must hold an earned graduate degree in a field relevant to the position description or must possess an appropriate combination of education and experience.

Degree or credential seeking interns or others in training must be qualified by enrollment in an appropriate field of study and relevant experience. These individuals must be trained and supervised adequately by professional staff members.

Student employees and volunteers must be carefully selected, trained, supervised, and evaluated. When their knowledge and skills are not adequate for particular situations, they must refer students or others in need of assistance to qualified professional staff.

The campus activities program must have secretarial and technical staff adequate to accomplish its mission. Such staff must be technologically proficient and qualified to perform activities including reception duties, office equipment operation, records maintenance, and mail handling.

Appropriate salary levels and fringe benefits for all staff members must be commensurate with those for comparable positions within the institution, in similar institutions, and in the relevant geographic area.

The campus activities program must intentionally employ a diverse staff to reflect the diversity of the institution's student population, to ensure the existence of readily identifiable role models for students and to enrich the campus community.

Affirmative action must occur in hiring and promotion practices to ensure diverse staffing profiles as required by institutional policies and local, state/provincial, and federal law.

Individuals such as part-time professionals, graduate assistants, practicum and internship students, hourly wage employees, and volunteers may support full-time professional staff and assist with campus activities programs.

The campus activities program must use a system of staff selection and evaluation consistent with institutional policies and procedures, and must provide continuing staff development opportunities including opportunities for participation in in-service training programs, professional conferences, workshops, and other continuing education activities.

Depending upon the scope of campus activities programs, the activities staff may include an activities director, a program coordinator, organization and program advisors, orientation and leadership specialists, and a financial officer.

Professional staff members should be qualified by experience and formal graduate studies including at least a master's degree in college student affairs, higher education administration, or a related program. Graduate studies should include courses in the behavioral sciences, management, recreation, student affairs, student development, and research techniques. Institutions may require particular training and experience appropriate to serving distinctive campus populations and specialized campus or community needs.

The primary functions of full-time professional staff members include the administration and coordination of campus activities programs; assessment of student interests and needs; planning, implementing, and evaluating programs for students; advising student groups; and advising student self-governance organizations.

At least one professional staff member should be assigned to be responsible for campus activities programs at each institution. Qualifications of campus activities staff members include:

- ability to collaborate with faculty, administrative, staff colleagues, students and all other constituencies;
- capacity to interpret student concerns and interests to the campus community; expertise in the developmental education of students;
- skill to create and deliver programs, activities, and services to students and to student groups;
- skill for promoting student leadership; capability of serving as a role model of ethical behavior; commitment to professional and personal development; and
- knowledge of group dynamics and abilities to work effectively with groups.

Thorough training should be provided for student employees and volunteers to enable them to carry out their duties and responsibilities and to enhance their personal experiences with campus activities programs.

Appropriate training should be offered for all staff members. Training in leadership, organizational planning, ethical decision making and communication skills should be emphasized. Staff members should develop resourcefulness, empathy, openness to serving a diverse student population, and creativity.

Joint ventures in staff development should be encouraged by colleagues in allied programs such as recreational sports, residence halls programming, special programs for students of traditionally under-represented groups and international students, regardless of whether they are administratively connected with campus activities programs.

Student participation in campus activities should be encouraged. Students should be trained in leadership concepts and skills, organizational development, ethical behavior, and other skill training particular to distinctive programming requirements, such as contracting for entertainment. training should emphasize mutual sensitivity, recognizing diverse and special student or community population needs.

# Part 6. FINANCIAL RESOURCES

The campus activities program must have adequate funding to accomplish its mission and goals. Priorities, whether set periodically or as a result of extraordinary conditions, must be determined within the context of the stated mission, goals, and resources.

Funds for campus activities programs may be provided through state appropriations, institutional budgets, activities fees, user fees, membership and other specialized fees, revenues from programming or fund-raising projects, grants, and foundation resources.

Funds may be supplemented by income from ticket sales, sales of promotional items, and individual or group gifts consistent with institutional policies.

Methods for collecting and allocating fees must be clear and equitable. The authority and processes for decisions relevant to campus activities fees must be clearly established and funds be spent consistent with established priorities.

Students who have fiscal responsibility must be provided with information and training regarding institutional regulations and policies that govern accounting and handling of funds.

Adequate funding should be available for campus activities programs including social, cultural, multicultural, intellectual, recreational, and campus governance programs.

Authority for decisions relevant to campus activities fees should rest in large part with students. Because of the amounts of money generated by campus activities and because of the transience of the student population, good business practice dictates that reasonable safeguards be established to ensure responsible management of and accounting for the funds involved. Student organizations may be required to maintain their funds with the institution's business office in which an account for each group is established and where bookkeeping and auditing services are provided. When possible, it is recommended that processes be established to permit individual student organizations to keep account of their own business transactions. Within this framework, the campus activities office works collaboratively with student organizations on matters of bookkeeping and budgeting, and other matters of fiscal accountability, including contract negotiations, consistent with institutional practices.

Mandatory activities fees normally are initiated by a vote of the student body. The fees, once approved through institutional processes, may be managed and allocations distributed by representative student governing bodies or by another allocations board or committee.

Finance committees of student organizations or student governments should work collaboratively with staff members to establish campus activities fees and priorities. Students and staff members should share responsibility for budget development and implementation according to mutually established program priorities.

Specialized fees, generally applicable to college unions and residence halls governing groups and administered by their representative governing bodies, can be considered as part of the overall funding of the range of student activities available.

Professional staff should educate students about the basics of financial management.

## Part 7. FACILITIES, TECHNOLOGY, and EQUIPMENT

Campus activities programs must have adequate, suitably located facilities and equipment to support its mission and goals. Facilities, technology, and equipment must be in compliance with relevant federal, state, provincial, and local requirements to provide for access, health and safety.

Facilities should be located conveniently and designed with flexibility to serve the wide variety of functions associated with campus activities. Appropriate facilities, accessible to all clients, should be provided including student organization offices and adequately equipped public performance spaces.

Campus activities programs may occur in college unions. [See Standards and Guidelines for College Unions.] In addition to their traditional programming, social and service facilities, unions typically house campus activities programs, student organization offices, and related meeting and work and storage rooms. Campus activities functions also may take place in the residence halls, recreation centers, fraternity and sorority houses, sports facilities, and other campus locations.

Staff and student space should be designed to encourage maximum interaction among students and between staff members and students.

## Part 8. LEGAL RESPONSIBILITIES

Campus activities staff members must be knowledgeable about and responsive to law and regulations that relate to their respective responsibilities. Sources for legal obligations and limitations include constitutional, statutory, regulatory, and case law; mandatory laws and orders emanating from federal, state, provincial and local governments; and the institution through its policies.

Staff members must use reasonable and informed practices to limit the liability exposure of the institution, its officers, employees, and agents. Campus activities staff members must be informed about institutional policies regarding personal liability and related insurance coverage options.

The institution must provide access to legal advice for staff members as needed to carry out assigned responsibilities.

The institution must inform staff and students, in a timely and systematic fashion, about extraordinary or changing legal obligations and potential liabilities.

## Part 9. EQUAL OPPORTUNITY, ACCESS, and AFFIRMATIVE ACTION

Campus activities staff members must ensure that services and programs are provided on a fair and equitable basis. Each program and service must be accessible. Hours of operation must be responsive to the needs of all students.

The campus activities program must adhere to the spirit and intent of equal opportunity laws.

The campus activities program must not be discriminatory on the basis of age, color, disability, gender, national origin, race, religious creed, sexual orientation, and/or veteran status. Exceptions are appropriate only where provided by relevant law and institutional policy.

Consistent with its mission and goals, The campus activities program must take affirmative action to remedy significant imbalances in student participation and staffing patterns.

## Part 10. CAMPUS and COMMUNITY RELATIONS

The campus activities program must establish, maintain, and promote effective relations with relevant campus offices and external agencies.

Campus activities programs should encourage faculty and staff members throughout the campus community to be involved in campus activities. Faculty members must serve as valuable resources related to their academic disciplines, especially as lecturers, performers, artists, and workshop facilitators. Faculty and staff members who serve as administrative advisors may work directly with organizations in program and leadership development and should be supported by the activities staff. Faculty, staff members, and administrators external to the institution may be important resources for activities programs. Faculty and staff members, administrators, and students may serve together on advisory boards to provide leadership for important initiatives.

Campus activities programs are highly visible to persons on and off campus and may be influential in forming public opinion about the institution and creating a positive environment for both communities. Cooperation between governmental and social organizations and campus activities programs on matters of mutual community concern strengthens the institution's role in the community, expands the resources available to both communities, and provides valuable developmental opportunities for students.

Appropriate programs and resources should be accessible to all members of the campus community. This accessibility should be supported by current information about the availability of artists, entertainers, and speakers.

41

The campus activities staff works with students and student groups in the translation of institutional policies and procedures in the provision of these programs. Staff members should coordinate policy and procedure implementation with the business office, campus safety, food services, physical plant, and other related campus service departments.

# Part 11. DIVERSITY

Within the context of the institution's unique mission, multi-dimensional diversity enriches the community and enhances the collegiate experience for all; therefore, campus activities must nurture environments where similarities and differences among people are recognized and honored.

The campus activities program must promote cultural educational experiences that are characterized by open and continuous communication, that deepen understanding of one's own culture and heritage, and that respect and educate about similarities, differences and histories of cultures.

Campus activities must address the characteristics and needs of a diverse population when establishing and implementing policies and procedures.

The campus activities program must provide educational activities that sensitize all constituencies to an appreciation and understanding of cultural diversity among people. Activities programs must emphasize self-assessment and personal responsibility for improving intercultural relations.

The campus activities program must provide educational programs that help students of traditionally under-represented groups identify their unique needs, set appropriate goals, and learn how to achieve them. All students must be oriented to the culture of the institution. The program must give special attention to students from traditionally under-represented groups to ensure their best chances of success.

# Part 12. ETHICS

All persons involved in the delivery of campus activities programs and services must adhere to the highest principles of ethical behavior. The campus activities program must develop or adopt and implement statements of ethical practice addressing the issues unique to campus activities work. Campus activities must publish these statements and insure their periodic review by all concerned.

Staff members must ensure that confidentiality is maintained with respect to all communications and records considered confidential unless exempted by law.

Information disclosed in individual counseling sessions must remain confidential, unless written permission to divulge the information is given by the student. However, all staff members must disclose to appropriate authorities information judged to be of an emergency nature, especially when the safety of the individual or others is involved. Information contained in students' educational records must not be disclosed to non-institutional third parties without appropriate consent, unless classified as "Directory" information or when the information is subpoenaed by law. Programs and services must apply a similar dedication to privacy and confidentiality to research data concerning individuals.

Staff members must be aware of and comply with the provisions contained in the institution's human subjects research policy and in other relevant institutional policies addressing ethical practices.

Campus activities staff members must recognize and avoid personal conflict of interest or appearance thereof in their transactions with students and others. Staff members must strive to insure the fair, objective, and impartial treatment of all persons with whom they deal.

When handling institutional funds, all staff members must ensure that such funds are managed in accordance with established and responsible accounting procedures.

Campus activities staff members must not participate in any form of harassment that demeans persons or creates an intimidating, hostile, or offensive campus environment.

Staff members must perform their duties within the limits of their training, expertise, and competence. When these limits are exceeded, individuals in need of further assistance must be referred to persons possessing appropriate qualifications.

Staff members must use suitable means to confront and otherwise hold accountable other staff members who exhibit unethical behavior.

Staff members must maintain the highest principles of ethical behavior in the use of technology.

Campus activities programs must be administered in compliance with these standards and with applicable statements of ethical and professional conduct published by relevant professional associations.

Applicable statements may include principles and standards pertaining to:

- civil and ethical conduct;
- accuracy of information (i.e., accurate presentation of institutional goals, services, and policies to the public and the college or university community, and fair and accurate representation in publicity and promotions);
- conflict of interest;
- role conflicts;

- fiscal accountability;
- fair and equitable administration of institutional policies; effective disclosure of and respect for relevant civil and criminal law;
- student involvement in related institutional decisions;
- free and open exchange of ideas through campus activities programs; and
- fulfillment of contractual arrangements and agreements.

# Part 13. ASSESSMENT and EVALUATION

**The campus activities program must regularly conduct systematic qualitative and quantitative evaluations of program quality to determine whether and to what degree the stated mission and goals are being met. Although methods of assessment vary, programs and services must employ a sufficient range of measures to insure objectivity and comprehensiveness. Data collected must include responses from students and other affected constituencies. Results of these evaluations must be used in revising and improving campus activities programs and services and in recognizing staff performance.**

Campus activities programs should be evaluated regularly and the findings should be disseminated to appropriate campus agencies and constituencies. Evaluation procedures should yield evidence relative to student success and retention, the achievement of program goals, quality and scope of program offerings, responsiveness to expressed interests, program attendance and effectiveness, cost effectiveness, quality and appearance of facilities, equipment use and maintenance, and staff performance. Data sources should include students, staff, alumni, faculty, administrators, community members, and relevant documents and records. Instrumentation and methods should be scientifically designed and implemented. Records of program evaluations should be maintained in the office of the administrative leader of campus activities programs and should be accessible to planners of subsequent programs.

© 1997 Council for the Advancement of Standards in Higher Education (CAS)

# THE ROLE of CAREER PLANNING and PLACEMENT
## CAS Standards Contextual Statement

The first evidence of assistance in job placement dates to the early 19th century, when commercial employment agencies began to place graduates of the nation's teacher-training programs. Over 200 such agencies existed by the late 1800s. By the turn of the century, an increasing number of institutions had begun to realize their responsibility to help their graduates find jobs. When the first institutional placement services were established, faculty members took responsibility for them, on a part-time basis. Soon, many institutions began to establish programs staffed by full-time directors. By 1920, approximately 75 percent of the normal schools had placement services. As a direct result of the increasing number of college-sponsored placement services, the number of external agencies decreased.

The first professional association related to job placement for college graduates, the National Institutional Teacher Placement Association, was established in 1924. (This organization later evolved into the American Association for Employment in Education.) In 1927, a group concerned with business and industry placement established the Eastern College Personnel Association; by the 1940s, seven other regional associations had been formed.

A forerunner to a comprehensive national association, the Association of School and College Placement was formed in 1941. The organization and its emphases were broadened in 1952 and its name was changed to the College Placement Publication Association. The name was changed again in 1956 to the College Placement Council. Reflecting its increasing employer membership, the Council was renamed the National Association of Colleges and Employers (NACE) in 1995.

On-campus recruiting of college graduates reached its apex by the mid-1950s; over 65 percent of the current placement offices were established between 1947 and 1960. Currently, the majority of colleges and universities provide placement services to their graduates. The 1970s saw many institutions adding career counseling components to the placement function and "office of career planning and placement" increasingly became the nomenclature of choice.

During the past two decades, the career planning and placement functions have increasingly been integrated with other student service areas. Newly developed programs include internships, cooperative education, peer career advising, and student part-time employment. These responsibilities, along with an increased emphasis on working with faculty, promoting services to both corporate and nonprofit employers, and providing career services to alumni have lead to a much broader definition of career planning and placement's role in higher education. This trend is reflected in recent name changes. To encompass this broader view of their mission, many departments concerned with career planning and placement are now "career services," "career development," and "career center."

## References, Readings and Resources

Frauzblau, A. (1980). *Fundamentals of college placement.* Bethlehem, PA: College Placement Council, Inc.

Gysbers, N. C., & Associates (1994). *Designing careers.* San Francisco: Jossey-Bass.

Kirts, D., & Powell, C. R. (1980). *Career services today.* Bethlehem, PA: College Placement Council, Inc.

McDaniels, C., & Gysbers, N. C. (1992). *Counseling for career development.* San Francisco: Jossey-Bass.

Woellner, R. (Ed.) (1955). *The dynamics of teacher placement.* Eugene, OR: University of Oregon Press.

American College Personnel Association, Commission VI, Career Development, One Dupont Circle, Suite 300, Washington, DC 20036-1110. (202) 835-2272; Fax (202) 296-3286. http://www.acpa.nche.edu; info@acpa.nche.edu

National Association of Colleges and Employers (NACE). 62 Highland Ave., Bethlehem, PA 18107. (610) 868-1421, Ext. 16; Fax (215) 868-0208. http://jobweb.org

# CAREER PLANNING and PLACEMENT
## CAS STANDARDS and GUIDELINES

## Part 1.  MISSION

The career planning and placement program must develop, record, disseminate, implement and regularly review its mission and goals. Mission statements must be consistent with the mission and goals of the institution and with the standards in this document.

Career planning is a developmental process and must be fostered during the entire period of a student's involvement with the institution.

The primary purpose of career planning and placement must be to aid students in developing, evaluating, and effectively initiating and implementing career plans.

Career planning and placement services should help students to

* engage in self-assessment;
* obtain occupational information;
* explore the full range of employment opportunities and/or graduate study;
* present themselves effectively as candidates; and
* obtain optimal placement in employment or further professional preparation.

Career planning and placement programs should also promote a greater awareness within the entire institutional community of the world of work and the need for and nature of career development over the life span.

In addition, the staff should give special attention to special populations such as mature persons returning to the labor market and those engaging in career changes.

## Part 2. PROGRAM

The formal education of students is purposeful, holistic, and consists of the curriculum and the co-curriculum.

The overall career planning and placement services program must be (a) intentional, (b) coherent, (c) based on theories and knowledge of learning and human development, (d) reflective of developmental and demographic profiles of the student population, and (e) responsive to special needs of individuals.

Career planning and placement services must promote learning and development in students by encouraging outcomes such as intellectual growth, ability to communicate effectively, realistic self-appraisal, enhanced self-esteem, clarification of values, appropriate career choices, leadership development, physical fitness, meaningful interpersonal relations, ability to work independently and collaboratively, social responsibility, satisfying and productive lifestyles, appreciation of aesthetic and cultural diversity, and achievement of personal goals.

Career planning and placement services must offer the following programs.

1. Career counseling, which assists students at any point in time to:

* analyze interests, aptitudes, abilities, previous work experience, personal traits, and desired life style to promote awareness of the interrelationship between self-knowledge and career choice;
* obtain occupational information including, where possible, exploratory experiences such as cooperative education, internships, externships, and summer and part-time jobs;
* make reasoned, well-informed career choices that are not based on race/sex stereotypes; and
* set short range and long range goals.

Career counseling includes teaching self-assessment techniques, including analysis of the individual's needs, interests, aptitudes, abilities, educational background, traits of temperament and academic achievement. Career counseling also provides opportunity for research of career information and vocational testing and interpretation.

Staff members should

* disseminate information on the availability of career counseling through (a) official college publications and catalogs, student handbooks career planning and placement publications, brochures, bulletin board announcements, and campus media; and (b) presentations to academic classes, departments, student services, administrators academic advisors, alumni associations, community organizations, high school students and employers;
* provide career counseling through regularly scheduled appointments with individuals and with groups, and through career planning courses, outreach, and special topical programs;
* provide career counseling to students at any point in their college experience;
* encourage students to take advantage of career services as early as possible;
* help students explore occupational areas through part-time and vacation work, cooperative education internships and externships, and informational interviews with practitioners;
* refer students to other counseling and resource agencies on and off campus if assistance needed is beyond the scope of career counseling;
* make career information available through planned programs and conferences;

- maintain a career resource facility that includes information on self-assessment career planning, occupations, prospective employers, organizational structure, employer expectations, and job market conditions, demands and trends;
- provide field visits through employer and alumni contacts; and
- collect and maintain records and staff notes for future work with the student (e.g., career needs analysis, academic records, vocational inventory, test results and evaluations, academic advisor and faculty comments, staff interview notes).

**2. Placement counseling and referral, which assists the student to**

- **clarify objectives and establish goals;**
- **explore the full range of life and work possibilities including graduate and professional preparations; prepare for the job search or further study;**
- **present oneself effectively as a candidate for employment or further study; and**
- **make the transition from education to the world of work.**

Placement counseling and referral staff members should

- disseminate information on the availability and use of placement services (including fee schedules) through catalogs, handbooks, and other institutional publications; through campus media, periodic career planning and placement publications, and announcements distributed throughout the campus community; through presentations to student and faculty groups; through regular orientation programs; and through presentations to professional, employer, civic and alumni groups;
- register students who wish to use the career planning and placement services;
- collect and maintain records, credentials, and earner information on candidates;
- schedule group sessions for presentation of information on placement counseling and referral services; conduct sessions on job-seeking techniques including: application correspondence and resumes, development of interview skills use of the on-campus recruiting schedule, and mail campaigns using various employment sources as well as employer information [such procedures should include discussions of ethical obligations of students, employers, and others involved in the employment process];
- arrange individual and group sessions to help students relate to and assess (a) the labor market; (b) their personal interests, aptitudes, abilities, attitudes, and needs; (c) their educational, experiential, and personal backgrounds; and (d) their preferred life styles;
- establish short range and long range career goals and implement action plans to achieve those goals through graduate or professional preparation or immediate employment;
- collect and provide information on current and projected employment opportunities and employers, including policies, products, locations, requirements, typical career paths, and corporate financial reports [such information

should be provided through various means such as arranged presentations by employers, alumni, and other groups and use of personal contacts, letters, TV, radio, press and other media;

- offer a variety of approaches to promote candidate/ employer contacts such as campus interviews, direct referrals, correspondence campaigns, personal contact campaigns, and use of publications and reference directories;
- provide information concerning graduate and professional academic programs as well as employer-sponsored graduate and special study programs; and
- conduct follow-up studies of graduates and disseminate this information to appropriate segments of the college and employer communities.

**3. Student employment, including part-time, vacation, and experiential education programs designed to assist students obtain work experiences, financial resources, and opportunity for academic credit.**

Staff members should

- disseminate information concerning the availability and use of student part-time and vacation employment cooperative education assignments, internships, and externships;
- identify and register students obtaining information concerning their skills, abilities, qualifications, and availability in order to facilitate their employment;
- make students aware of employment sources and job seeking procedures by offering a variety of approaches to promote student/employer contacts;
- career orientation and development; and
- develop comprehensive employment opportunities.

# Part 3. LEADERSHIP

**Effective and ethical leadership is essential to the success of all organizations. Institutions must appoint, position and empower leaders within the administrative structure to accomplish stated missions. Leaders at various levels must be selected on the basis of formal education and training, relevant work experience, personal attributes, and other professional credentials. Institutions must determine expectations of accountability for leaders and fairly assess their performance.**

**Leaders of career planning and placement programs must exercise authority over resources for which they are responsible to achieve their respective missions. Leaders must articulate a vision for their organization; set goals and objectives; prescribe and practice ethical behavior; recruit, select, supervise, and develop others in the organization; manage, plan, budget, and evaluate; communicate effectively; and marshal cooperative action from colleagues, employees, other institutional constituencies, and persons outside the organization. Career planning and placement leaders must address individual, organizational, or environmental conditions that inhibit goal achievement. Leaders must improve programs and services continuously in response to changing needs of students and institutional priorities.**

# Part 4. ORGANIZATION and MANAGEMENT

The career planning and placement program must be structured purposefully and managed effectively to achieve stated goals. Evidence of appropriate structure must include current and accessible policies and procedures, written performance expectations for all employees, functional work flow graphics or organizational charts, and service delivery expectations. Evidence of effective management must include clear sources and channels of authority, effective communication practices, decision-making and conflict resolution procedures, responsiveness to changing conditions, accountability systems, and recognition and reward processes.

Career planning must provide channels within the organization for regular review of administrative policies and procedures.

> The career planning function should be integrated with placement function. Career planning and placement should be organized so as to be closely related to the academic organizational structure to increase faculty/staff awareness of the career development process and current employment trends. Career planning and placement should serve as a key point of contact between the institution and its employers.

> Career planning and placement may be provided by a separate service unit or by other institutional units such as counseling, financial aid, or academic. Staff members should collaborate in career planning and placement activities that occur in other units.

> Responsibility for part-time and vacation placement and for experiential education (e.g., cooperative education internships and externships) should be included within the career planning and placement framework.

# Part 5. HUMAN RESOURCES

The career planning and placement program must be staffed adequately by individuals qualified to accomplish its mission and goals. Career planning must establish procedures for staff selection, training, and evaluation; set expectations for supervision; and provide appropriate professional development opportunities.

Professional career planning staff members must hold an earned graduate degree in a field relevant to the position description or must possess an appropriate combination of education and experience.

Degree or credential seeking interns or others in training must be qualified by enrollment in an appropriate field of study and relevant experience. These individuals must be trained and supervised adequately by professional staff members.

Student employees and volunteers must be carefully selected, trained, supervised, and evaluated. When their knowledge and skills are not adequate for particular situations, they must refer students or others in need of assistance to qualified professionals.

The career planning and placement program must have secretarial and technical staff adequate to accomplish its mission. Such staff must be technologically proficient and qualified to perform activities including reception duties, office equipment operation, records maintenance, and mail handling.

Appropriate salary levels and fringe benefits for all staff members must be commensurate with those for comparable positions within the institution, in similar institutions, and in the relevant geographic area.

Career planning must intentionally employ a diverse staff to reflect the diversity of the institution's student population to ensure the existence of readily identifiable role models for students and to enrich the campus community.

Affirmative action must occur in hiring and promotion practices to ensure diverse staffing profiles as required by institutional policies and local, state/provincial, and federal law.

Career planning services must have a regular system of staff selection and evaluation, and must provide continuing professional development opportunities for staff including inservice training and participation in professional conferences, workshops, and other continuing education activities.

Professional staff members must be skilled in career planning, placement, and counseling and must have the ability to function effectively with students, faculty, administrators, and employers.

> To ensure quality service to students, those providing career counseling should also attend to placement counseling and referral concerns.

> Appropriate graduate fields of study for staff members include, but are not limited to behavioral management science, counseling psychology, education, educational administration, guidance and counseling, industrial relations, personnel management, college student affairs administration, and college student personnel.

> Preparation in counseling techniques and methods of counseling also are necessary. Especially relevant to career planning and placement are courses such as career development theory, counseling theory and techniques, counseling internships and practica, interpretation of vocational tests and inventories, interviewing techniques, occupational information, occupational research and manpower employment trends, placement office operations, principles of administration and decision-making, theory and practice of organizational and fiscal management, socioeconomic ethnic, and legal implications, and group dynamics.

> Prior work experience may be of considerable value to the career counseling function.

A continuing program of professional self-development should be maintained by staff members to keep abreast of conditions and developments that affect the field. Such self-development includes participation in professional organizations, inservice training, and other professional development activities.

A well-organized and effectively administered program should have professional leaders who

- participate in making decisions about career planning and placement objectives and policies;
- prepare and control annual budgets;
- develop position descriptions and recruit staff members;
- plan and implement programs for staff development;
- establish effective procedures for carrying out policies and programs;
- maintain good public relations;
- assign and supervise the functions and responsibilities of staff members; and
- conduct staff meetings regularly.

The size of the clerical staff should be sufficient to perform the tasks of reception, secretarial, appointment and scheduling, maintenance and mailing of credentials and other files, maintenance of career information literature and facilities, compilation of statistics, preparation and mailing of publications, intermediate management and supervision, and other tasks required by the programs.

Staff aides, graduate assistants, research aides, and interns may be employed to provide career information, conduct research, or carry out other technical tasks. Similarly, graduate student interns may be employed to counsel students when professional supervision is available.

# Part 6. FINANCIAL RESOURCES

The career planning and placement program must have adequate funding to accomplish its mission and goals. Priorities, whether set periodically or as a result of extraordinary conditions, must be determined within the context of the stated mission, goals, and resources.

Funds should be provided for purchasing and maintaining career/employment information and for the preparation and maintenance of student placement credentials.

# Part 7. FACILITIES, TECHNOLOGY, and EQUIPMENT

The career planning program must have adequate, suitably located facilities and equipment to support its mission and goals. Facilities, technology, and equipment must be in compliance with relevant federal, state/provincial, and local requirements to provide for access, health, and safety.

It is recommended that space be provided for a reception area, staff offices, a private office for the unit head, private interview and counseling rooms, an employer lounge, a student registration and sign-up area, a career resource center, office equipment, bulletin boards, work and storage areas, secure record files, and rooms for group meetings and conferences.

Program space should be available that provides

- counseling rooms equal in number to the professional staff members who will be counseling students at any one time;
- enough individual interview rooms to meet the demand of employers for interviews;
- space for both recruiters and counselors that offer privacy, adequate ventilation and lighting, soundproofing, and power sources for audiovisual aids;
- adequate and convenient parking for visiting employers and graduate school representatives.

# Part 8. LEGAL RESPONSIBILITIES

Career planning and placement staff members must be knowledgeable about and responsive to law and regulations that relate to their respective program or service. Sources for legal obligations and limitations include constitutional, statutory, regulatory, and case law; mandatory laws and orders emanating from federal, state, provincial and local governments; and the institution through its policies.

Staff members must use reasonable and informed practices to limit the liability exposure of the institution, its officers, employees, and agents. Career planning staff members must be informed about institutional policies regarding personal liability and related insurance coverage options.

The institution must provide access to legal advice for staff members as needed to carry out assigned responsibilities.

The institution must inform staff and students, in a timely and systematic fashion, about extraordinary or changing legal obligations and potential liabilities.

# Part 9. EQUAL OPPORTUNITY, ACCESS, and AFFIRMATIVE ACTION

Career planning and placement staff members must ensure that services and programs are provided on a fair and equitable basis. Career programs and services must be accessible. Hours of operation must be responsive to the needs of all students. The career planning program must adhere to the spirit and intent of equal opportunity laws.

Career programs must not be discriminatory on the basis of age, color, disability, gender, national origin, race, religious creed, sexual orientation, and/or veteran status. Exceptions are appropriate only where provided by relevant law and institutional policy.

Consistent with its mission and goals, career planning and placement must take affirmative action to remedy significant imbalances in student participation and staffing patterns.

## Part 10. CAMPUS and COMMUNITY RELATIONS

Career planning and placement programs must establish, maintain, and promote effective relations with relevant campus offices and external agencies.

The career planning and placement service must

- develop job opportunities on a continuing basis from a variety of employers;
- provide all employers the opportunity to consider candidates for employment;
- maximize students' exposure to employers through a variety of programs;
- collect information on occupational trends and employer needs;
- encourage dialogue among employers, faculty, and administration concerning job needs and trends; and
- encourage employers to recognize career planning and placement services through public acknowledgment and other avenues of support.

The career planning and placement service should

- provide pertinent information to prospective employers including curricula, academic calendar, estimate of enrollment by degree and discipline, and recruiting and interviewing logistics;
- exchange information with employers concerning their respective operations through activities such as on-site visits and exchange programs;
- assist employers in setting and confirming interviewing dates well in advance;
- exchange with employer representatives detailed information concerning interview schedules, job descriptions, desired applicant qualifications, and other arrangements as needed;
- arrange for employer representatives to meet with faculty and administrative staff members in order to exchange information pertinent to the career planning and placement of graduates;
- schedule candidates for on-campus recruitment interviews;
- encourage employer compliance with ethical and legal obligations of the equal employment opportunity laws;
- encourage employer participation in programs such as career courses, conferences, and alumni career fairs;
- encourage employers to list staff needs on a continuing basis and to provide information concerning job offers, hires, and compensation; and
- encourage employer participation in off-campus activities relating to career counseling, placement, and employment including involvement in professional associations.

The career planning and placement service must

- develop a working relationship that encourages the academic administration and faculty to maximize and give active support to an effective program for students and graduates;
- promote better understanding between the institution and employers about the relationship of curricular and other activities to the career needs of and opportunities for students; and
- promote a systematic flow of information to faculty members and students from alumni concerning their academic preparation, and employment experiences.

The career planning and placement service should

- define the roles that academic administrators and faculty members can play in career planning and placement programs and discuss these roles at every appropriate opportunity;
- participate fully in such campus activities as faculty organizations and committees, general student orientation programs, classroom presentations, academic courses in career planning, and student club career programs;
- exchange with the academic administration and faculty information concerning work-force needs, labor market trends, specific jobs, and placements that may be related to academic planning and curriculum development:
- arrange appropriate programs that utilize alumni experience and expertise such as on-campus visits and participation in career planning seminars;
- prepare and disseminate annual and special reports including career planning and placement philosophy, goals and objectives, current programs, statistical and interpretive information, and graduate follow-up information; and
- create cooperative relationships including mutual referral for services, exchange of information, sharing of equipment and space, and other coordination with campus student services and administrative programs.

## Part 11. DIVERSITY

Within the context of each institution's unique mission, multi-dimensional diversity enriches the community and enhances the collegiate experience for all; therefore, career planning and placement must nurture environments where similarities and differences among people are recognized and honored.

Career planning must promote cultural educational experiences that are characterized by open and continuous communication, that deepen understanding of one's own culture and heritage, and that respect and educate about similarities, differences, and histories of cultures.

Career planning must address the characteristics and needs of a diverse population when establishing and implementing policies and procedures.

## Part 12. ETHICS

All persons involved in the delivery of career planning and placement must adhere to the highest principles of ethical behavior. Career planning and placement must develop or adopt and implement statements of ethical practice addressing the issues unique to each program and service. The career planning and placement program must publish these statements and insure their periodic review by all concerned.

Staff members must ensure that confidentiality is maintained with respect to all communications and records considered confidential unless exempted by law.

Information disclosed in individual counseling sessions must remain confidential, unless written permission to divulge the information is given by the student. However, all staff members must disclose to appropriate authorities information judged to be of an emergency nature, especially when the safety of the individual or others is involved. Information contained in students' educational records must not be disclosed to non-institutional third parties without appropriate consent, unless classified as "Directory" information or when the information is subpoenaed by law. Programs and services must apply a similar dedication for privacy and confidentiality to research data concerning individuals. Staff members must be aware of and comply with the provisions contained in the institution's human subjects research policy and in other relevant institutional policies addressing ethical practices.

Staff members must recognize and avoid personal conflict of interest or the appearance thereof in transactions with students and others. Staff members must strive to insure the fair, objective, and impartial treatment of all persons with whom they deal.

When handling institutional funds, career planning and placement staff members must ensure that such funds are managed in accordance with established and responsible accounting procedures.

Staff members must not participate in any form of harassment that demeans persons or creates an intimidating, hostile, or offensive campus environment.

Staff members must perform their duties within the limits of their training, expertise, and competence. When these limits are exceeded, individuals in need of further assistance must be referred to persons possessing appropriate qualifications.

Staff members must use suitable means to confront and otherwise hold accountable other staff members who exhibit unethical behavior.

Career planning staff members must maintain the highest principles of ethical behavior in the use of technology.

Referral of an employed graduate to another employer must be preceded by that person's request for referral.

Career planning and placement office personnel must use their best efforts to ensure that the student's selection of a career or a graduate school is protected from improper influence by faculty, administrators, placement staff, and employers.

Conditions of employment and salary offers made to an individual by an employer must not be divulged in a personally identifiable form by career planning and placement office staff members.

Unless permission is given by the student, information disclosed in individual counseling sessions as well as information contained in records must remain confidential.

## Part 13. ASSESSMENT and EVALUATION

The career planning and placement program must regularly conduct systematic qualitative and quantitative evaluations of program quality to determine whether and to what degree the stated mission and goals are being met. Although methods of assessment vary, career planning and placement must employ a sufficient range of measures to insure objectivity and comprehensiveness. Data collected must include responses from students and other affected constituencies. Results of these evaluations must be used in revising and improving career planning and placement programs and services and in recognizing staff performance.

# THE ROLE of COLLEGE UNIONS
## CAS Standards Contextual Statement

Today's college union is the campus community center, serving students, faculty, administration, staff, alumni, and guests. It is a unifying force that brings together diverse people, provides a forum for divergent viewpoints, and creates an environment where all feel welcome.

The college union—which may refer to an organization, a program, or a building—evolved from the debating tradition of British universities. The earliest college union, founded at Cambridge University in 1815, was literally a "union" of three debating societies. The first US college union was organized at Harvard in 1832; like its British predecessors, it existed primarily for debating purposes. By the late 1800s, the Harvard Union had embraced the concept of being a general club. The first building erected explicitly for union purposes was Houston Hall at the University of Pennsylvania. Built in 1896, it housed lounges, dining rooms, reading and writing rooms, an auditorium, game rooms, and student offices; it was given to the university by the Houston family as a "place where all may meet on common ground."

In the 1930s, the success of civic recreational and cultural centers influenced college union leaders to view the union as the campus counterpart of the "community center," with an educational and recreational mission to perform. The most extensive period of union building construction took place following World War II, as enrollments surged and colleges and universities sought to better fulfill the needs of students and faculty.

In the last half of this century, the college union movement has concentrated on building community, emphasizing its educational mission, and promoting student development and leadership.

The college union provides numerous educationally purposeful activities outside the classroom, which are "key to enhancing learning and personal development," according to ACPA's "The Student Learning Imperative" preamble. "The Role of the College Union" states that it is "an integral part of the educational mission of the college." The union contributes to the education of the student body at large through its cultural, educational, social, and recreational programs and by encouraging "self-directed activity, giving maximum opportunity for self-realization." But the union also educates the students involved in its governance and program boards and those it employs. The role statement defines the union as "a student centered organization that values participatory decision making. Through volunteerism, its boards, committees, and student employment, the union offers firsthand experience in citizenship and educates students in leadership, social responsibility, and values." These models of college union governance foster student/staff partnerships that form the foundation for student development and leadership training.

## References, Readings and Resources

McMillan, A., & Davis, N. T. (Eds.). (1989). *College unions: Seventy-five years.* Bloomington, IN: Association of College Unions International.

Butts, P. F. (1971). *The college union idea.* Bloomington, IN: Association of College Unions International.

Metz, N. D. (Ed.) (1996). *Student development in college unions and student activities.* Bloomington, IN: Association of College Unions International.

*The Bulletin,* the official ACUI publication, published bimonthly and available from the ACUI Central Office.

American College Personnel Association (ACPA), Commission IV. Students, Their Activities and Their Community. One Dupont Circle, N.W., Suite 300, Washington, DC 20036-1110. (202) 835-2272.

Association of College Unions International (ACUI) Central Office, One City Centre, Suite 200, 120 W. Seventh St., Bloomington, IN 47404-3925. (812) 855-8550.

National Association for College Activities (NACA), 13 Harbison Way, Columbia, SC 29212-3401. (803) 732-6222.

# COLLEGE UNIONS
## CAS STANDARDS and GUIDELINES

## Part 1.  MISSION

The College Union must develop, record, disseminate, implement and regularly review its mission and goals. Mission statements must be consistent with the mission and goals of the institution and with the standards in this document.

The primary goals of the college union must be to maintain facilities, provide services, and promote programs that are responsive to student developmental needs and to the physical, social, recreational, and continuing education needs of the campus community.

The college union is a center for the campus community and, as such, is an integral part of the institution's educational environment. The union represents a building, an organization, and a program; it provides services, facilities, and educational and recreational programs that enhance the quality of college life.

Through the work of its staff and various committees the college union can be a "laboratory" where students can learn and practice leadership, programming, management, social responsibility, and interpersonal skills. As a center for the academic community, the union provides a place for increased interaction and understanding among individuals from diverse backgrounds.

To meet its goals, college unions should provide:
- food services;
- leisure time and recreational opportunities;
- social, cultural, and intellectual programs;
- continuing education opportunities;
- retail stores;
- service agencies that are responsive to campus needs;
- student leadership development programs and opportunities;
- student employment; and
- student development programs.

## Part 2. PROGRAM

The formal education of students is purposeful, holistic, and consists of the curriculum and the co-curriculum.

College union programs and services must be (a) intentional, (b) coherent, (c) based on theories and knowledge of learning and human development, (d) reflective of developmental and demographic profiles of the student population, and (e) responsive to special needs of individuals.

The college union must promote learning and development in students by encouraging outcomes such as intellectual growth, ability to communicate effectively, realistic self-appraisal, enhanced self-esteem, clarification of values, appropriate career choices, leadership development, physical fitness, meaningful interpersonal relations, ability to work independently and collaboratively, social responsibility, satisfying and productive lifestyles, appreciation of aesthetic and cultural diversity, and achievement of personal goals.

The union's activities and services must be appropriate to the size and diversity of the campus and must provide opportunities for student, staff, and faculty participation, interaction, and collaboration on policy establishment, facility operation, and program activities. The college union program must strive to enhance intellectual and behavioral learning.

The program of college unions includes services, facilities and activity events. The college union should provide, in varying degrees, food services, meeting rooms student and administrative offices an information-reception center, lounge(s), a merchandise counter or store, a lobby, public telephones, recreation facilities, and rest rooms.

Additional services and facilities provided by most unions include music listening rooms, table game rooms, space for exhibits, parking facilities, and conference rooms.

The union should include a balanced variety of activities, such as art, performing arts, music, cinematic arts, games and tournaments, outdoor recreation, lecture and literary events, crafts and hobbies, social and dance events, and activities addressing social responsibility and human relations. Program events should be diverse reflecting the richness of the community's cultures.

## Part 3. LEADERSHIP

Effective and ethical leadership is essential to the success of all organizations. Institutions must appoint, position and empower leaders within the administrative structure to accomplish stated missions. Leaders at various levels must be selected on the basis of formal education and training, relevant work experience, personal attributes, and other professional credentials. Institutions must determine expectations of accountability for leaders and fairly assess their performance.

Leaders of the college union must exercise authority over resources for which they are responsible to achieve their respective missions. Leaders must articulate a vision for their organization; set goals and objectives; prescribe and practice ethical behavior; recruit, select, supervise, and develop others in the organization; manage, plan, budget, and evaluate; communicate effectively; and marshal cooperative action from colleagues, employees, other institutional constituencies, and persons outside the organization. College union leaders must address individual, organizational, or environmental conditions that inhibit goal achievement. Leaders must improve programs and services continuously in response to changing needs of students and institutional priorities.

## Part 4. ORGANIZATION and MANAGEMENT

The college union must be structured purposefully and managed effectively to achieve stated goals. Evidence of appropriate structure must include current and accessible policies and procedures, written performance expectations for all employees, functional work flow graphics or organizational charts, and service delivery expectations. Evidence of effective management must include clear sources and channels of authority, effective communication practices, decision-making and conflict resolution procedures, responsiveness to changing conditions, accountability systems, and recognition and reward processes.

The college union must provide channels within the organization for regular review of administrative policies and procedures.

The union must be organized to maintain its physical plant, to provide for cultural, intellectual, and recreational programming, to operate its business enterprises, and to deliver successfully the services inherent in the union's mission.

A variety of facilities, programs, and services may be incorporated within the building and operation. These include: food service; store and other revenue producing services; leisure time activities; social, cultural, and intellectual activities; building operations; and continuing education.

The college union must involve members of the campus community in its governance and programming structure and in the formulation of necessary union policies.

Operations involve day-to-day undertakings such as fiscal controls, maintenance of physical plant and equipment, provision of services supervision of personnel, planning, and public relations.

Involvement of the campus community should include students, faculty, staff, and alumni, as appropriate. Typically such involvement is through advisory, governing, and program boards. These boards might address issues such as (a) facility operating policies related to the use and/or rental of the union by campus and noncampus groups, (b) scheduling of controversial speakers and/or events, (c) budget planning and allocation of funds (d) employment policies, (e) space allocation priority setting, and (f) hours of operation.

## Part 5. HUMAN RESOURCES

The college union must be staffed adequately by individuals qualified to accomplish its mission and goals. The union must establish procedures for staff selection, training, and evaluation; set expectations for supervision, and provide appropriate professional development opportunities.

Professional staff members must hold an earned graduate degree in a field relevant to the position description or must possess an appropriate combination of education and experience.

Degree or credential seeking interns or others in training must be qualified by enrollment in an appropriate field of study and relevant experience. These individuals must be trained and supervised adequately by professional staff members.

Student employees and volunteers must be carefully selected, trained, supervised, and evaluated. When their knowledge and skills are not adequate for particular situations, they must refer students or others in need of assistance to qualified professional staff.

The college union must have secretarial and technical staff adequate to accomplish its mission. Such staff must be technologically proficient and qualified to perform activities including reception duties, office equipment operation, records maintenance, and mail handling.

Appropriate salary levels and fringe benefits for all staff members must be commensurate with those for comparable positions within the institution, in similar institutions, and in the relevant geographic area.

The college union must intentionally employ a diverse staff to reflect the diversity of the institution's student population to ensure the existence of readily identifiable role models for students and to enrich the campus community.

Affirmative action must occur in hiring and promotion practices to ensure diverse staffing profiles as required by institutional policies and local, state/provincial, and federal law.

The college union must employ qualified professional, technical, and support staff members who have the ability to meet the varied educational, service, social, leisure, and recreational requirements inherent in the union's mission.

Staff should include persons providing the necessary professional leadership to assume responsibility for the entire union as well as for specific programs.

Desirable qualities of staff members should include: (a) knowledge of and ability to use, management principles, including the effective management of volunteers; (b) skills in assessment, planning, training, and evaluation; (c) interpersonal skills; (d) technical skills; (e) understanding of union philosophy; (f) commitment to institutional mission; and (g) understanding of, and the ability to apply student development theory.

Graduate degrees should be earned in fields relevant to college unions including, but not limited to, student development business administration, higher education administration, and recreation leadership.

Specific aspects of the union's mission for which staff should be assigned include business operations (e.g., operations, program activities, cultural, recreational, theater, and arts and crafts), and special events.

There should be adequate technical and clerical personnel to provide the services and maintain the facilities of the union. Included may be cooks, dishwashers, projectionists, stage hands, maintenance personnel, secretaries bookkeepers, typists, attendants, receptionists, housekeepers, scheduling clerks, sales clerks, and cashiers.

Student employees and volunteers may be an important part of the union's operation. Their work experience can be an important part of their educational experience as well as a source of income. A thorough training program should be provided for part-time student helpers and volunteers and, depending on their assigned duties, might include leadership training, group facilitation skills, and communication skills. Volunteers should be adequately supervised and evaluated.

Graduate students pursuing advanced degrees in student development, business administration, higher education institutional management, and recreation are among those to whom an internship or practicum in the college union can be valuable. Such experiences should provide a variety of opportunities within the union operation. Graduate assistantships also may allow persons pursuing careers in specific areas of the union field to expand their expertise. Graduate students frequently serve as program advisors or assist operations, recreation or other department supervisors while pursuing advanced degrees. Others such as paraprofessional staff and volunteers, may fulfill specific needs. The union should utilize volunteers in a manner consistent with its mission.

# Part 6. FINANCIAL RESOURCES

The college union must have adequate funding to accomplish its mission and goals. Priorities, whether set periodically or as a result of extraordinary conditions, must be determined within the context of the stated mission, goals, and resources.

The institution's budget commitment to the union should be sufficient to support the achievement of its mission and to provide appropriate services, facilities, and programs deemed necessary to maintain standards and diversity of services commensurate with the image and reputation of the institution.

The union should have adequate financial resources to ensure reasonable pricing of services, adequate programming, adequate staffing, proper maintenance and professional development.

The institution should consider various methods and sources of financial support including, but not limited to: (a) income from sales, services, and rentals; (b) student activities or program fees; (c) fees for operation or debt service; and (d) direct institutional support (e.g., utilities subsidy, salary assistance, cleaning and maintenance, operating subsidy, and membership fees).

# Part 7. FACILITIES, TECHNOLOGY, and EQUIPMENT

The college union must have adequate, suitably located facilities technology, and equipment to support its mission and goals. Facilities, technology, and equipment must be in compliance with relevant federal, state/provincial, and local requirements to provide for access, health, and safety.

The physical plant should be proportional in size to the campus population. Generally a college union should contain approximately 10 square feet of gross space for each student enrolled. Smaller colleges may require more square feet per student; large colleges may require less. Also to be considered is the nature of the student body. Colleges with a large number of commuter and/or part time students or members of a special population might adjust facility requirements accordingly.

# Part 8. LEGAL RESPONSIBILITIES

College union staff members must be knowledgeable about and responsive to law and regulations that relate to their respective program or service. Sources for legal obligations and limitations include constitutional, statutory, regulatory, and case law; mandatory laws and orders emanating from federal, state, provincial and local governments; and the institution through its policies.

Staff members must use reasonable and informed practices to limit the liability exposure of the institution, its officers, employees, and agents. Staff members must be informed about institutional policies regarding personal liability and related insurance coverage options.

The institution must provide access to legal advice for union staff members as needed to carry out assigned responsibilities.

The institution must inform staff and students, in a timely and systematic fashion, about extraordinary or changing legal obligations and potential liabilities.

# Part 9. EQUAL OPPORTUNITY, ACCESS, and AFFIRMATIVE ACTION

College union staff members must ensure that services and programs are provided on a fair and equitable basis. The college union must be accessible. Hours of operation must be responsive to the needs of all students. The union must adhere to the spirit and intent of equal opportunity laws.

The college union must not be discriminatory on the basis of age, color, disability, gender, national origin, race, religious creed, sexual orientation, and/or veteran status. Exceptions are appropriate only where provided by relevant law and institutional policy.

Consistent with its mission and goals, the college union must take affirmative action to remedy significant imbalances in student participation and staffing patterns.

# Part 10. CAMPUS and COMMUNITY RELATIONS

The college union must establish, maintain, and promote effective relations with relevant campus offices and external agencies.

The success of the college union is dependent on the maintenance of good relationships with students, faculty, administrators, alumni, the community at large, contractors, and support agencies. Staff members must encourage participation in union programs by relevant groups.

Each member of the campus community is a potential patron of the union's services, a potential member of the union organization, including its governing board, and a potential participant in the union's programming.

Students are the principle constituency of the union. Much of the vitality, variety, and spontaneity of the union's activities stem from student boards and committees.

Student government and other groups should have ongoing involvement with the union's programs, services, and operations.

Student publications also may be important for communicating information about union programs. Communications with students should be continuous.

The involvement of faculty, staff, and alumni is essential to the vitality of union programs and services.

Faculty members should be involved in policy-making processes and program efforts of the union.

Alumni are potential sources of support and involvement financial and otherwise.

The administrative staff of the institution is important to day-to-day operations of the union. In some instances important union services such as food, cleaning, repairs, bookstore, or accounting may be administered by a department of the college rather than by union staff; relations with those department heads and their representatives must be cultivated carefully. The support of other student affairs agencies as well as chief campus officials is important.

Technical and clerical staff members can be important as customers, members of the various committees, and members of the governing board.

Positive relations with lessees and contractors, (e.g., barbershops, boutiques, food services, bookstores) require close and continuing attention.

# Part 11. DIVERSITY

Within the context of each institution's unique mission, multi-dimensional diversity enriches the community and enhances the collegiate experience for all; therefore, the college union must nurture environments where similarities and differences among people are recognized and honored.

The student union must promote cultural educational experiences that are characterized by open and continuous communication, that deepen understanding of one's own culture and heritage, and that respect and educate about similarities, differences and histories of cultures.

The college union must address the characteristics and needs of a diverse population when establishing and implementing policies and procedures.

# Part 12. ETHICS

All persons involved in the delivery of union programs and services must adhere to the highest principles of ethical behavior. The college union must develop or adopt and implement statements of ethical practice addressing the issues unique to its programs and services. The union must publish these statements and insure their periodic review by all concerned.

Staff members must ensure that confidentiality is maintained with respect to all communications and records considered confidential unless exempted by law.

Information disclosed in individual counseling sessions must remain confidential, unless written permission to divulge the information is given by the student. However, all staff members must disclose to appropriate authorities information judged to be of an emergency nature, especially when the safety of the individual or others is involved. Information contained in students' educational records must not be disclosed to non-institutional third parties without appropriate consent, unless classified as "Directory" information or when the information is subpoenaed by law. Programs and services must apply a similar dedication to privacy and confidentiality to research data concerning individuals. All staff members must be aware of and comply with the provisions contained in the institution's human subjects research policy and in other relevant institutional policies addressing ethical practices.

Staff members must recognize and avoid personal conflict of interest or appearance thereof in their transactions with students and others. Staff members must strive to insure the fair, objective, and impartial treatment of all persons with whom they deal.

When handling institutional funds, all staff members must ensure that such funds are managed in accordance with established and responsible accounting procedures.

Union staff members must not participate in any form of harassment that demeans persons or creates an intimidating, hostile, or offensive campus environment.

Staff members must perform their duties within the limits of their training, expertise, and competence. When these limits are exceeded, individuals in need of further assistance must be referred to persons possessing appropriate qualifications.

Staff members must use suitable means to confront and otherwise hold accountable other staff members who exhibit unethical behavior.

Union staff members must maintain the highest principles of ethical behavior in the use of technology.

# Part 13. ASSESSMENT and EVALUATION

The college union must regularly conduct systematic qualitative and quantitative evaluations of program quality to determine whether and to what degree the stated mission and goals are being met. Although methods of assessment vary, the union must employ a sufficient range of measures to insure objectivity and comprehensiveness. Data collected must include responses from students and other affected constituencies. Results of these evaluations must be used in revising and improving programs and services and in recognizing staff performance.

Evaluation of union facilities, staff, programs, services, and governance must be continuous and must be within the context of the union's mission.

Evaluation may include goal-related progress on such considerations as attendance at programs, cash flow, appearance of facilities, and vitality of volunteer groups.

Periodic reports, statistically valid research, and outside reviews should be utilized.

© Copyright 1997 Council for the Advancement of Standards in Higher Education

# THE ROLE of COMMUTER PROGRAMS and SERVICES
## CAS Standards Contextual Statement

Commuter students, defined as those who do not live in institution-owned housing on campus, accounted for over 87 percent of college enrollments in the US in the fall of 1996. Commuter students attend virtually every institution of higher education. Their numbers include full-time students who live at home with their parents and fully employed adults who live with their own families and attend college part time. Commuters may live near the campus or far away; they may commute by car, public transportation, walking, or bicycle. They may represent a small minority of students at a private, residential liberal arts college or the entire population of a community college or urban institution.

Regardless of differences in backgrounds and educational goals, commuter students share a common core of needs and concerns such as issues related to transportation that limit the time they spend on campus, multiple life roles, the importance of integrating their support systems into the collegiate world, and developing a sense of belonging on the campus. Whether they attend a predominantly residential or commuter institution, the fact that they commute to college profoundly affects the nature of their educational experience.

Despite the overwhelming numbers of commuter students, the long-standing residential tradition of American higher education has impeded effective, comprehensive institutional response to their presence on campus. Typically, the relationship of commuter students to the institution has been neither understood nor incorporated into the design of policies, programs, and practices. Too often, it has been assumed erroneously that what has worked for residential students will serve commuter students equally well.

To begin to correct the inequities that have been built into policies and programs, institutions must criti-cally and comprehensively examine their practices from the point of view of commuter students. The *CAS Standards and Guidelines for Commuter Student Programs and Services* provide a basis for institutional self-assessment and program development. In addition, because the commuter student population is so diverse and because each institution's commuter population is unique, it is important that each college and university regularly collect data about its commuter students and the nature of their college experience.

As the students pursuing higher education become more diverse and as diverse students attend a wider range of institutions, it will only become more necessary to assure that the institutions are responsive to the needs of commuter students.

## References, Readings and Resources

Chickering, A. W. (1974). *Commuting versus resident students.* San Francisco: Jossey-Bass.

Jacoby, B. (1989). *The student as commuter: Developing a comprehensive institutional response.* ASHE-ERIC Higher Education Report No. 7, Washington, DC: School of Education and Human Development, The George Washington University.

Jacoby, B., & Girrell, K. (Winter 1981). A model for improving services and programs for commuter students," *NASPA Journal,* 18. 38-41.

Schlossberg, N. K., Lynch, A.Q., & Chickering, A.W. (1989). *Improving higher education: Environments for adults.* San Francisco: Jossey-Bass.

Stewart, S. (ed.) (1983). *Commuter students: Enhancing their educational experience.* New Directions for Student Services No. 24, San Francisco: Jossey-Bass.

# COMMUTER STUDENT PROGRAMS
## CAS STANDARDS and GUIDELINES

## Part 1. MISSION

The commuter student program must develop, record, disseminate, implement and regularly review its mission and goals. Mission statements must be consistent with the mission and goals of the institution and with the standards in this document.

Commuter student programs and services must consider and respond to the diverse needs of commuting students and must help these students benefit from the institution's total educational process.

The goals of a commuter student program must be to:

- provide services and facilities to meet physical, personal safety, and educational needs of commuting students based on institutional assessment of their needs;
- ensure that the institution provides commuter students equal access to services and facilities; make available opportunities to assist commuting students in their individual development; and
- act as an advocate for commuter students.

Commuter students may range from a small minority to the entire student population. The commuting students in any higher educational institution are entitled to the full benefits of the curricular and cocurricular programs and services offered, regardless of their full-time or part-time status, whether they commute from near or far, are day or evening students, are living independently for the first time, or are returning after an extended interruption. Each commuter student is entitled to fair and reasonable access to institutional resources and full administrative support.

Commuter student services and programs should address:

- the unique needs of commuter students such as adequate parking, emergency assistance in parking lots, carpool programs, study space in classroom buildings, and mobile food service;
- developmental opportunities, such as tutoring for reentry students, assessment of prior experience, social programs for students to meet other students, and support groups for those experiencing major life transitions; and
- information to faculty and staff regarding commuter students such as lifestyle characteristics, head of household status, marital status, and employment status.

To respond to the student as commuter, many colleges and universities create a separate commuter-student area within the student affairs division. When that is the case, the standards outlined here apply. When no specific office is identified for the student as commuter, then all student affairs areas should be evaluated to ensure that quality services and programs exist to meet survival, esteem, and self-actualization needs of commuting students.

## Part 2. PROGRAM

The formal education of students is purposeful, holistic, and consists of the curriculum and the co-curriculum.

Commuter student programs must be (a) intentional, (b) coherent, (c) based on theories and knowledge of learning and human development, (d) reflective of developmental and demographic profiles of the student population, and (e) responsive to special needs of individuals.

Commuter student programs must promote learning and development in students by encouraging outcomes such as intellectual growth, ability to communicate effectively, realistic self-appraisal, enhanced self-esteem, clarification of values, appropriate career choices, leadership development, physical fitness, meaningful interpersonal relations, ability to work independently and collaboratively, social responsibility, satisfying and productive lifestyles, appreciation of aesthetic and cultural diversity, and achievement of personal goals.

Campus scheduling policies must accommodate commuters, including evening students, part-time students, and students who depend on fixed-transportation schedules.

If a commuter student program office exists, it must serve a wide variety of needs and interests, either through direct delivery of essential programs and services or by assisting other offices in meeting those needs.

Commuter student program staff must:

- assist students with transportation needs and serve as liaison with campus security and municipal transit agencies to communicate commuter needs;

  Transportation information and programs such as car pools, intracampus transit (depending on size), and transport between campus and local community should be available. Provisions should be made for parking; emergency services (including jumper cables, towing service, road aid); and walkway, bike path, and parking lot security.

- assist students in obtaining housing and dealing with landlord and/or community regulatory agencies;

  Off-campus housing programs should assist students in making informed choices about housing, and should include information about available housing, tenancy ordinances, tenants' rights, legal aid information, small claims court, parking, transportation to campus, and special lease provisions and limitations.

- **assist students to acquire needed information and receive accurate referrals;**

  Information about campus services, programs, and current events should be disseminated in a variety of formats, including calendars, campus and local newspapers and radio stations, telephone hotlines, electronic bulletin boards, fliers, and the World Wide Web. Access to processes such as course registration and advising should be available via computer and telephone as well as in traditional modes.

- **provide for educational, recreational, and social programs consistent with the needs of the diverse commuter population;**

  Staff members should provide commuter students programs that include daytime social and cultural activities, workshops on relevant topics (e.g., landlord/tenant issues, energy conservation for homes and apartments, banking and personal financial management), activities located in areas off campus that are densely populated by students, and family-oriented activities.

- **encourage representation of the commuter perspective at all appropriate levels of campus planning, budgeting, and governance;**

  Commuter student advocacy should focus on:

  - access to comprehensive academic advising, student support services, and sources of information;
  - recognition of the diverse subgroups of the commuter student population, including students that are older, married, fully employed, part-time, evening, veterans, or those living at home with parents;
  - fair ratio of fee burden for campus services for resident and commuter students;
  - fair representation of commuter students in areas of campus employment, internship placement, and financial aid awards;
  - working with faculty to enhance understanding of the demographic characteristics and unique needs of commuter students; and
  - inclusion of the commuter perspective in community decision making. Examples include transportation route changes and zoning changes.

- **provide for institutional research including the variables of residence, proximity to campus, age, and employment status so that institutional planners and decision makers can understand the complexity of the lifestyle of the commuter student.**

  Research efforts may include demographic studies, needs assessments, environmental assessments, longitudinal studies, and commuter/resident comparisons.

## Part 3. LEADERSHIP

Effective and ethical leadership is essential to the success of all organizations. Institutions must appoint, position and empower leaders within the administrative structure to accomplish stated missions. Leaders at various levels must be selected on the basis of formal education and training, relevant work experience, personal attributes, and other professional credentials. Institutions must determine expectations of accountability for leaders and fairly assess their performance.

Leaders of commuter student programs must exercise authority over resources for which they are responsible to achieve their respective missions. Leaders must articulate a vision for their organization; set goals and objectives; prescribe and practice ethical behavior; recruit, select, supervise, and develop others in the organization; manage, plan, budget, and evaluate; communicate effectively; and marshal cooperative action from colleagues, employees, other institutional constituencies, and persons outside the organization. Program leaders must address individual, organizational, or environmental conditions that inhibit goal achievement. Leaders must improve programs and services continuously in response to changing needs of students and institutional priorities.

## Part 4. ORGANIZATION and MANAGEMENT

Commuter student programs must be structured purposefully and managed effectively to achieve stated goals. Evidence of appropriate structure must include current and accessible policies and procedures, written performance expectations for all employees, functional work flow graphics or organizational charts, and service delivery expectations. Evidence of effective management must include clear sources and channels of authority, effective communication practices, decision-making and conflict resolution procedures, responsiveness to changing conditions, accountability systems, and recognition and reward processes.

Commuter student programs must provide channels within the organization for regular review of administrative policies and procedures.

The commuter student program shall play a principal role in implementing institutional programs developed in response to the assessed needs of commuter students.

  The administrative organization of the commuter student program shall be governed by the size, nature, and mission of the institution. Commuter student programs may function as autonomous student services units or may be housed as component units of other student services departments. In either instance, the commuter student program must be organized and administered in a manner that permits its stated mission to be fulfilled.

## Part 5. HUMAN RESOURCES

The commuter student program must be staffed adequately by individuals qualified to accomplish its mission and goals. Programs and services must establish procedures for staff selection, training, and evaluation; set expectations for supervision, and provide appropriate professional development opportunities.

**Professional staff members must hold an earned graduate degree in a field relevant to the position description or must possess an appropriate combination of education and experience.**

**Degree or credential seeking interns or others in training must be qualified by enrollment in an appropriate field of study and relevant experience. These individuals must be trained and supervised adequately by professional staff members.**

**Student employees and volunteers must be carefully selected, trained, supervised, and evaluated. When their knowledge and skills are not adequate for particular situations, they must refer students or others in need of assistance to qualified professional staff.**

**The commuter student program must have secretarial and technical staff adequate to accomplish its mission. Such staff must be technologically proficient and qualified to perform activities including reception duties, office equipment operation, records maintenance, and mail handling.**

**Appropriate salary levels and fringe benefits for all staff members must be commensurate with those for comparable positions within the institution, in similar institutions, and in the relevant geographic area.**

**Commuter student programs must intentionally employ a diverse staff to reflect the diversity of the institution's student population, to ensure the existence of readily identifiable role models for students and to enrich the campus community.**

**Affirmative action must occur in hiring and promotion practices to ensure diverse staffing profiles as required by institutional policies and local, state/provincial, and federal law.**

The professional staff should consist of individuals whose primary responsibility is to assist commuter students to accomplish their educational, personal, and social goals.

Professional staff should: (a) develop and implement programs and services; (b) counsel students; (c) conduct research and evaluation; (d) advocate for the improvement of the quality of life for students as commuters, and (e) perform developmental educational functions.

Technical and support staff should perform office and administrative functions, including reception, information-giving, problem identification, and referral.

The professional staff should possess the academic preparation, experience, abilities, professional interests, and competencies essential for the efficient operation of the office as charged, as well as the ability to identify additional areas of concern about the commuter student population.

Relevant graduate preparation programs include those in counseling and guidance, student development, and higher education administration.

Some courses of study relevant to professionals working in commuter student services are:

- research methodologies;
- the American college student;
- history of higher education;
- organizational behavior and change;
- interpersonal communication;
- social psychology;
- developmental theory and personality;
- the individual and society;
- counseling theories and techniques;
- environmental assessment;
- program evaluation;
- the adult learner; and
- management in higher education.

Staff development is an essential activity if staff members are to remain current and effective in an educational setting. Additional credit courses, seminars, professional conferences, access to published research and opinion, and to relevant other media are examples of staff-development activities.

Preprofessional, practicum, or intern student staff members should come from academic programs in counseling and guidance, student development, higher education administration, or comparable programs, and should be appropriately supervised.

Where student staff members are employed, they should be provided with clear and precise job descriptions, pre service training, and adequate supervision.

In the selection and training of technical and support staff members, special emphasis should be placed on skills in the areas of public relations, information dissemination, problem identification, and referral. A thorough knowledge of the institution and its various offices is important.

## Part 6. FINANCIAL RESOURCES

**The commuter student program must have adequate funding to accomplish its mission and goals. Priorities, whether set periodically or as a result of extraordinary conditions, must be determined within the context of the stated mission, goals, and resources.**

Services that are paid for with student fees should benefit the student population as a whole, and they should be accessible to all students or financed equitably through user fees or in some manner other than through a general fee.

Consideration should be given to an equitable fee burden/service ratio (i.e., the fees paid for the services delivered). This ratio should be related to the percentage of commuting students in the campus population and should be applied to obvious commuter services such as parking lots, lockers, and to more routine institutional offerings such as library hours, laboratories, recreational facilities, and programs.

## Part 7. FACILITIES, TECHNOLOGY, and EQUIPMENT

The commuter student program must have adequate, suitably located facilities and equipment to support its mission and goals. Facilities, technology, and equipment must be in compliance with relevant federal, state, provincial, and local requirements to provide for access, health, and safety. The campus must provide adequate free-time facilities for the use of commuter students, including recreational, study, and lounge space; computer work stations; lockers; and eating facilities.

Because commuter students do not have a residence on campus in which to spend time before, between, and after classes, it is important that a variety of comfortable free-time spaces be specifically designated for commuter student use. These spaces should be in classroom buildings, as well as in college union and student center buildings, and should include individual locker and campus mail facilities.

## Part 8. LEGAL RESPONSIBILITIES

Commuter student program staff members must be knowledgeable about and responsive to law and regulations that relate to their program or service. Sources for legal obligations and limitations include constitutional, statutory, regulatory, and case law; mandatory laws and orders emanating from federal, state, provincial and local governments; and the institution through its policies.

Staff members must use reasonable and informed practices to limit the liability exposure of the institution, its officers, employees, and agents. Staff members must be informed about institutional policies regarding personal liability and related insurance coverage options.

The institution must provide access to legal advice for commuter student program staff members as needed to carry out assigned responsibilities.

The institution must inform staff and students, in a timely and systematic fashion, about extraordinary or changing legal obligations and potential liabilities.

## Part 9. EQUAL OPPORTUNITY, ACCESS, and AFFIRMATIVE ACTION

Commuter student program staff members must ensure that services and programs are provided on a fair and equitable basis. The program must be accessible. Hours of operation must be responsive to the needs of all students. The program must adhere to the spirit and intent of equal opportunity laws.

Commuter student programs must not be discriminatory on the basis of age, color, disability, gender, national origin, race, religious creed, sexual orientation, and/or veteran status. Exceptions are appropriate only where provided by relevant law and institutional policy.

Consistent with their mission and goals, commuter student programs must take affirmative action to remedy significant imbalances in student participation and staffing patterns.

## Part 10. CAMPUS and COMMUNITY RELATIONS

Commuter student programs must establish, maintain, and promote effective relations with relevant campus offices and external agencies.

The commuter service program should maintain a high degree of visibility with the academic units through direct promotion and delivery of services, through involvement with cocurricular programs, and through staff efforts to increase understanding of the special needs of commuting students.

The commuter student program should be actively involved and informed about the activities of other offices whose efforts directly affect commuting students. These include such areas as campus safety and security, transportation and parking, public information, scheduling, and campus switchboard, as well as campus-wide committees that bear on these issues.

Staff should be particularly cognizant that for many commuting students the institution is only one facet of their lives. Many important needs of commuter students are met through interaction with community agencies and services.

The commuter service program should maintain active contacts with various community service agencies such as legal assistance, housing boards, and transportation services.

The commuter student service program should promote involvement in events and activities that may affect commuter students.

## Part 11. DIVERSITY

Within the context of each institution's unique mission, multi-dimensional diversity enriches the community and enhances the collegiate experience for all; therefore, commuter student programs must nurture environments where similarities and differences among people are recognized and honored.

Commuter student programs must promote cultural educational experiences that are characterized by open and continuous communication, that deepen understanding of one's own culture and heritage, and that respect and educate about similarities, differences and histories of cultures.

The commuter student programs must address the characteristics and needs of a diverse population when establishing and implementing policies and procedures.

## Part 12. ETHICS

All persons involved in the delivery of commuter student programs must adhere to the highest principles of ethical behavior. Commuter student programs must develop or adopt and implement statements of ethical practice addressing the issues unique to each program and service. The commuter student program must publish these statements and insure their periodic review by all concerned.

Staff members must ensure that confidentiality is maintained with respect to all communications and records considered confidential unless exempted by law.

Information disclosed in individual counseling sessions must remain confidential, unless written permission to divulge the information is given by the student. However, all staff members must disclose to appropriate authorities information judged to be of an emergency nature, especially when the safety of the individual or others is involved. Information contained in students' educational records must not be disclosed to non-institutional third parties without appropriate consent, unless classified as "Directory" information or when the information is subpoenaed by law. Commuter student programs must apply a similar dedication to privacy and confidentiality to research data concerning individuals. All staff members must be aware of and comply with the provisions contained in the institution's human subjects research policy and in other relevant institutional policies addressing ethical practices.

Staff members must recognize and avoid personal conflict of interest or appearance thereof in their transactions with students and others. Staff members must strive to insure the fair, objective, and impartial treatment of all persons with whom they deal.

When handling institutional funds, staff members must ensure that such funds are managed in accordance with established and responsible accounting procedures.

Commuter student program staff members must not participate in any form of harassment that demeans persons or creates an intimidating, hostile, or offensive campus environment.

Staff members must perform their duties within the limits of their training, expertise, and competence. When these limits are exceeded, individuals in need of further assistance must be referred to persons possessing appropriate qualifications.

Staff members must use suitable means to confront and otherwise hold accountable other staff members who exhibit unethical behavior.

Staff members must maintain the highest principles of ethical behavior in the use of technology.

# Part 13. ASSESSMENT and EVALUATION

Commuter student programs must regularly conduct systematic qualitative and quantitative evaluations of program quality to determine whether and to what degree the stated mission and goals are being met. Although methods of assessment vary, programs and services must employ a sufficient range of measures to insure objectivity and comprehensiveness. Data collected must include responses from students and other affected constituencies. Results of these evaluations must be used in revising and improving programs and services and in recognizing staff performance.

# THE ROLE of COUNSELING PROGRAMS
## CAS Standards Contextual Statement

College counseling represents the union of several movements in higher education and the integration of a helping profession activity and an educational environment. Knowledge of the college environment and its effect on students is an important tool for college counselors. Steenbarger (1990) noted that college counseling exemplifies the developmental framework that has produced a history of creative outreach and support work on campuses. College counseling is counseling in context that can best be illustrated through exploring the development of the field and the models that have influenced it.

Stimulated by the development of personnel and industrial psychology during and subsequent to World War I (Lloyd-Jones, 1929), the mental hygiene movement (Bragdon, 1929), and newly developing psychometric procedures and instruments (Williamson, 1939), together with advocacy for changes in philosophy of higher education (Mueller, Raphael, McKinney, Lloyd-Jones, & Cottrell, 1947), formal college counseling programs appeared as early as 1914 (Farnsworth, 1957). Following a period of slow but steady growth, counseling programs began rapid expansion immediately after World War II, largely in response to the need to assist returning veterans (Embree, 1950; Gaudet, 1949). By the late 1960s, two-thirds of country's colleges were providing programs of counseling (Oetting, Ivey, & Weigel, 1970).

Although service delivery varies, college counseling programs largely reflect the vocational, mental health, and student personnel models of counseling (Oetting et al., 1970; Whiteley, Mahaffey, & Geer, 1987; Heppner & Neal, 1983). Early counseling pioneers such as Parsons (1909) in vocational counseling, Beers (1908/1950) in mental health counseling, and Williamson (1939) in college counseling at the University of Minnesota initiated programs that foreshadowed more recent approaches to college counseling and testing programs and exerted significant influence on the development of counseling as a profession.

College counseling services work in concert with other student support services to promote students' personal and educational success through activities that complement formal academic programs. College counselors offer remedial, preventive, crisis, outreach, and consultative services, depending on the nature of the campus and the students it serves. Counseling services have changed and adapted over time along with shifts in student demographics. As the functions adapted after World War II to accommodate the needs of returning veterans, so have they continued to respond to the needs of increasingly diverse students and to complex societal issues.

College attendance creates a unique set of circumstances and stressors that can stimulate significant student growth and development, especially when the many student support functions are well coordinated and working together. As students experience change, they often need to address personal issues, work through challenges, and deal with the implications of growth and change. The presence and availability of counseling services on campus is an important support for the education and development of the whole person. Counseling, and counselors, can and do both effect and support student development.

The Counseling Programs and Services Standards and Guidelines that follow provide institutional leaders with criteria to judge the quality of the counseling programs and services offered.

## References, Readings and Resources

Beers, C. W. (1950). *A mind that found itself* (Rev. Ed.). New York: Doubleday, (Original work published in 1908).

Bragdon, H. D. (1929). *Counseling the college student.* Cambridge, MA: Harvard University Press.

Dean, L. A., & Meadows, M. E. (1995). College counseling: Union and intersection. *Journal of Counseling and Development, 74,* 139-142.

Embree, R. B. (1950). Developments in counseling bureaus and clinics. *Educational and Psychological Measurement, 10,* 465-475.

Farnsworth, D. L. (1957). *Mental health in college and university.* Cambridge, MA: Harvard University Press.

Gaudet, F. J. (1949). The Veterans Administration advisement and guidance program. *School and Society, 69,* 251-254.

Heppner, P. P., & Neal, G. W. (1983). Holding up the mirror: Research on the roles and functions of counseling centers in higher education. *Counseling Psychologist,* 11, 81-98.

Lloyd-Jones, E. (1929). *Student personnel work.* New York: Harper.

Mueller, K. H., Raphael, T., McKinney, F., Lloyd-Jones, E., & Cottrell, L. (1947). Counseling for mental health. *American Council on Education Studies,* 11 (Serial No. 8).

Oetting, E. R., Ivey, A.E., & Weigel, R. G. (1970). *The college and university counseling center* (ACPA Monograph No. 11). Washington, DC: American Personnel and Guidance Association.

Parsons, F. (1909). *Choosing a vocation.* Boston: Houghton-Mifflin.

Steenbarger, B. N. (1990). Toward a developmental understanding of the counseling specialty. *Journal of Counseling and Development,* 68, 435-437.

Whiteley, S. M., Mahaffey, P. J., & Geer, C. (1987). The campus counseling center: A profile of staffing patterns and services. *Journal of College Student Personnel,* 28, 71-81.

Williamson, E. G. (1939). *How to counsel students.* New York: McGraw-Hill.

# COUNSELING PROGRAMS and SERVICES
## CAS STANDARDS and GUIDELINES

## Part 1. MISSION

The counseling programs and services must develop, record, disseminate, implement and regularly review its mission and goals. Mission statements must be consistent with the mission and goals of the institution and with the standards in this document.

The mission of counseling services is to assist students to define and accomplish personal and academic goals. To accomplish the mission, the goals of counseling services must include:

- high quality individual and group counseling services to students who may be experiencing psychological or behavioral difficulties;

- programming focused on the developmental needs of college students to maximize the potential of students to benefit from the academic environment and experience; and

- consultative services to the institution to make the environment as beneficial to the intellectual, emotional, and physical development of students as possible.

A wide variety of counseling, consultative, evaluative, and training functions may be performed by the counseling services as an expression of their institutional mission.

While there are basic similarities in the overall goals of various types of institutions, differences in student populations and institutional priorities may affect emphases of functions within individual counseling services. For these reasons, a given counseling service may emphasize different combinations of personal counseling, academic counseling, or student development services.

Counseling services programs should mirror the diversity of institutional structures and priorities. Accordingly, some functions or programs that may not typically be organized as a part of the counseling services are included. Conversely, some services or programs typically associated with counseling services may be the responsibility of other units.

To effectively respond to the educational needs of the institution and the personal and academic needs of students, the counseling services should have the following complementary functions:

- *Developmental.* The developmental function is to help students, both well-adjusted and disturbed, enhance their growth. The aim of developmental interventions is to help students benefit from the academic environment. To do so, the counseling services promote student growth by encouraging positive and realistic self-appraisal, intellectual development, appropriate personal and occupational choices, the ability to relate meaningfully and mutually with others, and the capacity to engage in a personally satisfying and effective style of living.

- *Remedial.* The remedial function recognizes that some students experience significant personal adjustment problems that require immediate professional attention. This function includes assisting students in overcoming current specific personal and educational problems and, in some cases, remedying current academic skill deficiencies.

- *Preventive.* The preventive function role is to anticipate environmental conditions that may negatively influence student welfare and initiate interventions that will neutralize such conditions.

## Part 2. PROGRAM

The formal education of students is purposeful, holistic, and consists of the curriculum and the co-curriculum.

Counseling programs and services must be (a) intentional, (b) coherent, (c) based on theories and knowledge of learning and human development, (d) reflective of developmental and demographic profiles of the student population, and (e) responsive to special needs of individuals.

The counseling program must promote learning and development in students by encouraging outcomes such as intellectual growth, ability to communicate effectively, realistic self-appraisal, enhanced self-esteem, clarification of values, appropriate career choices, leadership development, physical fitness, meaningful interpersonal relations, ability to work independently and collaboratively, social responsibility, satisfying and productive lifestyles, appreciation of aesthetic and cultural diversity, and achievement of personal goals.

To effectively fulfill its mission, the counseling services must provide directly or through referral, or collaborate in the provision of:

- individual counseling and/or psychotherapy in areas of personal, educational, career development/vocational choice, interpersonal relationships, family, and social problems;

- group counseling and/or psychotherapy to help students establish satisfying personal relationships and to become more effective in areas such as interpersonal processes, communication skills, decision-making concerning personal and educational/career matters, and the establishment of personal values;

- psychological testing and other assessment techniques, when appropriate, to foster client self-understanding and decision making;

65

- outreach efforts to address developmental concerns of students;

- counseling support to help students assess and overcome specific deficiencies in educational preparation or skills;

- crisis intervention and emergency coverage, as appropriate, and in relationship to other available mental health resources; and

- staff and faculty professional development programs.

In those cases where other campus agencies provide similar services, such as career counseling and educational counseling, the counseling services should establish cooperative relationships and maintain mutual referrals. In those cases where significant and needed expertise is not available within the counseling services, staff members should make full and active use of referral resources within the institution and the local community.

The counseling services should play an active role in interpreting and, when appropriate, advocating the needs of students to administration, faculty and staff of the institution. The counseling services can provide a needed perspective for campus administrative leaders, reflecting an appropriate balance between administrative requirements and the special needs and interests of students. The counseling services should interpret the institutional environment to students and intervene to either improve the quality of the environment or facilitate the development of a better person-environment interaction. The counseling services should be sensitive to the needs of traditionally underserved populations such as ethnic and cultural minorities and nontraditional students.

The counseling services may contribute studies of student characteristics and needs and follow-up studies of student progress in various programs. The counseling services should provide consultation, supervision, and inservice professional development services for faculty members, administrators, student staff members, and paraprofessionals.

The counseling services may assist students and faculty who conduct individual research on student characteristics or on the influence of specific student development programs.

Although training and supervision of paraprofessionals, practicum students, and interns is an appropriate and desirable responsibility of the counseling services, the training functions should be secondary in importance to primary service functions.

## Part 3. LEADERSHIP

Effective and ethical leadership is essential to the success of all organizations. Institutions must appoint, position and empower leaders within the administrative structure to accomplish stated missions. Leaders at various levels must be selected on the basis of formal education and training, relevant work experience, personal attributes, and other professional credentials. Institutions must determine expectations of accountability for leaders and fairly assess their performance.

The leaders of counseling programs must exercise authority over resources for which they are responsible to achieve their respective missions. Leaders must articulate a vision for their organization; set goals and objectives; prescribe and practice ethical behavior; recruit, select, supervise, and develop others in the organization; manage, plan, budget, and evaluate; communicate effectively; and marshal cooperative action from colleagues, employees, other institutional constituencies, and persons outside the organization. Counseling program leaders must address individual, organizational, or environmental conditions that inhibit goal achievement. Leaders must improve counseling programs and services continuously in response to changing needs of students and institutional priorities.

## Part 4. ORGANIZATION and MANAGEMENT

Counseling programs and services must be structured purposefully and managed effectively to achieve stated goals. Evidence of appropriate structure must include current and accessible policies and procedures, written performance expectations for all employees, functional work flow graphics or organizational charts, and service delivery expectations. Evidence of effective management must include clear sources and channels of authority, effective communication practices, decision-making and conflict resolution procedures, responsiveness to changing conditions, accountability systems, and recognition and reward processes.

Counseling programs and services must provide channels within the organization for regular review of administrative policies and procedures.

Because institutional perceptions of the counseling services will define its resources, use, referrals, and overall impact on the community, it is important that these services be perceived as central to the overall mission of the institution.

Counseling services provide a highly unique service on campuses not typically offered by any other student and academic agency.

The director of the counseling services should be positioned within the administrative structure so as to be able to effectively interact with significant unit heads, as well as with the chief student affairs administrator and chief academic affairs administrator.

Every effort should be made to assure that counseling services function independently of units directly responsible for making decisions concerning students' official matriculation status, such as judicial actions, academic probation, and admission or readmission actions.

## Part 5. HUMAN RESOURCES

The counseling program must be staffed adequately by individuals qualified to accomplish its mission and goals. Counseling programs and services must establish procedures for staff selection, training, and evaluation; set expectations for supervision; and provide appropriate professional development opportunities.

Professional counselors and other staff members must hold an earned graduate degree in a field relevant to the position they hold or must possess an appropriate combination of education and experience to meet the position description.

Degree or credential seeking interns or others in training must be qualified by enrollment in an appropriate field of study and relevant experience. These individuals must be trained and supervised adequately by professional staff members.

Student employees and volunteers must be carefully selected, trained, supervised, and evaluated. When their knowledge and skills are not adequate for particular situations, they must refer students or others in need of assistance to qualified professional staff.

The counseling program must have secretarial and technical staff adequate to accomplish its mission. Such staff must be technologically proficient and qualified to perform activities including reception duties, office equipment operation, records maintenance, and mail handling.

Appropriate salary levels and fringe benefits for all staff members must be commensurate with those for comparable positions within the institution, in similar institutions, and in the relevant geographic area.

Counseling programs and services must intentionally employ a diverse staff to reflect the diversity of the institution's student population to ensure the existence of readily identifiable role models for students and to enrich the campus community.

Affirmative action must occur in hiring and promotion practices to ensure diverse staffing profiles as required by institutional policies and local, state/provincial, and federal law.

The counseling services program must have a regular system of staff selection and evaluation, and must provide continuing professional development opportunities for staff including inservice training programs, participation in professional conferences, workshops, and other continuing education activities.

The counseling function must be performed by professionals from disciplines such as counseling and clinical psychology, counseling and personnel services, psychiatry, social work, and by others with appropriate training and supervised experience.

Professional counseling staff members should be accorded all the responsibilities, rights, and privileges of faculty or professional staff. This may include the opportunity to secure academic rank, tenure, and representation on institutional governing bodies. Sabbatical or educational leaves should be available to counseling services staff members in the same way that such opportunities are available to other comparable institutional personnel.

**The director of counseling services must have an appropriate combination of graduate coursework, formal training, and supervised experience.**

The director of counseling services should have (a) a doctoral degree in counseling psychology, clinical psychology, or other related discipline from an accredited institution or (b) a minimum of a master's degree in the behavioral or other social sciences with emphasis in whatever counseling areas characterize the functions undertaken by the counseling services.

- The director should have personal attributes that enable effective interaction with administrators, faculty and staff members, students, and colleagues in the counseling services and should possess all the general qualifications of a professional staff member.
- It is highly desirable that the director have a minimum of three years experience as a staff member or administrator in a counseling services agency.
- The director should have supervised experience (either pre- or post-doctoral) with college-age students.
- The director should hold or be eligible for state licensure or certification, where such exist.
- The director should demonstrate involvement and commitment to educational and professional development.

The responsibilities of the director should include:

- overall administration and coordination of counseling activities;
- coordination, recruitment, training, supervision, development, and evaluation of professional and support staff personnel;
- preparation and administration of budget;
- preparation of annual reports;
- provision of counseling information and services to students, faculty, and staff;
- provision of consultation/leadership in policy formation and program development; and
- education of staff members regarding legal issues governing the delivery of counseling and psychological services.

**The professional counseling staff must have an appropriate combination of graduate coursework, formal training, and supervised experience.**

The minimum qualification for a professional counseling staff member should be a master's degree from disciplines such as counseling psychology, clinical psychology, counseling and personnel services, mental health counseling, and social work, with appropriate supervised experience.

Professional staff members should have personal attributes that enable effective interaction with administrators, faculty, students, and colleagues.

Professional staff members should have appropriate coursework and training in psychological assessment, theories of personality, abnormal psychology or psychopathology, legal issues in psychology, and learning theory. Professional staff members should also demonstrate knowledge of principles of organizational development and consultation.

Professional staff members should have a supervised practicum/internship at the graduate level in the counseling of college-age students.

Professional staff members should hold, or be eligible for, state licensure or certification, where such exist.

In cases where staff members are responsible for the supervision of colleagues or of graduate student trainees, staff members should have doctoral degrees or have appropriate experience in the training of other professionals.

The counseling services should maintain an in-service training program and a staff development program which includes supervision, case presentations, research reports, and discussion of relevant professional issues.

Teaching of courses in academic departments should be encouraged, where appropriate.

Staff members should participate in appropriate professional organizations and should have the budgetary support to do so.

Staff members should be encouraged to participate in community activities related to their profession.

Professional trainees, such as practicum students and interns (doctoral level trainees working at least half-time), as well as paraprofessional assistants, may perform, under supervision, various functions in the counseling services, where appropriate.

The size of a counseling services agency is a critical factor in determining the ability of the staff to meet objectives. Ratios for professional and support staff should be established and reviewed frequently with regard to enrollment, service demands, user surveys, diversity of services offered, institutional resources, and other mental health and student services that may be available on the campus and in the local community.

In addition to providing direct services, it is important that in accordance with individual qualifications and task assignments, staff time be allowed for preparation of interviews and reports, updating institutional information, research, faculty and staff contacts, staff meetings, training and supervision, personal and professional development, consultation, and walk-in and emergency counseling interventions.

Similarly, teaching, administration, research, and other such responsibilities are legitimate functions and where appropriate should be so recognized in the determination of individual workloads.

Clerical employees who deal directly with students should be carefully selected, since they play an important role in the students' impressions of the counseling services and often must make some preliminary client-related decisions.

**Support and clerical staff must be adequate to perform receptionist, secretarial, and testing duties necessary for the effective functioning of the agency such that professional staff members spend the preponderance of their time on professional duties.**

# Part 6. FINANCIAL RESOURCES

**The counseling services must have adequate funding to accomplish its mission and goals. Priorities, whether set periodically or as a result of extraordinary conditions, must be determined within the context of the stated mission, goals, and resources.**

# Part 7. FACILITIES, TECHNOLOGY, and EQUIPMENT

**The counseling services must have adequate, suitably located facilities and equipment to support its mission and goals. Facilities, technology, and equipment must be in compliance with relevant federal, state/provincial, and local requirements to provide for access, health, and safety.**

Providers of counseling services should promote the maintenance of a physical and social environment that facilitates optimal human functioning.

- Counseling services, when feasible, should be physically separate from administrative offices, campus police, and judicial units.

- Individual offices for professional staff members should be provided and appropriately equipped.

The offices should be designed to accommodate the functions performed by staff members. For example:

- There should be a reception area that provides a comfortable and private waiting area for clients;

- The counseling services should maintain or have ready access to a professional library;

- In instances where counseling services include a career development unit, there should be a reading room which holds institutional catalogs and occupation/care information;

- An area suitable for individual and group testing procedures should be available;

- The counseling services should maintain, or have ready access to, group meeting space;

- The counseling services should maintain, or have access to, equipment that is capable of providing modern technical approaches to research, record keeping, media presentations, and treatment; and

- Counseling services with training components should have adequate audiovisual recording facilities and, where possible, direct observation facilities.

# Part 8. LEGAL RESPONSIBILITIES

**Professional counselors and other staff members must be knowledgeable about and responsive to law and regulations that relate to their respective program or service. Sources for legal obligations and limitations include constitutional, statutory, regulatory, and case law; mandatory laws and orders emanating from federal, state, provincial and local governments; and the institution through its policies.**

Counselors and staff members must use reasonable and informed practices to limit the liability exposure of the institution, its officers, employees, and agents. Counselors and staff members must be informed about institutional policies regarding personal liability and related insurance coverage options.

The institution must provide access to legal advice for counselors and staff members as needed to carry out assigned responsibilities.

The institution must inform staff and students, in a timely and systematic fashion, about extraordinary or changing legal obligations and potential liabilities.

## Part 9. EQUAL OPPORTUNITY, ACCESS, and AFFIRMATIVE ACTION

Counselors and staff members must ensure that counseling services and programs are provided on a fair and equitable basis. The counseling program must be accessible. Hours of operation must be responsive to the needs of all students. The program must adhere to the spirit and intent of equal opportunity laws.

Counseling programs and services must not be discriminatory on the basis of age, color, disability, gender, national origin, race, religious creed, sexual orientation, and/or veteran status. Exceptions are appropriate only where provided by relevant law and institutional policy.

Consistent with its mission and goals, the counseling services must take affirmative action to remedy significant imbalances in student participation and staffing patterns.

## Part 10. CAMPUS and COMMUNITY RELATIONS

The counseling services must establish, maintain, and promote effective relations with relevant campus offices and external agencies.

It is desirable that the counseling services develop close cooperation with campus referral sources and with potential consumers of counseling services consultations. The counseling services should also work closely with other services and academic personnel whose goal is the promotion of psychological and emotional development.

The counseling services should work closely with the chief student affairs and chief academic affairs administrators to ensure the meeting of institutional goals and objectives.

Within the campus community, the counseling services should establish close cooperation with career planning and placement services, special academic support units (e.g., reading and study skills programs, learning assistance programs) and specialized student services (e.g., handicapped students, international and minority students, academically disadvantaged students, women, veterans, and returning adult students).

The counseling services should establish and maintain a close working relationship with student health services as counseling services staff are often called upon to refer clients for medical concerns or hospitalization, or to serve as consultants to, or to seek consultation from, health services professionals.

The counseling services should foster relationships with academic units and with campus professionals in admissions, registrar's office, student activities, athletics, and residence halls, where appropriate.

Where adequate mental health resources are not able on campus, the counseling services must establish and maintain close working relationships with institutional community mental health resources.

The counseling services should have procedures for the referral of students who require professional help beyond the scope of the institutional counseling services.

The counseling services should establish effective relationships with the institutional legal staff and the staffs of relevant professional organizations in order to effectively respond to pertinent legal issues and precedents which underlie the delivery of counseling and psychological services.

## Part 11. DIVERSITY

Within the context of the host institution's unique mission, multi-dimensional diversity enriches the community and enhances the collegiate experience for all; therefore, counseling programs and services must nurture environments where similarities and differences among people are recognized and honored.

The counseling services must promote cultural educational experiences that are characterized by open and continuous communication, that deepen understanding of one's own culture and heritage, and that respect and educate about similarities, differences and histories of cultures.

Counseling services must address the characteristics and needs of a diverse population when establishing and implementing policies and procedures.

## Part 12. ETHICS

All persons involved in the delivery of counseling services must adhere to the highest principles of ethical behavior. The counseling program must develop or adopt and implement statements of ethical practice addressing the issues unique to its institutional functions. The counseling program must publish these statements and insure their periodic review by all concerned.

Counselors and other staff members must ensure that confidentiality is maintained with respect to all communications and records considered confidential unless exempted by law.

Information disclosed in individual counseling sessions must remain confidential, unless written permission to divulge the information is given by the student. However, counselors must disclose to appropriate authorities information judged to be of an emergency nature, especially when the safety of the individual or others is involved. Information contained in students' educational records must not be disclosed to non-institutional third parties without appropriate consent, unless classified as "Directory" information or when the information is subpoenaed by law. Programs and services must apply a similar dedication to privacy and confidentiality to research data concerning individuals. All staff members must be aware of and comply with the provisions contained in the institution's human subjects research policy and in other relevant institutional policies addressing ethical practices.

Counselors must recognize and avoid personal conflict of interest or appearance thereof in their transactions with students and others. Counselors and other staff members must strive to insure the fair, objective, and impartial treatment of all persons with whom they deal.

When handling institutional funds, counselors and staff members must ensure that such funds are managed in accordance with established and responsible accounting procedures.

Counselors and staff members must not participate in any form of harassment that demeans persons or creates an intimidating, hostile, or offensive campus environment.

Counselors must perform their duties within the limits of their training, expertise, and competence. When these limits are exceeded, individuals in need of further assistance must be referred to persons possessing appropriate qualifications.

Counselors and staff members must use suitable means to confront and otherwise hold accountable other staff members who exhibit unethical behavior.

Counselors and other staff members must maintain the highest principles of ethical behavior in the use of technology.

The counseling services staff members must he familiar with, adhere to, and perform in a manner consistent with relevant ethical standards in the field, including particularly the preparation, use, and distribution of psychological tests.

When the condition of a client is indicative of clear and imminent danger to the client or to others, counseling services professionals must take reasonable personal action that may involve informing responsible authorities, and when possible, consulting with other professionals. In such cases, counseling services professionals must be cognizant of pertinent ethical principles, state or federal statutes, and local mental health guidelines that stipulate the limits of confidentiality.

Information should be released only at the written request or concurrence of a client who has full knowledge of the nature of the information that is being released and of the parties to whom it is released. Instances of limited confidentiality should be clearly articulated. Implementation of limited confidentiality procedures should only occur after careful consideration.

Consultation regarding individual students, as requested or needed with faculty and other campus personnel, is offered in the context of preserving the student's confidential relationship with the counseling services. Consultation with parents, spouses, and public or private agencies that bear some responsibility for particular students may occur, but the confidentiality of the counseling relationship should be maintained.

## Part 13. ASSESSMENT and EVALUATION

The counseling service must regularly conduct systematic qualitative and quantitative evaluations of program quality to determine whether and to what degree the stated mission and goals are being met. Although methods of assessment vary, counseling programs and services must employ a sufficient range of measures to insure objectivity and comprehensiveness. Data collected must include responses from students and other affected constituencies. Results of these evaluations must be used in revising and improving programs and services and in recognizing staff performance.

# THE ROLE of DISABILITY SUPPORT SERVICE PROGRAMS
## CAS Standards Contextual Statement

Beginning in the early 1970s, access to higher education by students with disabilities began to change dramatically. As the result of sweeping legislation, colleges and universities receiving Federal funds were required to provide nondiscriminatory access to programs and facilities for students with disabilities. The decade of the 1990s brought even more significant legislation prescribing what many have heralded as "Civil Rights" for individuals with disabilities. The primary national legislation was identified as the Americans with Disabilities Act (ADA).

The early professionals providing support services for students with disabilities came from established campus departments, such as student life, counseling, and affirmative action. As growing numbers of students with disabilities enrolled in higher education at increasing rates, the roles of disability service providers expanded to include those of educator, administrator, advocate, and counselor. Professional help providers were especially challenged as goals were set to promote full participation in the educational experience while supporting students to become independent and personally responsible learners. As both the numbers requiring service and the needs of disabled students grew, a uniquely challenged and experienced cadre of professional disability service providers developed.

In support of students' needs and aspirations, disability service professionals strive to create institutional accommodations that make education fully accessible. To assure the general acceptance and success of students with diverse needs, disability service professionals seek to enhance awareness in all areas of campus life through advocacy and education.

The founding of the Association on Higher Education and Disability, which was originally organized as the Association on Handicapped Student Services Programs in Post-Secondary Education (AHSSPPE), led to the identity of professionals in the field of disability support service. Following an ethical code promoting integrity in practice, these professionals support the success of students with disabilities within the mission of each campus.

Services for students with disabilities has become an integral component of institutions of higher education. The promotion of a holistic educational experience for students with disabilities adds to the diversity of our campuses and the success of all students.

## References, Readings and Resources

American Council on Education (1994). *Educating students with disabilities on campus: Strategies of successful projects.* Washington, DC: Author.

American Council on Education. (1995). *College freshmen with disabilities: A triennial statistical profile.* Washington, DC: Author.

*Disability Compliance for Higher Education Newsletter.* Dan Gephart, Managing Editor, LRP Publications, Horsheim, PA.

Heyward, S. M. (1996). *Frequently asked questions: Postsecondary education and disability.* Cambridge, MA: Heyward, Lawton and Associates.

Kroeger, S., & Schuck, J. (eds.) (1993). *Responding to disability issues in student affairs,* no. 64. New Directions For Student Services. San Francisco: Jossey-Bass.

Latham, J. D., & Latham, P. H. (1996). *Documentation and the law for professionals concerned with ADD/LD and those they serve.* Washington, DC: JKL Communications.

Ryan, D, & McCarthy, M. (eds.) (1994). *A student affairs guide to the ADA and disability issues,* Monograph 17. Washington, DC: National Association of Student Personnel Administrators.

Walling, L. L. (ed.) (1996). *Hidden abilities in higher education: New college students with disabilities.* Monograph series no. 21, National Resource Center for the Freshman Year Experience and Students in Transition. Columbia, SC: University of South Carolina.

Association on Higher Education and Disability (AHEAD), P.O. Box 21192, Columbus, OH 43221-0192 (V/TDD) (614) 488-4972; esuddath@magnus.acs.ohio-state.edu

*Information from HEATH,* National Clearinghouse on Postsecondary Education for Individuals with Disabilities Newsletter. American Council in Education, Washington, DC.

*Journal of Postsecondary Education and Disability.* Association on Higher Education and Disability, Columbus, OH.

# DISABILITY SUPPORT SERVICES
## CAS STANDARDS and GUIDELINES

## Part 1. MISSION

The disability support services program must develop, record, disseminate, implement and regularly review its mission and goals. Mission statements must be consistent with the mission and goals of the institution and with the standards in this document.

Two primary purposes of the disability support services program are to improve the educational development of students with disabilities and to enhance understanding and support within the campus community.

> The mission should be accomplished through direct and indirect assistance to students with disabilities, encouragement of independence, creation and maintenance of an accessible physical environment and a supportive psychological environment.

The services must assume a major role in ensuring that the campus community is knowledgeable about and in compliance with legal requirements for access such as under Section 504 of the Rehabilitation Act of 1973 and The Americans with Disabilities Act (ADA) of 1990.

To ensure fulfillment of the mission, the services must have a clear set of objectives that reflect the institution's characteristics and that:

**1. Assure that qualified students with disabilities have equal access to all institutional programs and services.**

> Attention should be given to ensure that each qualified individual receives equal access to services regardless of the type, extent, or duration of the disability.

> Assistance to students should take various forms depending on the specific population to be served and the services available elsewhere, both on and off campus. Commonly provided services may include the provision of specialized assistance or equipment.

> Institution staff should be led and encouraged toward developing positive attitudes toward individuals with disability.

**2. Advocate responsibly the needs of students with disabilities to the campus community.**

> Responsible advocacy is necessary to ensure that the campus community is sufficiently aware of disabled students' needs so it is appropriately responsive to them.

## Part 2. PROGRAM

The formal education of students is purposeful, holistic, and consists of the curriculum and the co-curriculum.

The disability support services program must be (a) intentional, (b) coherent, (c) based on theories and knowledge of learning and human development, (d) reflective of developmental and demographic profiles of the student population, and (e) responsive to special needs of individuals.

The services must promote learning and development in students by encouraging outcomes such as intellectual growth, ability to communicate effectively, realistic self-appraisal, enhanced self-esteem, clarification of values, appropriate career choices, leadership development, physical fitness, meaningful interpersonal relations, ability to work independently and collaboratively, social responsibility, satisfying and productive lifestyles, appreciation for aesthetic and cultural diversity, and achievement of personal goals.

> Special attention should be given to making effective use of existing resources to avoid costly duplication of services and to ensure that all campus offices/services are able to meet the needs of students with disabilities.

> The disability support services program should assist students in addressing specific personal, physical, or educational problems or skill deficiencies.

The disability support services program must identify environmental conditions that negatively influence students' welfare and propose interventions that are designed to neutralize such conditions.

The program must provide those physical and/or academic support services that cannot be provided adequately or developed by other campus departments or services. However organized, the following components must be among those offered:

**1. The identification of students with disabilities who are eligible for services; and in consultation, with the student, the determination of appropriate services.**

> The staff should make continuous efforts to identify all eligible students with disabilities and to encourage self-disclosure.

> Each student requesting services should be screened in an intake interview. Documentation of the disability should be requested from qualified professionals. Information on the student's disability and its effect on academic performance and participation in campus life should be evaluated to provide adequate and appropriate services.

**2. Direct assistance to individual students with disabilities.**

> A primary responsibility of the program is to provide direct support services to qualified students with disabilities to ensure access to institutional programs and services as well as to meet the accessibility requirements of the Rehabilitation Act of 1973 and the ADA. The services provided may vary

among institutions based on the disabilities represented on the campus and on the services available elsewhere on the campus and in the community.

Professional staff members should assist students with disabilities to accomplish their educational, personal, and social goals. Assistance should include: (a) developing and implementing programs and services; (b) consulting with faculty and staff on matters of academic adjustments and modifications; and (c) advocating for the improvement of the quality of life of students with disabilities.

The following types of direct support services should be available on most campuses: aides, testing services, readers, scribes, sign language and oral interpreters, and note takers. Assistive devices such as print enlargers, tape recorders, adaptations of standard equipment and adaptive computing technology should be available.

Personal assistance for independent living is not required by relevant federal law. However, attendant care and equipment for private use may be considered for inclusion in the program.

### 3. Individual and group counseling and advising to students with disabilities.

Counseling and advising services offered should address the unique needs of students with disabilities and particularly focus on those strategies needed by individuals with disabilities to cope with and succeed in a college environment.

### 4. Consultative and/or training assistance to campus and community agencies.

Staff members with expertise should provide consultation and technical assistance to departmental units and faculty to increase awareness and knowledge of disabled students' limitations and abilities. The services should also provide information on various academic accommodations including alternative teaching and testing techniques.

The staff should provide information and technical assistance, including professional development activities, to campus agencies that serve students, so that they can assist students with disabilities.

The services may be available as a campus training resource for students in human services disciplines. Designated staff members may serve as practicum instructors or intern supervisors.

### 5. Dissemination to the campus community of information about needs and legal rights of students with disabilities.

Information regarding the availability of services for students with disabilities should be included in all campus publications such as bulletins, student handbooks, recruitment materials, and class schedules. Publications should identify a contact point where persons with disabilities can obtain accessibility information. Persons with disabilities should be acknowledged in the institution's nondiscrimination statements.

Policies and procedures such as life safety and evacuation plans should address and accommodate the needs of students with disabilities.

The services should ensure that published materials, such as brochures, student and faculty handbooks, and maps (including access information) are available and properly distributed to students with disabilities.

Publications should be reviewed regularly and revised to reflect the level of current services and populations served. The information should be provided in print and alternate formats such as large print, Braille or tape recordings, publications etc.

### 6. Coordinate actions, policies, and procedures that affect students with disabilities.

## Part 3. LEADERSHIP

Effective and ethical leadership is essential to the success of all organizations. The institution must appoint, position and empower leaders within the administrative structure to accomplish stated missions. Leaders at various levels must be selected on the basis of formal education and training, relevant work experience, personal attributes, and other professional credentials. Institutions must determine expectations of accountability for leaders and fairly assess their performance.

Leaders of the disability support services program must exercise authority over resources for which they are responsible to achieve their respective missions. Leaders must articulate a vision for their organizations and set goals and objectives; prescribe and practice ethical behavior; recruit, select, supervise and develop others in the organization; manage plan, budget, and evaluate; communicate effectively; and marshal cooperative action from colleagues, employees, other institutional constituencies, and persons outside the organization. Leaders must address individual, organizational, or environmental conditions that inhibit goal achievement. Leaders must improve programs and services continuously in response to changing needs of students and institutional priorities.

## Part 4. ORGANIZATION and MANAGEMENT

The disability support services program must be structured purposefully and managed efficiently to achieve stated goals. Evidence of appropriate structure must include current and accessible policies and procedures, written performance expectations for all employees, functional work flow graphics or organizational charts, and service delivery expectations. Evidence of effective management must include clear sources and channels of authority, effective communication practices, decision making and conflict resolution procedures, responsiveness to changing conditions, accountability systems, and recognition and reward processes. Disability support services must provide channels within the organization for regular review of administrative policies and procedures.

The disability support services program should be situated within administrative structures in order to develop and direct program activities effectively. Such services normally function within the divisions of student affairs or academic affairs. The services should involve advisory bodies which include students, faculty and staff members with disabilities.

## Part 5. HUMAN RESOURCES

The disability support services program must be staffed adequately by individuals qualified to accomplish its mission and goals. These services must establish procedures for staff selection, training and evaluation; set expectations for supervision, and provide appropriate professional development opportunities.

Professional staff members must hold an earned graduate degree in a field relevant to the position description or must possess an appropriate combination of education and experience.

Degree or credential seeking interns or others in training must be qualified by enrollment in an appropriate field of study and relevant experience. These individuals must be trained and supervised adequately by professional staff members.

Student employees and volunteers must be carefully selected, trained, supervised, and evaluated. When their knowledge and skills are not adequate for particular situations, they must refer students or others in need of assistance to qualified professional staff.

The disability support services program must have secretarial and technical staff adequate to accomplish its mission. Such staff must be technologically proficient and qualified to perform activities such as reception duties, office equipment operation, records maintenance, and mail handling.

Appropriate salary levels and fringe benefits for all staff members must be commensurate with those for comparable positions within the institution, in similar institutions, and in the relevant geographic area.

The disability support services program must intentionally employ a diverse staff to reflect the diversity of the institution's student population, to ensure the existence of readily identifiable role models for students and to enrich the campus community.

Affirmative action must occur in hiring and promotion practices to ensure diverse staffing profiles as required by institutional policies and local, state/provincial, and federal law.

Support staff such as interpreters, readers, aides, scribes, lab assistants, test proctors, and office assistants should possess the academic preparation, experience, abilities, professional interest, and competencies essential for the efficient operation of services.

Support staff may include undergraduate or graduate students. Adequate training and supervision are essential.

Sign language and oral interpreters should have appropriate certification.

Clerical and support staff should possess special knowledge and training in use of equipment unique to students with disabilities. Staff assignments should take into account the benefits of employing persons with disabilities.

## Part 6. FINANCIAL RESOURCES

The disability support services program must have adequate funding to accomplish its mission and goals. Priorities, whether set periodically or as a result of extraordinary conditions, must be determined within the context of the stated missions, goals resources, and obligations under Section 504 of the Rehabilitation Act of 1973 and the Americans with Disabilities Act of 1990.

In addition to normal budget categories, the disability support services program may have special budgetary requirements. These may include the purchase and maintenance of special equipment necessary to provide for access for students with disabilities to institutional programs. Necessary equipment may include telephone communication devices for the deaf (TDD) for office use, screen readers and voice synthesizer, reading machines, devices for enlarging print, braillers, and variable speed tape recorders. This does not include personal equipment such as wheelchairs, hearing aids, or braces. The number and nature of devices that are provided should be governed by the needs of the disabled student population and the capacity of the institution to provide them. The institution should recognize that the service needs and associated costs can vary from term to term.

## Part 7. FACILITIES, TECHNOLOGY, and EQUIPMENT

The disability support services program must have adequate, suitably located facilities and equipment to support its mission and goals. Facilities, technology, and equipment must be in compliance with relevant federal, state, provincial, and local requirements to provide for access, health and safety.

The facilities for disabilities support services program should include, or the program should have access to, the following: private offices or private spaces for counseling, interviewing, or other meetings of a confidential nature; tape recording, space for testing, reception, storage, conference room and meeting space sufficient to accommodate assigned staff, supplies, equipment, and library resources.

The services must be conveniently located on campus and readily accessible to students with disabilities.

All furniture, space, and equipment should be accessible. Particular concern should be given to such things as rest rooms, water fountains, signage, elevators, and corridors. In addition, such facilities should:

(1) Provide access to appropriate space for counseling, reading, writing, test administration and other activities that require confidentiality or intense concentration;

(2) Provide adequate space at appropriate campus locations for assistive devices such as tape recorders, braillers, word processors, closed circuit devices for enlarged print, and equipment with speech output (e.g., computers, calculators, and reading machines) for student use; facilities and equipment must be in compliance with relevant federal, state, provincial, and local requirements to provide for access, health, and safety including minimally (a) have an identifiable and accessible information area; (b) have adequate accessible parking as near as possible to an accessible entrance; and (c) have adequate warning devices such as strobe/buzzer fire alarms for emergencies.

## Part 8. LEGAL RESPONSIBILITIES

Disability support service staff members must be knowledgeable about and responsive to law and regulations that relate to their respective program or service. Sources for legal obligations and limitations include constitutional, statutory, regulatory, and case law; mandatory laws and orders emanating from federal, state, provincial and local governments; and the institution through its policies.

Staff members must use reasonable and informed practices to limit the liability exposure of the institution, its officers, employees, and agents. Staff members must be informed about institutional policies regarding personal liability and related insurance coverage options.

The institution must provide access to legal advice for staff members as needed to carry out assigned responsibilities.

The institution must inform staff and students, in a timely and systematic fashion, about extraordinary or changing legal obligations and potential liabilities.

The institution must appoint an American with Disabilities Act of 1990 compliance officer.

The institution must make available a published set of grievance procedures to students with disabilities as required by the ADA.

## Part 9. EQUAL OPPORTUNITY, ACCESS, and AFFIRMATIVE ACTION

Disability support service staff members must ensure that the disability support services program is provided on a fair and equitable basis. Hours of operation must be responsive to the needs of all students. Each program and service must adhere to the spirit and intent of equal opportunity laws.

The Disability support service program must not be discriminatory on the basis of age, color, disability, gender, national origin, race, religious creed, sexual orientation, and/or veteran status. Exceptions are appropriate only where provided by relevant law and institutional policy.

Consistent with their mission and goals, the disability support services program must take affirmative action to remedy significant imbalances in student participation and staffing patterns.

## Part 10. CAMPUS and COMMUNITY RELATIONS

The disability support services program must establish, maintain, and promote effective relations with campus offices and external agencies.

The services must maintain good working relationships with campus and community service agencies to ensure that disabled students receive necessary and equitable services.

The services should take an active role in the coordination of the institution's response to the needs of disabled students. This is essential to ensure continuity of services, resource management, consistent institutional policies, and the integration of students with disabilities into the total campus experience.

The services should maintain a high degree of visibility with the academic units through the promotion and delivery of services, through involvement in determining what constitutes reasonable accommodation, and through promoting increased understanding of the special needs of students with disabilities.

The services should be informed about, and actively involved in, influencing and affecting the policies and practices of other agencies which directly affect students with disabilities. These include areas such as admissions, orientation, academic advising, counseling, career planning and placement, housing, transportation and parking, financial aid, health services, safety and security, scheduling, and public information as well as campus-wide committees that bear on these agencies and their services.

Disability support service staff members should be particularly cognizant of the fact that for many students with disabilities the institution is only one part of their support system. Some important needs of students with disabilities are met through interaction with community agencies such as state vocational rehabilitation, veterans administration, social security, and other social service agencies. Staff members should act as liaisons between student services, academic services, and community services on the behalf of students with disabilities.

## Part 11. DIVERSITY

Within the context of the institution's mission, multidimensional diversity enriches the community and enhances the collegiate experience for all; therefore, the disability support services program must nurture environments where similarities and differences among people are recognized and honored.

The services must promote cultural education experiences that are characterized by open and continuous communication, that deepen understanding of one's own culture and heritage, and that respect and educate about similarities, differences and histories of cultures.

The services must address the characteristics and needs of a diverse population when establishing and implementing policies and procedures.

# Part 12. ETHICS

All persons involved in the delivery of disability support services must adhere to the highest principles of ethical behavior. The services must develop or adopt and implement statements of ethical practice addressing the issues unique to the program. The disability support services must publish these statements and insure their periodic review by all concerned.

Staff members of the disabilities support services program must ensure that confidentiality is maintained with respect to all communications and records considered confidential unless exempted by law. Information disclosed in individual counseling sessions must remain confidential, unless written permission to divulge the information is given by the student. However, all staff members must disclose to the appropriate authorities information judged to be of legally sufficient an emergency nature, especially when the safety of the individual or others is involved. Information contained in the students' educational records must not be disclosed to non-institutional third parties without appropriate consent, unless classified as "Directory" information or when the information is subpoenaed by law. The services must apply a similar dedication to privacy and confidentiality to research data concerning individuals. Disability support service staff members must be aware of and comply with the provisions contained in the institution's human subjects research policy and in other relevant institutional policies addressing ethical practices.

Staff members must recognize and avoid personal conflict of interest or appearance thereof in their transactions with students and others. Staff members must strive to ensure the fair, objective, and impartial treatment of all persons with whom they deal.

When handling institutional funds, disability support services staff members must ensure that such funds are managed in accordance with established and responsible accounting procedures.

Staff members must not participate in any form of harassment that demeans persons or creates an intimidating, hostile, or offensive campus environment.

Staff members must perform their duties within the limits of their training, expertise, and competence. When these limits are exceeded, individuals in need of further assistance must be referred to persons possessing appropriate qualifications.

Disability support services staff members must use means to confront and otherwise hold accountable other staff members who exhibit unethical behavior.

Staff members must maintain the highest principles of ethical behavior in the use of technology.

# Part 13. ASSESSMENT and EVALUATION

The disability support services program must regularly conduct systematic qualitative and quantitative evaluations of program quality to determine whether and to what degree the stated mission and goals are being met. Although methods of assessment vary, programs and services must employ a sufficient range of measures to ensure objectiveness and comprehensiveness. Data collected must include responses from students and other affected constituencies. Results of these evaluations must be used in revising and improving programs and services and in recognizing staff performance.

Disability support services should be the primary source of information about programming for students with disabilities. Efforts should be made to develop multiple means of disseminating information to ensure access and to reduce attitudinal barriers.

Assessments may be formal or informal, based on ongoing experience with disabled students and units with which they interact. Systematic and periodic assessments should be conducted to address the academic, social, and physical needs of students as well as the psychological and physical environments of the campus. In turn, campus findings should be used to influence how present services should change for future development.

To determine the effectiveness of the organization and administration of the services a data collection system should be implemented. Program evaluation should be obtained from designated staff members, student users, and faculty members.

Analyses of population characteristics and trends in the use of services should be performed regularly. Data should be compiled annually on attrition and graduation rates of students using the services.

# THE ROLE of STUDENT FINANCIAL AID PROGRAMS
## CAS Standards Contextual Statement

Student aid from federal, state, and institutional sources increased by 75 percent in the last decade, topping $50 billion in 1995-96. This aid assisted some 8.5 million students—57 percent of those enrolled in postsecondary education—and most of the aid was administered by institutional personnel.

Concomitant with the tremendous growth of student aid has been growth in federal paperwork and reporting requirements for participating institutions. The number of pages of legislation governing the Title IV federal student aid programs alone has more than doubled in the last decade, and federal regulations promulgated to implement the law now contain more than 7,000 sections, according to a January 1995 study of "Federal Regulations Affecting Higher Education" by the National Association of Independent Colleges and Universities. While states and institutions are important sources of aid, the federal government provides three-fourths of the total aid, and therefore imposes the strongest imperative for accountability.

The mission of the financial aid office focuses on service to students and stewardship of funds. Practically speaking, the financial aid office assumes primary responsibility on behalf of the institution for compliance with federal requirements. This responsibility is reflected in the Institutional Participation Agreement between the institution and the Department of Education. To uphold this agreement, federal regulations require specific standards of administrative capability (34 CFR 668.16):

> "To begin and to continue to participate in any Title IV, HEA program, an institution shall demonstrate to the Secretary that the institution is capable of adequately administering that program under each of the standards established in this section. The Secretary considered an institution to have that administrative capability if the institution—
>
> (a) Administers the Title IV, HEA programs in accordance with all statutory provisions of or applicable to Title IV of the HEA, all applicable regulatory provisions prescribed under that statutory authority, and all applicable special arrangements, agreements, and limitations entered into under the authority of statues applicable to Title IV of the HEA;

> (b) (1) Designates a capable individual to be responsible for administering all the Title IV, HEA programs in which it participates and for coordinating those programs with the institution's other Federal and nonfederal programs of student financial assistance. The Secretary considered an individual to be "capable" under this paragraph if the individual is certified by the State I which the institution is located, if the State requires certification of financial aid administrators. The Secretary may consider other factors in determining whether an individual is capable, including, but not limited to, the individual's successful completion of Title IV, HEA program training provided or approved by the Secretary, and previous experience and documented success in administering the Title IV, HEA programs properly;
>
> (2) Uses an adequate number of qualified persons to administer the Title IV, HEA programs in which the institution participates. The Secretary considers the following factors to determine whether an institution uses an adequate number of qualified persons—
>
> (i)   The number and types of programs in which the institution participates;
>
> (ii)  The number of applications evaluated;
>
> (iii) The number of students who received any student financial assistance at the institution and the amount of funds administered;
>
> (iv)  The financial aid delivery system used by the institution;
>
> (v)   The degree of office automation used by the institution in the administration of the Title IV, HEA programs;
>
> (vi)  The number and distribution of financial aid staff; and
>
> (vii) The use of third-party servicers to aid in the administration of the Title IV, HEA programs; . . . ."

An effective and comprehensive aid program must be supported by leaders at the institution who understand the increasing administrative and operational responsibilities and obligations and the potential liabilities that accompany participation in federal aid programs, and who are aware of the challenges and conflicts imposed on the administration of aid and the delivery of quality services to their students. Leaders can take several steps to ensure that the financial aid program advances the goals of the institution without compromising service quality or program integrity. The consistency between institutional goals and those of the aid program can be evaluated by examining the level of commitment of internal resources, the composition of aid packages, the levels of unmet need, and the extent of commitment to need-based aid.

The establishment and support of goals and measures that ensure high-quality financial aid operations should be a high priority for all institutions. Of equal importance is the leaders' responsibility for educating the institution's community about its goals and mission and the role of financial aid in defining and meeting them. Communicating the importance of financial aid to both internal and external constituencies is critical. Presidents, trustees, and others must understand and support the policies of their financial aid programs and serve as effective advocates at the institutional, state, and federal levels. These advocacy efforts should:

- Provide opportunities for representatives from all academic and administrative areas of the institution to discuss and help formulate institutional goals.

- Coordinate with the financial aid office to develop mission statements and strategic goals that consider its relationship with other offices and present its philosophy, purpose, goals, and strategies, and the principles governing financial aid awards; disseminate these statements to demonstrate the leadership's support of them and their complementary relationship to broader objectives of the institution.

- Provide forums to make known the impact of pending federal and state developments on the institution and the financial aid office.

- Communicate widely the criteria by which financial aid policies are defined and evaluated, and create opportunities to highlight program successes and the positive impact they have on students and the broader community.

Institutions committed to these strategies draw upon tools provided by the government, the National Association of Student Financial Aid Administrators, and other non-governmental entities. Regional and state associations of financial aid administrators support and augment the activities of national entities to provide the technical training and professional development needed to ensure the viability of financial aid operations.

# References, Readings and Resources

National Association of Independent Colleges and Universities (1995). *Federal regulations affecting higher education.* Washington, DC: Author.

National Association of Student Financial Aid Administrators (NASFAA). 1920 L Street, NW, Suite 200, Washington, DC 20036-5020. (202) 785-0453; Fax (202) 785-1487.

# FINANCIAL AID PROGRAMS
## CAS STANDARDS and GUIDELINES

## Part 1. MISSION

The financial aid program must develop, record, disseminate, implement and regularly review its mission and goals. Mission statements must be consistent with the mission and goals of the institution and with the standards in this document.

The financial aid program shall develop, review, and disseminate financial resources to students to assist them in achieving their educational goals from pre-enrollment through graduation. Many aspects of financial aid are mandated by federal and state entities that define the parameters within which institutional programs must operate. In a manner consistent with the goals of the institution the mission and goals of the financial aid program must address the following.

### Students in Transition.

Such students move from secondary to postsecondary education, from one postsecondary institution to another including undergraduate to graduate school, and return from a period of non-enrollment to formal learning or re-enrollment in the institution.

### Awarding Practices.

Such practices establish, promulgate, and implement financial aid criteria that accurately represent the financial needs of the applicant pool, set priorities within this group, and respond with funding to the extent possible.

### Financial Counseling.

Such counseling provides high quality services to students for (a) the purpose of providing better understanding of financial aid, (b) financial guidance, (c) individual review of situations that may require special consideration, and (d) guidance in academic and financial matters especially as they relates to satisfactory academic progress.

### Goal Integration.

Goals should be consistent with the mission, goals, policies, procedures and characteristics of the institution and be compatible with the ability of the institution to provide adequate resources to meet the needs and educational goals of the students.

### Review of Goals.

Institutional goals for financial aid should be developed and reviewed regularly. Such goals should be consistent with statements of good practices articulated by relevant and appropriate professional associations such as the National Association of Student Financial Aid Administrators and the Canadian Association of Student Financial Aid Administrators.

## Part 2. PROGRAM

The formal education of students is purposeful, holistic, and consists of the curriculum and the co-curriculum.

Co-curricular programs and services must be (a) intentional, (b) coherent, (c) based on theories and knowledge of learning and human development, (d) reflective of developmental and demographic profiles of the student population, and (e) responsive to special needs of individuals.

The financial aid program must assist students by addressing financial issues that may serve as barriers to the achievement of educational goals.

The financial aid program must promote learning and development in students by encouraging outcomes such as intellectual growth, ability to communicate effectively, realistic self-appraisal, enhanced self-esteem, clarification of values, appropriate career choices, leadership development, physical fitness, meaningful interpersonal relations, ability to work independently and collaboratively, social responsibility, satisfying and productive lifestyles, appreciation of aesthetic and cultural diversity, and achievement of personal goals.

The financial aid program must

- comply with federal and state law, provincial statutes, and institutional policies;

- promote and maintain integrity, accuracy, and timeliness in the delivery of financial aid;

- provide adequate information for students and parents to make informed decisions regarding the financing of their education; and

- promote and provide equal access to eligible students interested in pursuing an education at the institution.

## Part 3. LEADERSHIP

Effective and ethical leadership is essential to the success of all organizations. Institutions must appoint, position and empower leaders within the administrative structure to accomplish stated missions. Leaders at various levels must be selected on the basis of formal education and training, relevant work experience, personal attributes, and other professional credentials. Institutions must determine expectations of accountability for leaders and fairly assess their performance.

Administrators of financial aid programs must exercise authority over resources for which they are responsible to achieve their respective missions. Leaders must articulate a vision for their organization; set goals and objectives; prescribe and practice ethical behavior; recruit, select, supervise, and develop others in the organization; manage, plan, budget, and evaluate; communicate effectively; and marshal cooperative action from colleagues, employees, other institutional constituencies, and persons outside the organization. Leaders must address individual, organizational, or environmental conditions that inhibit goal achievement. Leaders must improve programs and services continuously in response to changing needs of students and institutional priorities.

> The institution should designate a well-qualified senior administrator with appropriate financial aid experience and training to effectively lead the financial aid program staff.

The senior financial aid administrator must be able to advocate for and to represent the financial needs of students, the operation and staffing of the financial aid program, and the institution.

The senior financial aid administrator must insure the development of

- a set of policies and procedures that includes descriptions of the administrative processes;
- clearly stated criteria used in the decision making process for financial aid and the source of authority for the criteria employed;
- steps for appealing evaluating, or revising policies and procedures;
- a statement of the institution's mission, goals, and objectives for the financial aid programs;
- an effective system to manage the programs, services, and personnel of the financial aid program;
- an assessment plan for its programs and services;
- means for coordinating the financial aid program with other institutional agencies; and
- develop criteria for selecting qualified staff and ensuring adequate opportunities for staff development.

# Part 4. ORGANIZATION and MANAGEMENT

The financial aid program must be structured purposefully and managed effectively to achieve stated goals. Evidence of appropriate structure must include current and accessible policies and procedures, written performance expectations for all employees' functional work flow graphics or organizational charts, and service delivery expectations. Evidence of effective management must include clear sources and channels of authority, effective communication practices, decision-making and conflict resolution procedures, responsiveness to changing conditions, accountability systems, and recognition and reward processes.

The financial aid program must provide channels within its organization for regular review of administrative policies and procedures.

# Part 5. HUMAN RESOURCES

The financial aid program must be staffed adequately by individuals qualified to accomplish its mission and goals. The program must establish procedures for staff selection, training, and evaluation; set expectations for supervision, and provide appropriate professional development opportunities.

Continued training is essential for all financial aid staff. It is imperative to be alert to change within the field and to be able to integrate changes into daily practice.

> Every financial aid staff members should be
>
> - familiar with federal, state/provincial, and institutional regulations, policies, and practices regarding the awarding of financial aid funds;
> - willing to seek out and implement new ideas;
> - able to translate new ideas into practical methods for improving the overall operation of the financial aid program;
> - respectful of the confidential nature of the profession;
> - willing to seek out and use new conceptual frameworks and equipment that bring information to students more clearly and effectively; and
> - aware of relevant developments in the higher education and be able to incorporate these developments.
>
> Financial aid staff members should have knowledge and understanding of the mission, programs and services of the institution. Institutional training should be provided for all staff members to include
>
> - a thorough tour of the campus;
> - familiarization with publications, academic programs, admission policies, and services of the institution; and
> - rights and responsibilities as an employee of the institution.
>
> Job descriptions with the duties and responsibilities for each staff member should be developed.

Professional staff members must hold an earned graduate degree in a field relevant to the position description or must possess an appropriate combination of education and experience.

> Suggested formal training in preparation for professional financial aid employment include such fields as business administration, computer sciences, information systems, college student personnel, higher education administration, counseling and other human behavior disciplines; course work may include computer literacy, research and statistical methods, counseling, legal issues of higher education, and leadership and management.

Professional staff members should be competent to provide assistance to students that May include but not be limited to, the following

- careful and concerned analysis of each student's need;
- knowledgeable guidance and counseling on all financial aid issues and concern;
- explanation of federal and state, and, if appropriate, provincial statues of Canada; and
- interpretation of institutional policies and procedures.

**Graduate students, interns, and others in training must be instructed and supervised adequately by professional staff members.**

**Student employees and volunteers must be carefully selected, trained, supervised, and evaluated. When their knowledge and skills are not adequate for particular situations, they must refer students or others in need of assistance to qualified professional staff members.**

Student employees and volunteers should be trained in public relations, referral techniques, peer counseling, and dissemination of information. They should be knowledgeable in their individual job assignments and understand the confidential nature of their positions.

**The financial aid program must have secretarial and technical staff adequate to accomplish its mission. Such staff must be technologically proficient and qualified to perform activities including reception duties, office equipment operation, records maintenance, and mail handling.**

Support staff members should be skilled in interpersonal communications, public relations, referral techniques and dissemination of information. support staff members with higher technical responsibilities should posses the academic background and experience for effective performance. support staff members should understand the confidential nature of their job.

**Appropriate salary levels and fringe benefits for all staff members must be commensurate with those for comparable positions within the institution, in similar institutions, and in the relevant geographic area.**

**To reflect the diversity of the student population, to ensure the existence of readily identifiable role models for students and to enrich the campus community, institutions must intentionally employ a diverse staff.**

**Affirmative action must occur in hiring and promotion practices as required to ensure diverse staffing profiles.**

## Part 6. FINANCIAL RESOURCES

**The financial aid program must have adequate funding to accomplish its mission and goals. Priorities, whether set periodically or as a result of extraordinary conditions, must be determined within the context of the stated mission, goals, and resources.**

Funding for the financial aid program should cover staff salaries; purchases and maintenance of office furnishings and equipment, including state of the art technology; purchases of supplies and materials; telephone, fax, electronic communication and postage costs; printing and media costs; institutional membership in appropriate professional organizations; relevant subscriptions and necessary library resources; attendance at professional association meetings, conferences, workshops and other professional development activities. In addition to institutional commitment of general funds, other funding sources ma be considered including state appropriations, federal resources, student fees, fines, donations and contributions.

**The financial aid program budget must be properly prepared, clearly detailed and defined, continually monitored and adequately funded for full program support.**

## Part 7. FACILITIES, TECHNOLOGY, and EQUIPMENT

**The financial aid program must have adequate, suitably located facilities, technology, and equipment to support its mission and goals. Facilities and equipment must be in compliance with relevant federal, state/provincial, and local requirements to provide for access, health and safety.**

The program should have facilities or have access to

- private office or space for confidential counseling, interviewing, and other meetings;
- office, reception, and storage space and security sufficient to accommodate assigned staff, supplies, equipment, library resources, and machinery; and
- conference room or meeting space.

The financial aid program should be readily accessible, included on campus maps, and have highly visible signage.

## Part 8. LEGAL RESPONSIBILITIES

**Financial aid program staff members must be knowledgeable about and responsive to law and regulations that relate to their respective program or service. Sources for legal obligations and limitations are constitutional, federal, statutory, regulatory, and case law; mandatory laws and orders emanating from federal, state/provincial and local governments; and the institution through its policies.**

**Financial aid staff members must use reasonable and informed practices to limit the liability exposure of the institution, its officers, employees, and agents. Staff members must be informed about institutional policies regarding personal liability and related insurance coverage options.**

**The institution must provide access to legal advice for staff members as needed to carry out assigned responsibilities.**

**The institution must inform staff and students, in a timely and systematic fashion, about extraordinary or changing legal obligations and potential liabilities.**

Financial aid staff members must be aware of the legal and ethical limits and standards relevant to their roles and perform any counseling or guidance functions accordingly.

## Part 9. EQUAL OPPORTUNITY, ACCESS, and AFFIRMATIVE ACTION

Financial aid staff members must ensure that services and programs are provided on a fair and equitable basis. Each program and service must be accessible. Hours of operation must be responsive to the needs of all students. Each program and service must adhere to the spirit and intent of equal opportunity laws.

> The program should ensure that its programs, services, and facilities are accessible to and provide hours of operation that respond to the needs of special populations, including traditionally under-represented, evening, part-time and commuter students.

The financial aid program must not be discriminatory on the basis of age, color, disability, gender, national origin, race, religious creed, sexual orientation, and/or veteran status. Exceptions are appropriate only where provided by relevant law and institutional policy.

Consistent with its mission and goals, the financial aid program must take affirmative action to remedy significant imbalances in student participation and staffing patterns in keeping with court mandated, institutional, local, state/provincial, and federal laws.

Institutional and financial aid publications must reflect relevant federal and state law, Provincial Statutes, if applicable, and institutional policies and practices.

## Part 10. CAMPUS and COMMUNITY RELATIONS

The financial aid program must establish, maintain, and promote effective relations with relevant campus offices and external agencies.

> Institutional functions and constituencies linked to financial aid typically include admissions, registration and records, athletics, business services, academic advising, counseling services, student affirmative action, outreach programs, educational opportunity programs, career planning and placement, institutional development and faculty and alumni affairs.

Financial aid documents must be accurate and their confidentiality maintained by all offices at the institution.

> Financial aid and admission decisions should be made independently. However, the financial aid program should have access to appropriate information in the student's admission file to assure compliance with applicable rules and regulations.

> The financial aid program should maintain relationships with interested groups within the community regarding general and

institutional financial aid practices. The community may include grant and scholarship agencies, high schools, and other community outreach programs.

## Part 11. DIVERSITY

Within the context of each institution's unique mission, multi-dimensional diversity enriches the community and enhances the collegiate experience for all; therefore, programs and services must nurture environments where similarities and differences among people are recognized and honored.

The financial aid program must promote cultural educational experiences that are characterized by open and continuous communication, that deepen understanding of one's own culture and heritage, and that respect and educate about similarities, differences and histories of cultures.

The financial aid program must address the characteristics and needs of a diverse population when establishing and implementing policies and procedures.

> Financial aid staff members should be particularly sensitive to the needs of traditionally under-represented students and students with special needs.

## Part 12. Ethics

Students must be provided access to financial aid programs and services on a fair and equitable basis.

All persons involved in the delivery of financial aid must adhere to the highest principles of ethical behavior. Programs and services must develop or adopt and implement statements of ethical practice addressing the issues unique to each program and service. Programs and services must publish these statements and insure their periodic review by all concerned.

> In the formulation of these standards, ethical standards statements adopted by the profession at large or relevant professional associations may be of assistance and should be considered.

Financial aid staff members must ensure that confidentiality is maintained with respect to all communications and records considered confidential unless exempted by law. Information disclosed in individual counseling sessions must remain confidential, unless written permission to divulge the information is given by the student. However, all staff members must disclose to appropriate authorities information judged to be of an emergency nature, especially when the safety of the individual or others is involved. Information contained in students' educational records must not be disclosed to non-institutional third parties without appropriate consent, unless classified as "Directory" information or when the information is subpoenaed by law. The financial aid program must apply a similar dedication to privacy and confidentiality to research data concerning individuals. All staff members must be aware of and comply with the provisions contained in the institution's human subjects research policy and in other relevant institutional policies addressing ethical practices.

Financial aid staff members must recognize and avoid personal conflict of interest or appearance thereof in their transactions with students and others. Staff members must strive to insure the fair, objective, and impartial treatment of all persons with whom they deal.

When handling institutional funds, all staff members must ensure that such funds are managed in accordance with established and responsible accounting procedures.

Financial aid staff members must maintain the highest principles of ethical behavior in the use of technology.

Financial aid staff members must not participate in any form of harassment that demeans persons or creates an intimidating, hostile, or offensive campus environment.

Staff members must perform their duties within the limits of their training, expertise, and competence. When these limits are exceeded, individuals in need of further assistance must be referred to persons possessing appropriate qualifications.

Financial aid staff members must use suitable means to confront and otherwise hold accountable other staff members who exhibit unethical behavior.

Financial aid administrators must insure timely and fair administration of policies regarding financial aid decisions and proper notification.

Publications and written communications should include a financial aid deadlines and information on opportunities for financial aid.

Financial aid must be awarded in compliance with applicable rules and regulations governing financial aid.

When appropriate, the senior financial aid administrator and professional staff members may need to exercise professional judgment in making exceptions to established financial aid policies. These decisions should be made in a fair and objective manner with supporting documentation.

## Part 13. ASSESSMENT and EVALUATION

Programs and services must regularly conduct systematic qualitative and quantitative evaluations of program quality to determine whether and to what degree the stated mission and goals are being met. Although methods of assessment vary, programs and services must employ a sufficient range of measures to insure objectivity and comprehensiveness. Data collected must include responses from students and other affected constituencies. Results of these evaluations must be used in revising and improving programs and services and in recognizing staff performance.

Publications such as the *Institutional Guide for Financial Aid Self-Evaluation,* published by the National Association of Student Financial Aid Administrators, may be used to evaluate financial aid programs and services.

# THE ROLE of FRATERNITY and SORORITY ADVISING
## CAS Standards Contextual Statement

Full-time fraternity and sorority advisors have been a part of the professional staff of colleges and universities since the 1950s. With the unprecedented growth in membership in fraternity and sorority organizations in the 1960s, many universities decided to formally define the relationship between the campus chapters and the host institution. In 1976, at the bicentennial celebration of the establishment of the country's first Greek chapter, the Association of Fraternity Advisors (AFA) was established. During the past 20 years, institutions and fraternity/sorority advising professionals have moved toward a model that further defines the role of fraternity/sorority advisor as administrator and advisor.

Advising fraternities and sororities is a unique experience for many new professionals. In most instances, the fraternity/sorority advisor acts as an external monitor of Greek organizations, depending significantly on the quality of chapter leadership and alumni/ae involvement in effecting changes within individual chapters. For the fraternity/sorority system on a campus, the advisor functions as a counselor, advisor, and educational programmer responsible for carrying out such programs as date rape awareness, time management, team building, and leadership training, and serving as institutional representative responsible for enforcing policy. Similarly, the advisor must understand business management and know how to handle public relations with the community.

At this point in higher education's evolution, the mystery that once shrouded fraternity and sorority membership is disappearing. Students no longer feel the need to join a Greek organization to obtain social approval. Nevertheless, fraternity and sorority membership has grown to more than 12 million members in more than 23,000 chapters nationwide. Some contend that fraternities and sororities exert a great deal of actual and potential force for contributing positively to higher education and to individual student development. Sanford (1964) wrote that fraternities (and sororities) serve some very genuine, legitimate needs of students. They meet the need of students to have close associates who can be trusted and for whom sacrifices can be made. In concert with the role fraternity/sorority membership plays in meeting the social needs of students, the fraternity/sorority advising professional can achieve remarkable student learning and development.

Many new students require a supported structure and a personal atmosphere; fraternity and sorority organizations provide both. Through their emphasis on tradition and ritual, these organizations offer new members structure; they also provide a safe forum for exchanging ideas and for interpersonal interactions.

Besides providing a personal and supportive atmosphere, Greek organizations also emphasize leadership. Today, a broad array of purposeful opportunities designed to facilitate student development are provided to promote growth during college. Exposure to new contacts, resources, and issues stimulates student growth and development.

The fraternity/sorority advisor can strengthen fraternities and sororities by helping the campus system, chapter leadership, and individual students understand the rights and responsibilities associated with a commitment to membership. By explaining rights and responsibilities, detailing services, and adhering to student development theory, fraternity/sorority advisors create a model for quality education and student learning. The standards and guidelines that follow provide comprehensive guidance for institutions that include fraternity and sorority organizations in the campus culture.

## References, Readings and Resources

Johnson, C. S. (1972). *Fraternities in our colleges.* New York: National Interfraternity Foundation.

Sanford, N. (Ed.). (1964) *College and character.* New York: John Wiley & Sons.

Winston, R. B., Jr., Nettles, W. R., III, & Opper, J. H., Jr. (Eds.) (1987). *Fraternities and sororities on the contemporary college campus.* New Directions for Student Services, No. 40. San Francisco: Jossey-Bass.

# FRATERNITY and SORORITY ADVISING
## CAS STANDARDS and GUIDELINES

## Part 1. MISSION

The institution and the fraternity and sorority advising program must develop, review, and disseminate regularly their own specific goals for student services/development. These goals must be consistent with the nature and goals of the institution and with the standards in this document.

The fraternity and sorority advising program must have a mission which facilitates the growth and development of students who choose to affiliate with Greek letter groups, and promotes the Greek system as an integral and productive part of the institution.

To accomplish the mission, the goals of the program must include:

- promoting the intellectual, social, recreational, spiritual, moral, and career development of students;
- providing training in leadership and other personal and social skills;
- promoting student involvement in cocurricular activities;
- promoting sponsorship of and participation in community service projects;
- providing training in group processes;
- promoting loyalty to the organization and the institution;
- promoting positive educational outcomes;
- promoting an appreciation for different lifestyles and cultural heritages, and
- recognizing the positive cultural traditions in a diversity of Greek organizations.

Participation in a fraternity or sorority chapter represents one of several group affiliation options for college students. Greek affiliation may include: a selection process, pledge/associate member education, initiation (formal induction into the organization), and lifelong membership. Professional staff members should promote student development in all affiliation processes.

Staff members should develop a coherent program to promote the education and welfare of participating students, coordinating the use of resources and Greek life activities with others in the campus community.

## Part 2. PROGRAM

The formal education of students is purposeful, holistic, and consists of the curriculum and the co-curriculum.

Fraternity and sorority advising programs must be (a) intentional, (b) coherent, (c) based on theories and knowledge of learning and human development, (d) reflective of developmental and demographic profiles of the student population, and (e) responsive to special needs of individuals.

Fraternity and sorority advising programs must promote learning and development in students by encouraging outcomes such as intellectual growth, ability to communicate effectively, realistic self-appraisal, enhanced self-esteem, clarification of values, appropriate career choices, leadership development, physical fitness, meaningful interpersonal relations, ability to work independently and collaboratively, social responsibility, satisfying and productive lifestyles, appreciation of aesthetic and cultural diversity, and achievement of personal goals.

Fraternity and sorority advising programs must include at least the following elements:

- **Educational programming that enhances member's knowledge, understanding, and skills essential for academic success, personal development, and the exercise of leadership.**

  Educational programming should complement the academic curriculum. Activities which improve the student's chances of academic success arc particularly important. There should be programs that address the maturation and development of students.

  Staff members should provide for programs that encourage faculty and administrator involvement and interaction with students.

  Leadership programs should be designed to help the individual effectively understand and manage group processes, particularly the relevant aspects of group self-governance.

  Citizenship programs should assist students to become responsible and involved community members.

- **Social and recreational programming to enhance members' knowledge, understanding, and skills necessary for social success and the productive use of leisure time.**

  Social skills programs should assist individuals to develop more complex and satisfying interpersonal relationships.

  Recreation programs should be designed to promote recreational sports participation and other constructive leisure time activities, addressing the psychological as well as the physical well-being of each individual.

- **Advocacy within the college administration for Greek life experiences and organizations as appropriate; and promotion, both within and beyond the Greek system, of broad understanding of Greek life**

**members' rights and responsibilities. Such are properly defined by both the institution's rules and regulations and the individual's fraternity or sorority.**

Professional staff members should help students function productively within the institution and to fully understand individual and group rights and responsibilities. This may include such activities as: interpreting institutional policies, administrating a disciplinary system that safeguards due process, conducting performance evaluations, and providing outreach programming to familiarize other departments and community agencies with Greek Life. Staff members should avoid social situations that pose conflicts of interest.

- **Educating fraternity and sorority members about the risks involved in the use of alcohol and other drugs.**
- **Enforcement of federal, state, and local laws as well as institutional policy against hazing.**
- **Programs must be designed to educate student members about issues of sexual harassment, racism, intolerance based on religion or sexual orientation. and other practices and attitudes, such as hazing, that diminish human dignity.**
- **Advising Greek life groups, their individual members, and their chapter officers with regard to their leadership roles and responsibilities.**

Advising services may include:

- monitoring scholastic standing of chapters and chapter members and recommending programs for improvement;
- providing workshops, programs, retreats, and seminars on relevant topics (e.g., substance abuse, human relations, human sexuality, and eating disorders);
- meeting with chapter leaders to discuss individual goals and developmental needs as well as chapter goals and developmental needs;
- assisting student members to understand their responsibilities to the group and to the future of the organization;
- attending individual chapter meetings on a periodic basis;
- disseminating information via monthly meetings, newsletters, and/or information bulletins to the various groups involved in Greek Life (e.g., chapter advisors, house corporation members, chapter presidents, and institutional administrators);
- coordinating the scheduling of service projects of individual chapters;
- encouraging chapter members' attendance at regional and national conferences;
- evaluating chapter development and recommending programs for improvement;
- advising the fraternity and sorority campus councils to enhance leadership development;
- providing assistance and advice in the planning of both Greek system and individual chapter programs (e.g., Greek Week, fund raising, and fiscal management);
- assisting chapters to identify and gain access, where appropriate, to institutional services (e.g., printing, bulk

mailing, legal assistance, alumni affairs, and computer services);

- providing a membership directory of chapter officers and a calendar of events for all chapters;
- publishing a newsletter that focuses on current events, leadership opportunities, and Greek life information;
- developing a speaker's directory that focuses on educational programs for distribution to fraternity/sorority chapters;
- conducting annual fire prevention and energy conservation programs in conjunction with local agencies;
- coordinating cooperative buying efforts on behalf of the local chapters; and
- monitoring of membership statistics and academic retention by chapter and system.

# Part 3. LEADERSHIP

Effective and ethical leadership is essential to the success of all organizations. Institutions must appoint, position and empower leaders within the administrative structure to accomplish stated missions. Leaders at various levels must be selected on the basis of formal education and training, relevant work experience, personal attributes, and other professional credentials. Institutions must determine expectations of accountability for leaders and fairly assess their performance.

Leaders of fraternity and sorority advising programs must exercise authority over resources for which they are responsible to achieve their respective missions. Leaders must articulate a vision for their organization; set goals and objectives; prescribe and practice ethical behavior; recruit, select, supervise, and develop others in the organization; manage, plan, budget, and evaluate; communicate effectively; and marshal cooperative action from colleagues, employees, other institutional constituencies, and persons outside the organization. Program leaders must address individual, organizational, or environmental conditions that inhibit goal achievement. Leaders must improve programs and services continuously in response to changing needs of students and institutional priorities.

# Part 4. ORGANIZATION and MANAGEMENT

Fraternity and sorority advising programs must be structured purposefully and managed effectively to achieve stated goals. Evidence of appropriate structure must include current and accessible policies and procedures, written performance expectations for all employees' functional work flow graphics or organizational charts, and service delivery expectations. Evidence of effective management must include clear sources and channels of authority, effective communication practices, decision-making and conflict resolution procedures, responsiveness to changing conditions, accountability systems, and recognition and reward processes.

Fraternity and sorority advising programs must provide channels within the organization for regular review of administrative policies and procedures.

> Many models for organizing fraternities and sororities exist. The size and philosophy of the system with the institution will determine its organizational parameters. It may include separate living arrangements with various levels of affiliation with the college. However, the Greek life system should be a fully integrated component of the institution's student development program. Staff members who work with fraternities and sororities commonly report to the chief student affairs officer or designee.

## Part 5. HUMAN RESOURCES

Fraternity and sorority advising programs must be staffed adequately by individuals qualified to accomplish its mission and goals. Programs and services must establish procedures for staff selection, training, and evaluation; set expectations for supervision, and provide appropriate professional development opportunities.

Professional staff members must hold an earned graduate degree in a field relevant to the position description or must possess an appropriate combination of education and experience.

> Specific coursework helpful in a graduate program may include organizational behavior and development, speech, communication, research and evaluation, ethics, appraisal of educational practices, group dynamics, budgeting, counseling techniques, leadership development, learning and human development theories, administration, performance appraisal and supervision, administrative uses of computers, higher education, and student affairs functions.

Degree or credential seeking interns or others in training must be qualified by enrollment in an appropriate field of study and relevant experience. These individuals must be trained and supervised adequately by professional staff members.

Student employees and volunteers must be carefully selected, trained, supervised, and evaluated. When their knowledge and skills are not adequate for particular situations, they must refer students or others in need of assistance to qualified professional staff.

The fraternity and sorority advising program must have secretarial and technical staff adequate to accomplish its mission. Such staff must be technologically proficient and qualified to perform activities including reception duties, office equipment operation, records maintenance, and mail handling.

Appropriate salary levels and fringe benefits for all staff members must be commensurate with those for comparable positions within the institution, in similar institutions, and in the relevant geographic area.

The fraternity and sorority advising program must intentionally employ a diverse staff to reflect the diversity of the institution's student population, to ensure the existence of readily identifiable role models for students and to enrich the campus community.

Affirmative action must occur in hiring and promotion practices to ensure diverse staffing profiles as required by institutional policies and local, state/provincial, and federal law.

The fraternity and sorority advising program must have adequate and qualified professional staff to fulfill its mission and to implement all aspects of the program.

The fraternity and sorority advising program must have a system of staff selection and evaluation, and must provide continuing professional development opportunities for staff including inservice training programs, participation in professional conferences, workshops, and other continuing education activities.

> Administrative expertise is critical to the success of the program, with effective management required in the areas of housing, dining, accounting, safety and risk management, alumni relations, and programming.
>
> There should be sufficient professional staff resources to allow for the coordination of chapter and system developmental activities, including planning, implementation, and evaluation. Staff should be qualified to work with various internal and external agencies in formulating the goals and directions of the chapters and system, consistent with institutional policies.
>
> A Greek life advisor should have experience in development and implementation of educational programs for students.
>
> Staff should coordinate the information gathering and dissemination processes relative to Greek life and serve as an immediate information resource for students, alumni, and other administrators.
>
> The use of graduate assistants and interns may be a way to expand staff capabilities and to provide valuable experience for young professionals who have an interest in the Greek life advising function.
>
> When appropriate, student employees or volunteers may be utilized and assigned responsibilities for specific projects that are administered or coordinated within the program. Students can lend a valuable perspective to educational programming efforts. (See also Campus and Community Relations in this Standard.)

## Part 6. FINANCIAL RESOURCES

The fraternity and sorority advising program must have adequate funding to accomplish its mission and goals. Priorities, whether set periodically or as a result of extraordinary conditions, must be determined within the context of the stated mission, goals, and resources.

When any special institutional or Greek system funding or expenditure accounts are used, professional staff members should provide for the collection and disbursement of such funds, utilizing the accounting procedures of the institution.

## Part 7. FACILITIES, TECHNOLOGY, and EQUIPMENT

The fraternity and sorority advising program must have adequate, suitably located facilities and equipment to support its mission and goals. Facilities, technology, and equipment must be in compliance with relevant federal, state, provincial, and local requirements to provide for access, health and safety.

Houses or common rooms that are owned, rented, or otherwise assigned to fraternities or sororities for their use must be managed in accordance with all applicable regulatory and statutory requirements of the host institution and relevant government authorities.

> To effectively carry out the activities, services, and programs of the Greek life advising functions, adequate space should be provided for private consultations, a work area for support staff, and a resource library. Any office provided should be accessible to students served by the program, and should be integrated with other institutional student support services.

## Part 8. LEGAL RESPONSIBILITIES

Fraternity and sorority advising staff members must be knowledgeable about and responsive to law and regulations that relate to their respective responsibilities. Sources for legal obligations and limitations include constitutional, statutory, regulatory, and case law; mandatory laws and orders emanating from federal, state, provincial and local governments; and the institution through its policies.

Staff members must use reasonable and informed practices to limit the liability exposure of the institution, its officers, employees, and agents. Staff members must be informed about institutional policies regarding personal liability and related insurance coverage options.

The institution must provide access to legal advice for staff members as needed to carry out assigned responsibilities.

The institution must inform staff and students, in a timely and systematic fashion, about extraordinary or changing legal obligations and potential liabilities.

## Part 9. EQUAL OPPORTUNITY, ACCESS, and AFFIRMATIVE ACTION

Staff members must ensure that the fraternity and sorority advising program is provided on a fair and equitable basis. The program must be accessible. Hours of operation must be responsive to the needs of all students. The program must adhere to the spirit and intent of equal opportunity laws.

Fraternity and sorority advising programs must not be discriminatory on the basis of age, color, disability, gender, national origin, race, religious creed, sexual orientation, and/or veteran status. Exceptions are appropriate only where provided by relevant law and institutional policy.

Consistent with its mission and goals, the fraternity and sorority advising program must take affirmative action to remedy significant imbalances in student participation and staffing patterns.

## Part 10. CAMPUS and COMMUNITY RELATIONS

The fraternity and sorority advising program must establish, maintain, and promote effective relations with relevant campus offices and external agencies.

To enhance the potential for student development and to properly represent institutional governance concerns, the advisor must seek to utilize multiple resources in the delivery of services and programs. These include, minimally, the national headquarters staff, alumni, the chapter officers and the membership, faculty members, and other institutional administrators.

> Faculty members are valuable as chapter advisors and role models for students. They serve on committees that focus on institutional issues affecting the Greek system. Further, faculty members can help shape the institutional policy with regard to the Greek system. Effective and consistent communication between faculty members and Greek chapter members will increase the chances for success in creating a meaningful living/learning environment. This communication will enhance the possibility of improving the academic success of each Greek life student and increase understanding of educational goals.

> Alumni can serve as valuable resources. The Greek life program should encourage and enlist a productive level of involvement of alumni and should assist with information exchange activities and with alumni-sponsored program efforts.

> The Greek life advisor is normally the principal representative of the administration to the Greek life community. Also, the advisor is normally the principle advocate for the Greek system within the administration.

Institutions must clearly articulate their relationships to Greek life organizations.

> Relationship statements should include, but are not necessarily limited to: (a) a description of the system; (b) historical relationships; (c) educational role of fraternities and sororities; (d) conditions and responsibilities of affiliation; (e) housing/ facilities; (f) support and program orientation; (g) governance and authority [e.g., national organization affiliation, expansion, etc.]; (h) reference to comprehensive policy documents; (i) expectations of the institution and the Greek system; and (j) accountability to other student governing bodies.

When chapter houses are located in community neighborhoods, good working relationships with merchants and community leaders must be maintained to promote cooperative solutions to problems that may arise.

> Chapters may have access to and be governed by local government community services and agencies. The Greek life advisor should assist students to maintain responsible community living patterns. Commonly, issues such as fire safety, noise control, parking, and security require ongoing attention.

> Philanthropic activities and community volunteer involvement, which have been traditional components of Greek life programs, should be developed, maintained, and enhanced.

The fraternity and sorority advising program staff must maintain effective contact with national headquarters officers.

> A team approach in working with students in the local chapters should be a common goal of Greek life advisors, alumni, and national offices.

## Part 11. DIVERSITY

Within the context of the institution's unique mission, multi-dimensional diversity enriches the community and enhances the collegiate experience for all; therefore, the fraternity and sorority advising program must nurture environments where similarities and differences among people are recognized and honored.

The program must promote cultural educational experiences that are characterized by open and continuous communication, that deepen understanding of one's own culture and heritage, and that respect and educate about similarities, differences and histories of cultures.

The program must address the characteristics and needs of a diverse population when establishing and implementing policies and procedures.

The institution's fraternity and sorority advising program must provide to members of its majority and minority cultures educational efforts that focus on awareness of cultural differences, self-assessment of possible prejudices, and desirable behavioral changes.

The fraternity and sorority advising program must provide educational programs that enable under represented groups to identify their needs and meet them to the degree that numbers of students, facilities, and their resources permit. The program must orient students of historically underrepresented groups to the culture of the institution and promote and deepen their understanding of their own culture and heritage.

The fraternity and sorority advising program must enhance students' knowledge, understanding, and skills for being a member of a pluralistic society.

> The fraternity and sorority advising program should include outreach to underrepresented populations in membership recruitment activities.

## Part 12. ETHICS

All persons involved in the delivery of fraternity and sorority advising programs for students must adhere to the highest principles of ethical behavior. Programs must develop or adopt and implement statements of ethical practice addressing the issues unique to each program and service. Programs and services must publish these statements and insure their periodic review by all concerned.

Staff members must ensure that confidentiality is maintained with respect to all communications and records considered confidential unless exempted by law.

Information disclosed in individual counseling sessions must remain confidential, unless written permission to divulge the information is given by the student. However, all staff members must disclose to appropriate authorities information judged to be of an emergency nature, especially when the safety of the individual or others is involved. Information contained in students' educational records must not be disclosed to non-institutional third parties without appropriate consent, unless classified as "Directory" information or when the information is subpoenaed by law. Fraternity and sorority advising programs must apply a similar dedication to privacy and confidentiality to research data concerning individuals. All staff members must be aware of and comply with the provisions contained in the institution's human subjects research policy and in other relevant institutional policies addressing ethical practices.

Staff members must recognize and avoid personal conflict of interest or appearance thereof in their transactions with students and others. Staff members must strive to insure the fair, objective, and impartial treatment of all persons with whom they deal.

When handling institutional funds, all staff members must ensure that such funds are managed in accordance with established and responsible accounting procedures.

Fraternity and sorority advising staff members must not participate in any form of harassment that demeans persons or creates an intimidating, hostile, or offensive campus environment.

Staff members must perform their duties within the limits of their training, expertise, and competence. When these limits are exceeded, individuals in need of further assistance must be referred to persons possessing appropriate qualifications.

Staff members must use suitable means to confront and otherwise hold accountable other staff members who exhibit unethical behavior.

Fraternity and sorority advising staff members must maintain the highest principles of ethical behavior in the use of technology.

Staff members must demonstrate a high level of ethical conduct. The Greek system must adopt a statement of ethics which strives to:

- treat fairly all students who wish to affiliate;

- eliminate illegal discrimination in selection of members; and

- uphold applicable standards of conduct expressed by respective national organizations.

# Part 13. ASSESSMENT and EVALUATION

Fraternity and sorority advising programs must regularly conduct systematic qualitative and quantitative evaluations of program quality to determine whether and to what degree the stated mission and goals are being met. Although methods of assessment vary, Greek life programs must employ a sufficient range of measures to insure objectivity and comprehensiveness. Data collected must include responses from students and other affected constituencies. Results of these evaluations must be used in revising and improving programs and services and in recognizing staff performance.

Evaluation of Greek life goals and objectives should be sought from relevant administrative units, community agencies, alumni, students, faculty, and national headquarters staff. Selected critical aspects of evaluations should be recorded and maintained by the institution.

Evaluations should address the following:

• The Greek system, programs, services, and activities

Evaluations should be made to determine the strength of leadership, the system's purposes and priorities, individual chapters' congruence with institutional and system purposes, the effectiveness of programs, and the availability and stability of resources.

• Chapter needs, goals, and objectives

The vitally of each chapter needs to be evaluated on a periodic basis. Evaluation of each group's leadership, self sufficiency, productive activities, and relative status within the campus community should be undertaken regularly.

• The living environment of each chapter

Periodic yearly safety, sanitation, and quality of life inspections should be conducted of all housing facilities. Kitchens, building electrical systems, heating systems, and fire control equipment require special attention.

© Copyright 1997 Council for the Advancement of Standards in Higher Education [CAS]

# THE ROLE of COLLEGE and UNIVERSITY STUDENT HOUSING
## CAS Standards Contextual Statement

Although American institutions of higher learning have provided student housing in one form or another since the first colleges were founded (Frederiksen, 1993), the professionalization of those employed in housing was greatly enhanced when the Association of College and University Housing Officers-International (ACUHO-I) held its first annual conference in 1949. This meeting marked a significant step forward in the development of college and university student housing programs as a profession.

Until the middle of this century, college and university residence halls were administered by "housemothers," often under the supervision of deans of men or women. These staff members assumed parental responsibility (*in loco parentis*) for the students housed in the residence halls. During the 1960s, dramatic changes in laws and education produced changes in the operation of residence halls. Housemothers were replaced by full-time staff with professional training in counseling and administration. These student affairs professionals focused on using the residence hall environment as a tool to complement formal classroom education. Since the 1960s, student housing has become increasingly more specialized and complex. However, the concept of utilizing residence halls as combined living-learning environments to enhance classroom learning has remained constant.

Many college and university student housing operations employ staff members with wide varieties of skills and functions. Areas administered by institutional housing and residence life programs include such functions as:

- Administration of various electronic media (residential cable TV channels, network access, internal movie and information channels, electronic access systems)
- Apartment housing
- Conference housing
- Education (e.g., leadership development, student government advising, student conduct, joint programs with faculty and academic departments, community and individual development)
- Facilities maintenance
- Financial and program planning and administration
- Food services (including catering and cash food operations)
- Marketing
- Off campus rental referral
- Planning and administration of the construction of new facilities
- Research, evaluation and assessment
- Safety and security

Most institutional student housing operations are self-supported auxiliaries that do not receive financial support from the institution or other public sources; in effect, student housing is an education "business." Because of the wide scope and function of student housing, planning is usually initiated institution-wide. Likewise, although housing encompasses many functions, most administrations agree that students are best served when all housing and residence life functions fall under the responsibility of a single administrator, usually the director of housing.

Group living influences maturation by exposing students to a variety of experiences. What distinguishes group living in campus residence from most other forms of housing is the involvement of both professional and paraprofessional staff members in providing intentional, as opposed to random, educational experiences for students. Students living in residence halls participate in more extracurricular, social, and cultural events; are more likely to graduate; and exhibit greater positive gains in psychosocial development, intellectual orientation, and self concept than students living at home or commuting. In addition, they demonstrate significantly greater increases in aesthetic, cultural, and intellectual values; social and political liberalism; and secularism (Schroeder & Mable, 1993).

Residence halls contribute significantly to a student's educational experience. The standards and guidelines that follow provide guidance to those who work in this field and accountability to the public they serve.

# References, Readings and Resources

Association of College and University Housing Officers-International (ACUHO-I) (1992). *Ethical principles and standards for college and university housing Professionals.* Columbus, OH: Author.

Frederiksen, C. F. (1993). A brief history of collegiate housing. In R. B. Winston, Jr. & S. Anchors, *Student housing and residential life: A handbook for student affairs professionals committed to student development goals.* pp. 167-183. San Francisco: Jossey-Bass.

Schroeder, C. C., Mable, P., & Associates. (1993). *Realizing the educational potential of residence halls.* San Francisco: Jossey-Bass.

Winston, R. B, Jr., Anchors, S., & Associates (1993). *Student housing and residential life: A handbook for student affairs professionals committed to student development goals.* San Francisco: Jossey-Bass.

*The Journal of College and University Student Housing.* Published by the Association of College and University Housing Officers-International (ACUHO-I), 101 Curl Dr., Suite 140, Columbus, OH 43210. (614) 292-0099; Fax (614) 292-0305; gschwarz@magnus.acs.ohio-state.edu

# HOUSING and RESIDENTIAL LIFE PROGRAMS
## CAS STANDARDS and GUIDELINES

## Part 1. MISSION

The housing and residential life program must develop, record, disseminate, implement and regularly review its mission and goals. Mission statements must be consistent with the mission and goals of the institution and with the standards in this document.

The housing and residential life program is an integral part of the educational purpose of the institution. Its mission must include provision for educational programs and services, residential facilities, management services, and, where appropriate, food services.

To accomplish the mission, the goals of the program must provide:

- a residential community that encourages both individual and community development and learning;
- reasonably priced safe and secure facilities that are clean, attractive, well maintained, and comfortable;
- management services that ensure the orderly and effective administration and operation of all aspects of the program; and where appropriate,
- food, dining facilities, and related services that effectively meet institutional and residential life program goals.

## Part 2. PROGRAM

The formal education of students is purposeful, holistic, and consists of the curriculum and the co-curriculum.

The housing and residential life program must be (a) intentional, (b) coherent, (c) based on theories and knowledge of learning and human development, (d) reflective of developmental and demographic profiles of the student population, and (e) responsive to special needs of individuals.

Housing and residential life programs must promote learning and development in students by encouraging outcomes such as intellectual growth, ability to communicate effectively, realistic self-appraisal, enhanced self-esteem, clarification of values, appropriate career choices, leadership development, physical fitness, meaningful interpersonal relations, ability to work independently and collaboratively, social responsibility, satisfying and productive lifestyles, appreciation of aesthetic and cultural diversity, and achievement of personal goals.

To fulfill its mission and goals effectively, the housing and residential life program must provide the following.

**Individual and group educational and developmental opportunities.**

Opportunities should include activities and/or experiences in:
- understanding and managing personal health, finances, and time;
- living cooperatively with others;
- improving interpersonal relationships and communication skills;
- promoting and demonstrating responsible social behavior such as avoiding participation in racial and sexual exploitation and discrimination;
- developing leadership skills;
- exploring and managing leisure time;
- promoting and demonstrating a proper understanding of the results of alcohol and other drug use and abuse; and
- promoting a sense of responsibility for the security of the community environment.

Educational programming, advising, and supervisory activities provided by the housing and residential life staff should address developmental objectives and should vary in accordance with local needs. Examples include:
- introduction and orientation of students to facilities, services, staff members and functions, and community norms and expectations;
- education of students on safety, security, and emergency precautions and procedures and on taking responsibility for their safety and security; .
- explanation of institutional and residential living policies, procedures, and expectations;
- development of an atmosphere conducive to educational pursuits;
- assessment of needs of both general and specific student populations including identified special interests;
- encouragement of student participation in institutional and residence hall programs, activities, groups, and organizations;
- encouragement of campus professionals' collaboration in conducing support activities such as learning strategies, time management, and study groups and workshops;
- provision of information to students about academics, institutional judicial system policies and procedures, and relevant civil and criminal laws;
- provision of training to aid staff members in recognizing problem behaviors, creating interventions, and making appropriate referrals;
- development of appropriate social, recreational, educational, cultural, and community service programs;
- provision of individual and group advising and counseling support; and
- encouragement of students to develop a sense of community responsibility through exposure to education about

93

inappropriate and disruptive behavior and participation activities such as (a) developing policies and making decisions, (b) mediating conflict within the community, (c) assessing fair charges to individuals responsible for damages, and (d) evaluating various aspects of the housing and residential life program.

**Where applicable, specialized functions, such as conference administration, apartment housing, and off-campus housing services.**

Any specialized functions should be effectively managed and administered in a manner consistent with the mission and goals of the institution. Such operations should be managed so as not to impair student housing operations when student residential facilities are used for conferences.

Off-campus housing services should include referrals to available housing opportunities, information about leases and landlord/tenant law, and other related information.

**Where applicable, food services that provide high-quality, nutritious, and reasonably priced meals and support the programmatic and education mission of the institution.**

Food services should include:

- menu planning to provide optimum nutrition and variety;
- purchase of high quality food products;
- recipes and processes which ensure appetizing food preparation and presentation;
- safety features and sanitary conditions;
- attention to students' varied schedules, cultural differences, and special dietary needs;
- management policies and practices that ensure timely delivery of services and products;
- good customer relations;
- adequate space and a pleasant environment in dining areas;
- involvement in educational programming which supports program goals;
- materials which educate students about nutrition; and
- solicitation of input from diners regarding menu selection and satisfaction with the dining program.

## Part 3. LEADERSHIP

**Effective and ethical leadership is essential to the success of all organizations. Institutions must appoint, position and empower leaders within the administrative structure to accomplish stated missions. Leaders at various levels must be selected on the basis of formal education and training, relevant work experience, personal attributes, and other professional credentials. Institutions must determine expectations of accountability for leaders and fairly assess their performance.**

**Leaders of housing and residential life programs must exercise authority over resources for which they are responsible to achieve their respective missions. Leaders must articulate a vision for their organization; set goals and objectives; prescribe and practice ethical**

behavior; recruit, select, supervise, and develop others in the organization; manage, plan, budget, and evaluate; communicate effectively; and marshal cooperative action from colleagues, employees, other institutional constituencies, and persons outside the organization. Housing leaders must address individual, organizational, or environmental conditions that inhibit goal achievement. In addition, housing leaders must improve programs and services continuously in response to changing needs of students and institutional priorities.**

## Part 4. ORGANIZATION and MANAGEMENT

**The housing and residential life program must be structured purposefully and managed effectively to achieve stated goals. Evidence of appropriate structure must include current and accessible policies and procedures, written performance expectations for all employees' functional work flow graphics or organizational charts, and service delivery expectations. Evidence of effective management must include clear sources and channels of authority, effective communication practices, decision-making and conflict resolution procedures, responsiveness to changing conditions, accountability systems, and recognition and reward processes.**

**Housing programs and services must provide channels within the organization for regular review of administrative policies and procedures. Where the management of the housing and residential life program is divided among different offices within the institution, it is the responsibility of institutional leaders and involved staff organizations to establish and maintain productive working relationships.**

Ideally, a unified organizational structure, including all housing and residential life functions, should be employed. In this way, the organization can function to meet all the campus housing needs of students, rather than coordinating through multiple and separate organizational lines of communication and authority.

**To fulfill its mission and goals effectively, the housing and residential life program must maintain well structured management functions, including planning, personnel, property management, purchasing, contract administration, financial control, and information systems.**

- short- and long-range planning should be adequate to project and accommodate immediate and future needs. The management role should be defined to include adequate time for planning as well as program implementation.
- purchasing and property management procedures should be designed to ensure value for money spent, security for supplies and furnishings, and maintenance of proper inventories.
- there should be a clear and complete written agreement between the resident and the institution, which conveys

mutual commitments and responsibilities. There should be clear communication to students, other interested members of the campus community, and potential residents of the procedures and priorities for obtaining housing and/or meal options.

- procedures for canceling, subleasing, or being released from the housing and/or dining agreement should be written and distributed, if there is provision for such release.

# Part 5. HUMAN RESOURCES

**The housing and residential life program must be staffed adequately by individuals qualified to accomplish its mission and goals. Programs and services must establish procedures for staff selection, training, and evaluation; set expectations for supervision, and provide appropriate professional development opportunities.**

**Professional staff members must hold an earned graduate degree in a field relevant to the position description or must possess an appropriate combination of education and experience.**

**Degree or credential seeking interns or others in training must be qualified by enrollment in an appropriate field of study and relevant experience. These individuals must be trained and supervised adequately by professional staff members.**

**Student employees and volunteers must be carefully selected, trained, supervised, and evaluated. When their knowledge and skills are not adequate for particular situations, they must refer students or others in need of assistance to qualified professional staff.**

**The housing and residential life program must have secretarial and technical staff adequate to accomplish its mission. Such staff must be technologically proficient and qualified to perform activities including reception duties, office equipment operation, records maintenance, and mail handling.**

**Appropriate salary levels and fringe benefits for all staff members must be commensurate with those for comparable positions within the institution, in similar institutions, and in the relevant geographic area.**

**The housing and residential life program must intentionally employ a diverse staff to reflect the diversity of the institution's student population, to ensure the existence of readily identifiable role models for students, and to enrich the campus community.**

**Affirmative action must occur in hiring and promotion practices to ensure diverse staffing profiles as required by institutional policy or local, state/provincial, and federal law.**

**The housing and residential life program must provide to each staff member appropriate training, supervision, and resources to accomplish assigned tasks.**

**The housing and residential life program must provide procedures for filing, processing, and hearing employee grievances.**

**All staff members must be aware of and support the goals, objectives, and philosophy of housing and residential life.**

Housing professional staff members should strive to develop and maintain staff relations in a climate of mutual respect, support, trust, and interdependence, recognizing the strengths and limitations of each professional colleague.

The housing and residential life staff consists of professionally trained staff members, paraprofessionals, and technical, clerical, and other support staff members. Qualifications for housing and residential life officer positions may be gained through formal academic preparation, workshops, self-study, work experience, participation in professional organizations, and in-service training .

The chief housing officer should have attained a graduate degree in higher education, business administration, a behavioral science, or possess an appropriate combination of education and experience.

The chief housing officer should have knowledge of and experience with human behavior and business management. Recommended concentration areas for preparation are (a) human behavior (e.g., learning theory philosophical foundations, social psychology, the college student, contemporary issues, multicultural studies) and (b) business management (e.g., accounting, statistics, marketing, budgeting and report analysis, computers, and business management functions such as planning, organization, staffing, and supervision).

The administrator in charge of facilities should possess at least a bachelor's degree and/or related experience in engineering and maintenance. This officer should coordinate residential staff and students' interactions with all construction, maintenance, and custodial work. These functions should be carried out in support of educational goals. Recommended academic study related to preparation for this position includes (a) architecture and design principles, (b) construction and engineering principles, and (c) preventive maintenance theory and practice.

It is the responsibility of the food services administrator to manage those functions that are necessary to provide wholesome, appetizing, and nutritious meals. The functions should be carried out with food services staff and in support of educational goals. Preparation for this position may include courses in (a) dietetics and menu planning, (b) principles of public health and sanitation, (c) institutional food services management, and (d) employee training and supervision.

The administrator in charge of educational programming should possess the minimum of a master's degree in college student affairs, counseling, or a closely related field or should possess an appropriate combination of education and experience.

Educational programming should provide for interaction with faculty members so that students' living experiences complement and reinforce classroom learning. Recommended courses for preparation for programming positions may include: (a) developmental psychology, (b) group theory, (c) the college student, (d) contemporary issues, (e) multicultural studies, and (f) principles of management.

Residential life operations are highly dependent upon the use of part-time student employees (the most common example being resident assistants) for the implementation of programs that affect student residents. Resident assistants and other paraprofessionals are expected to contribute to the accomplishment of the following functions: (a) educational programming, (b) administration, (c) group and activity advising, (d) leadership development, (e) discipline, (f) role modeling, (g) individual assistance and referral, and (h) providing information.

Desirable characteristics for both professional and paraprofessional staff members include demonstrated skills on leadership and communication, maturity, a well-developed sense of responsibility, sensitivity to individual differences, a positive self-concept, academic success, enthusiasm for working with students, and an understanding of issues facing students.

# Part 6. FINANCIAL RESOURCES

The housing and residential life program must have adequate funding to accomplish its mission and goals. Priorities, whether set periodically or as a result of extraordinary conditions, must be determined within the context of the stated mission, goals, and resources.

Housing and residential life fees must be dedicated to the support and improvement of housing and residential life programs and facilities.

It is not appropriate to use fees generated by an auxiliary to support operations not directly related to that auxiliary. Many campus housing and dining programs are auxiliary operations which are supported solely by fees charged to those using the service.

Financial reports must be available to appropriate offices, providing accurate, and timely data. Information must be available to the campus community and to other appropriate constituencies.

Funding must be adequate to provide continuous upkeep of facilities, major maintenance and renovation of facilities, educational programming, and services to residents. Adequate reserves for essential repairs, replacements, and capital improvements must exist.

- student governance units (e.g., hall or campus-wide residential councils) should have access to accounting offices and services to effectively carry out their functions. Dues collected from students for programs and services should be managed within the institution.

- representatives of the residence hall and apartment housing communities should be given opportunities to comment on proposed rate increases and operating budgets. Rate increases should be announced and discussed well in advance of their effective date.

- the budget should be used as a planning and goal-setting document which reflects commitment to the mission and goals of housing and residential life and of the institution.

# Part 7. FACILITIES, TECHNOLOGY, and EQUIPMENT

The housing and residential life program must have adequate, suitably located facilities, technology, and equipment to support its mission and goals. Facilities, technology, and equipment must be in compliance with relevant federal, state/provincial, and local requirements to provide for access, health and safety.

Facilities must provide sufficient and appropriate space to accommodate program goals and objectives and meet students needs for safety and security. Facilities must be maintained at optimal levels of cleanliness, repair, and decor.

Spaces provided must include adequate areas for study, office functions, lounging, recreation, and group meetings.

Individual rooms must be adequately furnished to accommodate all assigned occupants.

All community bathrooms and other public areas should be cleaned at least daily on weekdays. Ramps, bathrooms, elevators, room fixtures, and other appropriate special provisions to accommodate mobility-impaired students should be well maintained and clearly marked and their availability thoroughly communicated to current and potential students. Public and common areas such as study rooms, exercise rooms, TV rooms, computer rooms, and kitchens should be adequately furnished. Sufficient space for maintenance work and storage should be available in close proximity to the assigned area of the maintenance and custodial staff. Laundry facilities should be provided within or in close proximity to living areas.

Residential facilities must be accessible, clean, attractive, reasonably priced, properly designed, well-maintained, comfortable, and conducive to study and must have safety and security features.

Functions associated with this goal should include new construction, maintenance and renovation, equipment replacement, custodial care, energy conservation, and grounds care.

- Any new construction projects should be responsive to the current and future needs of residents.

- Decisions about new construction should be based upon institutional need and consistent with the mission of the institution.

- Maintenance/renovation programs should be implemented in all housing operations and may include: (a) a preventive maintenance program designed to extend the life of the equipment and facilities, (b) a program designed to repair in a timely manner equipment and building systems as they become inoperable, and (c) a renovation program that modifies physical facilities and building systems to make them more effective, attractive, efficient, and safe.

- Systematically planned equipment replacement programs should exist for furnishings, mechanical and electrical systems, maintenance equipment, carpeting, draperies, and dining and kitchen equipment, where applicable.

- Regularly scheduled cleaning of public areas should be provided.

- Recycling and energy conservation efforts should be implemented through educational programs, as well as through timely renovation and replacement of inefficient equipment and obsolete facilities.

- Grounds, which may include streets, walks, and parking lots, should be clean and attractively maintained, with attention given to safety features. There should be planned maintenance and renewal procedures.

## Part 8. LEGAL RESPONSIBILITIES

Housing staff members must be knowledgeable about and responsive to law and regulations that relate to their respective program or service. Sources for legal obligations and limitations are constitutional, statutory, regulatory, and case law; mandatory laws and orders emanating from federal, state/provincial and local governments; and the institution through its policies.

Staff members must use reasonable and informed practices to limit the liability exposure of the institution, its officers, employees, and agents. Staff members must be informed about institutional policies regarding personal liability and related insurance coverage options.

The institution must provide access to legal advice for housing staff members as needed to carry out assigned responsibilities.

The institution must inform housing and residential life staff and students, in a timely and systematic fashion, about extraordinary or changing legal obligations and potential liabilities.

## Part 9. EQUAL OPPORTUNITY, ACCESS, and AFFIRMATIVE ACTION

Housing staff members must ensure that services and programs are provided on a fair and equitable basis. Housing programs and services must be accessible. Hours of operation must be responsive to the needs of all students. The housing and residential life program must adhere to the spirit and intent of equal opportunity laws.

The housing program must not be discriminatory on the basis of age, color, disability, gender, national origin, race, religious creed, sexual orientation, and/or veteran status. Exceptions are appropriate only where provided by relevant law and institutional policy.

Consistent with its mission and goals, the housing program must take affirmative action to remedy significant imbalances in student participation and staffing patterns.

## Part 10. CAMPUS and COMMUNITY RELATIONS

Programs and services must establish, maintain, and promote effective relations with relevant campus offices and external agencies.

Particular efforts should be made by the staff to develop positive relationships with campus and off-campus agencies responsible for judicial affairs, student counseling services, student health services, student activities, security and safety, academic advising, admissions, campus mail and telephone services, physical plant services, institutional budgeting and planning, computer center, vendors and suppliers of products used in residence and dining halls, and private and commercial housing operators.

Housing and residential life staff members should be particularly aware of and supportive of the role of faculty. Faculty members should be encouraged to become involved in the residential program by presenting workshops, lectures, symposia, or by other means. Possibilities for faculty members to reside for a scheduled time in the residence halls as a community building activity or to accomplish a specific program objective should exist.

## Part 11. DIVERSITY

Within the context of the institution's unique mission, multi-dimensional diversity enriches the community and enhances the collegiate experience for all; therefore, the housing program must nurture environments where similarities and differences among people are recognized and honored.

The housing and residential life program must promote cultural educational experiences that are characterized by open and continuous communication, that deepen understanding of one's own culture and heritage, and that respect and educate about similarities, differences and histories of cultures.

Housing programs and services must address the characteristics and needs of a diverse population when establishing and implementing policies and procedures.

## Part 12. ETHICS

All persons involved in the delivery of housing and residential life programs and services must adhere to the highest principles of ethical behavior. The housing program must develop or adopt and implement statements of ethical practice addressing the issues unique to its existence. The housing program must publish these statements and insure their periodic review by all concerned.

Housing staff members must ensure that confidentiality is maintained with respect to all communications and records considered confidential unless exempted by law.

Information disclosed in individual counseling sessions must remain confidential, unless written permission to divulge the information is given by the student. However, all staff members must disclose to appropriate authorities information judged to be of an emergency nature, especially when the safety of the individual or others is involved. Information contained in students' educational records must not be disclosed to non-institutional third parties without appropriate consent, unless classified as "Directory" information or when the information is subpoenaed by law. Programs and services must apply a similar dedication to privacy and confidentiality to research data concerning individuals. All staff members must be aware of and comply with the provisions contained in the institution's human subjects research policy and in other relevant institutional policies addressing ethical practices.

Housing staff members must recognize and avoid personal conflict of interest or appearance thereof in their transactions with students and others. Staff members must strive to insure the fair, objective, and impartial treatment of all persons with whom they deal.

When handling institutional funds, staff members must ensure that such funds are managed in accordance with established and responsible accounting procedures.

Housing staff members must not participate in any form of harassment that demeans persons or creates an intimidating, hostile, or offensive campus environment.

Staff members must perform their duties within the limits of their training, expertise, and competence. When these limits are exceeded, individuals in need of further assistance must be referred to persons possessing appropriate qualifications.

Staff members must use suitable means to confront and otherwise hold accountable other staff members who exhibit unethical behavior.

Staff members must maintain the highest principles of ethical behavior in the use of technology.

Each housing and residential life professional staff member should accept students as individuals, each with rights and responsibilities, each with goals and needs, and with this in mind, should seek to create and maintain a group living environment that enhances learning and personal development.

## Part 13. ASSESSMENT and EVALUATION

The housing and residential life program must regularly conduct systematic qualitative and quantitative evaluations of its quality to determine whether and to what degree the stated mission and goals are being met. Although methods of assessment vary, the housing program must employ a sufficient range of measures to insure objectivity and comprehensiveness. Data collected must include responses from students and other affected constituencies. Results of these evaluations must be used in revising and improving programs and services and in recognizing staff performance.

# THE ROLE of the INTERNATIONAL STUDENT ADVISER
## CAS Standards Contextual Statement

In 1996, more than 450,000 international students from over 150 countries were studying at US colleges and universities. These students were pursuing undergraduate and graduate degrees as well as English-language training, and are drawn to this country because of the high quality programs and the wide range of academic options offered in the US. International students bring with them rich experiences and unique cross-cultural perspectives that help to internationalize the campus and give American students first-hand opportunities to learn about the world. International students face unique challenges as they attempt to adjust to American campus life and culture, master written and spoken English, comply with immigration regulations, meet the requirements of their academic programs, and prepare to return home to begin careers.

International student advisers work with these students providing information, advising, programs, and services designed to make their US experience as positive and productive as possible. They frequently serve as the liaison between international students and all those with whom these students come into contact, including American faculty, students, and staff; local citizens; officials of US and foreign government agencies; and the student's sponsor or family at home, representing the students' best interests and advising them accordingly.

International student advisers have a wide range of responsibilities, including advising on immigration, academic, and personal matters; orientation programming offered both at the beginning of the academic term and/or throughout the year; social and cultural programming to help international students learn more about American culture and develop friendships with American students; liaison and problem-solving with offices and groups on and off campus; crisis intervention in case of illness or serious legal, financial, or personal problems; and planning, budgeting, and office management.

International student advisers should be knowledgeable and articulate about American culture and how it differs from the cultures of other countries and should understand the social and psychological processes of cross-cultural adjustment. They should be familiar with the educational systems and political, economic, historical, and social issues and trends framing the contexts of the countries from which their students come. International student advisers must also be up to date on the intricacies of US immigration law and regulations, have good counseling and advising skills, understand how to develop effective and creative programming, and be good at setting priorities, managing time and resources, and communicating effectively with others. International student advisers must also enjoy helping people from diverse cultural backgrounds and learning about cultural differences.

## References, Readings and Resources

Althen, G. (Ed.) (1994). *Learning across cultures.* Cranberry Township, PA: NAFSA Publications.

Althen, G. (1983). *The handbook of foreign student advising.* Yarmouth, ME: Intercultural Press.

Althen, G. *Foreign student advising 101* [videotape]. Cranberry Township, PA: NAFSA Publications.

Gooding, J. (1995) *The faculty member's guide to immigration law.* Cranberry Township, PA: NAFSA Publications.

Hall, E. T. (1976). *Beyond culture.* Yarmouth, ME: Intercultural Press.

Hall, E. T. (1981). *The dance of life.* Yarmouth, ME: Intercultural Press.

Hall, E. T. (1982). *The hidden dimension.* Yarmouth, ME: Intercultural Press.

Ogami, N. (1987). *Cold water* [videotape]. Yarmouth, ME: Intercultural Press.

Yenkin, A (Ed.) (1996). *Adviser's manual of federal regulations affecting international students and scholars.* Cranberry Township, PA: NAFSA Publications.

NAFSA Publications, P.O. Box 1604, Cranberry Township, PA 16066, (800) 836-4994

Intercultural Press, P.O. Box 700, Yarmouth, ME 04096, (207) 846-5168

# INTERNATIONAL STUDENT PROGRAMS and SERVICES
## CAS STANDARDS and GUIDELINES

## Part 1.  MISSION

International student programs and services in higher education must develop, record, disseminate, implement and regularly review their mission and goals. Mission statements must be consistent with the mission and goals of the institution and with the standards in this document.

> The provision of international student programs and services should reflect a strong institutional commitment to the education of international students.

Programs and services must promote the academic and personal growth and development of international students. To accomplish the mission, international student programs and services must:

- Assess the needs of international students, set priorities among those needs, and respond to the extent that the number of students, facilities, and resources permit;
- Provide thorough information on immigration regulations and procedures to advise international students effectively, assure institutional adherence to those regulations and procedures, and interpret host country immigration policy to the campus community;
- Provide professional services to students in the areas of counseling, advising, and assistance in complying with government regulations;
- Orient international students to the policies and expectations of the institution, its culture, the host country educational system, and the host country in general;
- Foster an international dimension within the institution and the community at large;
- Promote positive interaction among international students, and between international and host country students, the academic community, and the community at large;
- Facilitate the enrollment and retention of international students; and
- Facilitate re-entry and cultural re-adjustment related to the student's return home.

> International student programs and services should facilitate institutional sensitivity to the cultural needs of international community members (e.g., social, religious, dietary, and housing).

> International student programs and services should be coordinated with academic units and other institutional functional areas that provide programs and services to students, faculty, and staff.

## Part 2. PROGRAM

The formal education of students is purposeful, holistic, and consists of the curriculum and the co-curriculum.

International student co-curricular programs and services must be (a) intentional, (b) coherent, (c) based on theories and knowledge of learning and human development, (d) reflective of developmental and demographic profiles of the student population, and (e) responsive to special needs of individuals.

International student programs and services must promote learning and development in students by encouraging outcomes such as intellectual growth, ability to communicate effectively, realistic self-appraisal, enhanced self-esteem, clarification of values, appropriate career choices, leadership development, physical fitness, meaningful interpersonal relations, ability to work independently and collaboratively, social responsibility, satisfying and productive lifestyles, appreciation of aesthetic and cultural diversity, and achievement of personal goals.

International student programs and services must provide opportunities for discussion and understanding to minimize cultural conflict and to deal with conflict.

International student programs and services must include the following elements:

- Counseling and advising in immigration regulations, financial matters, employment, health insurance and health care, personal concerns, and English-language needs;
- Educational programs to enhance positive interaction between domestic and international students, to develop faculty and staff sensitivity to cultural differences and international student needs, and to assist in the understanding of and adjustment to a host country's educational system and culture;
- Special orientation programs to enhance knowledge and understanding of the institution, the host country's educational system, and the culture of the host country in general, as well as programs to address issues related to re-entry to the student's home country;
- Assessment of the educational goals; personal development levels; and social, emotional, and cultural needs of international students;
- Appropriate and timely referrals to other service and program agencies;
- Cross-cultural programs addressing cultural problems and issues for faculty, staff, teaching assis-

tants, and students, and dependents of international students;

- Liaison with appropriate student organizations; and,
- Advocacy within the institution for the needs of international students.

# Part 3. LEADERSHIP

Effective and ethical leadership is essential to the success of all organizations. Institutions must appoint, position and empower leaders within the administrative structure to accomplish stated missions. Leaders at various levels must be selected on the bases of formal education and training, relevant work experience, personal attributes, and other professional credentials. Institutions must determine expectations of accountability for leaders and fairly assess their performance.

Leaders of international student programs and services must exercise authority over resources for which they are responsible to achieve their respective missions. Leaders must articulate a vision for their organization; set goals and objectives; prescribe and practice ethical behavior; recruit, select, supervise, and develop others in the organization; manage, plan, budget, and evaluate; communicate effectively; and marshal cooperative action from colleagues, employees, other institutional constituencies, and persons outside the organization. Leaders must address individual, organizational, or environmental conditions that inhibit goal achievement. Leaders must improve programs and services continuously in response to changing needs of students and institutional priorities.

# Part 4. ORGANIZATION and MANAGEMENT

International student programs and services must be structured purposefully and managed effectively to achieve stated goals. Evidence of appropriate structure must include current and accessible policies and procedures, written performance expectations for all employees, functional work flow graphics or organizational charts, and service delivery expectations. Evidence of effective management must include clear sources and channels of authority, effective communication practices, decision-making and conflict resolution procedures, responsiveness to changing conditions, accountability systems, and recognition and reward processes.

International student programs and services must provide channels within the organization for regular review of administrative policies and procedures.

Institutions enrolling international students must designate a specific office or service unit to coordinate programs and services for this student population.

# Part 5. HUMAN RESOURCES

International student programs and services must be staffed adequately by individuals qualified to accomplish the mission and goals. Programs and services must establish procedures for staff selection, training, and evaluation, set expectations for supervision, and provide appropriate professional development opportunities.

Wherever possible, staff members should be representative of the various cultures served in the student population.

Professional staff members must hold an earned graduate degree in a field relevant to the position description or must possess an appropriate combination of education and experience. They must be knowledgeable about research and practice in areas related to international student programs and services and stay abreast of developments in policies, laws, and regulations affecting international students.

Professional staff members should be competent in skills such as group facilitation, leadership training and development, crisis intervention, workshop design, report writing, public speaking, social and interpersonal development, individual and group counseling and their cross-cultural aspects. Generally, these competencies are found in persons who graduate from student personnel, counseling, and other higher education graduate programs, as well as from programs such as cross-cultural communication, international studies, and anthropology.

Specific study in the following areas is desirable: multicultural theory, organizational development, counseling theory and practice, group dynamics, leadership development, human development, and research and evaluation. Proficiency in a language other than English and extended travel and/or living experience abroad are also helpful.

Degree or credential seeking interns or others in training must be qualified by enrollment in an appropriate field of study and relevant experience. These individuals must be trained and supervised adequately by professional staff members.

The use of graduate assistants and interns in international student programs and services should be encouraged. These individuals expand staff abilities, provide peer role models, and gain valuable preprofessional experience. Particular attention should be given to preparing assistants and interns to be especially sensitive to cultural differences and the special needs of international students.

Student employees and volunteers must be carefully selected, trained, supervised, and evaluated. When their knowledge and skills are not adequate for particular situations, they must refer students or others in need of assistance to qualified professional staff.

International student programs and services must have secretarial and technical staff adequate to accomplish their mission. Such staff must be technologically proficient and qualified to perform activities including reception duties, office equipment operation, records maintenance, and mail handling.

Appropriate salary levels and fringe benefits for all staff members must be commensurate with those for comparable positions within the institution, in similar institutions, and in the relevant geographic area.

International student programs and services must intentionally employ a diverse staff to reflect the diversity of the institution's student population, to ensure the existence of readily identifiable role models for students and to enrich the campus community,

Affirmative action must occur in hiring and promotion practices to ensure diverse staffing profiles as required by institutional policies and local, state/provincial, and federal law.

## Part 6. FINANCIAL RESOURCES

International student programs and services must have adequate funding to accomplish the mission and goals. Priorities, whether set periodically or as a result of extraordinary conditions, must be determined within the context of the stated mission, goals, and resources.

> Institutions considering special student fees as a means of supporting international student services and programs should review carefully the ethical issues involved in implementing such fees.

## Part 7. FACILITIES, TECHNOLOGY, and EQUIPMENT

International student programs and services must have adequate, suitably located facilities and equipment to support its mission and goals. Facilities, technology, and equipment must be in compliance with relevant federal, state, provincial, and local requirements to provide for access, health and safety.

## Part 8. LEGAL RESPONSIBILITIES

Staff members in international student programs and services must be knowledgeable about and responsive to law and regulations that relate to their respective program or service. Sources for legal obligations and limitations include constitutional, statutory, regulatory, and case law; mandatory laws and orders emanating from federal, state, provincial and local governments; and the institution through its policies.

> Further, staff should also be familiar with constitutional issues of due process and rights of freedom of expression as applicable to residents of the United States and Canada.

Staff members must use reasonable and informed practices to limit the liability exposure of the institution, its officers, employees, and agents. Staff members must be informed about institutional policies regarding personal liability and related insurance coverage options.

The institution must provide access to legal advice for staff members as needed to carry out assigned responsibilities.

The institution must inform staff and students, in a timely and systematic fashion, about extraordinary or changing legal obligations and potential liabilities.

## Part 9. EQUAL OPPORTUNITY, ACCESS, and AFFIRMATIVE ACTION

Staff members must ensure that international student services and programs are provided on a fair and equitable basis. Each program and service must be accessible. Hours of operation must be responsive to the needs of all students.

Each program and service must adhere to the spirit and intent of equal opportunity laws.

Programs and services must not be discriminatory on the basis of age, color, disability, gender, national origin, race, religious creed, sexual orientation, and/or veteran status. Exceptions are appropriate only where provided by relevant law and institutional policy.

Consistent with the mission and goals, programs and services must take affirmative action to remedy significant imbalances in student participation and staffing patterns.

## Part 10. CAMPUS and COMMUNITY RELATIONS

International student programs and services must establish, maintain, and promote effective relations with relevant campus offices and external agencies. Professional staff members must coordinate, or where appropriate, collaborate with faculty and staff in providing services and programs for international students.

## Part 11. DIVERSITY

Within the context of the institution's unique mission, multi-dimensional diversity enriches the community and enhances the collegiate experience for all; therefore, international student programs and services must nurture environments where similarities and differences among people are recognized and honored.

International student programs and services must promote cultural educational experiences that are characterized by open and continuous communication, that deepen understanding of one's own culture and heritage, and that respect and educate about similarities, differences and histories of cultures.

International student programs and services must address the characteristics and needs of a diverse population when establishing and implementing policies and procedures. Programs and services must orient international students to the culture of the host country and promote and deepen international students' understanding of cross-cultural differences.

All institutional units that provide services to students should share responsibility for meeting the needs of international students. Coordinated efforts to promote multicultural sensitivity and the elimination of prejudicial behaviors in all functional areas on campus should be encouraged.

## Part 12. ETHICS

All persons involved in the delivery of programs and services for international students must adhere to the highest principles of ethical behavior. Programs and services must develop or adopt and implement statements of ethical practice addressing the issues unique to their functions. International student programs must publish these statements and insure their periodic review by all concerned.

Staff members must ensure that confidentiality is maintained with respect to all communication and records considered confidential unless exempted by law.

Information disclosed in individual counseling sessions must remain confidential, unless written permission to divulge the information is given by the student. However, all staff members must disclose to appropriate authorities information judged to be of an emergency nature, especially when the safety of the individual or others is involved. Information contained in student's educational records must not be disclosed to non-institutional third parties without appropriate consent, unless classified as "directory" information, or when the information is subpoenaed by law, or (in the case of non-immigrant international students studying in the United States) as mandated by regulations from the US Immigration and Naturalization Service or the US Information Agency. Programs and services must apply a similar dedication to privacy and confidentiality to research data concerning individuals. All staff members must be aware of and comply with the provisions contained in the institution's human subjects research policy and in other relevant institutional policies addressing ethical practices.

Staff members must recognize and avoid personal conflict of interest or appearance thereof in their transactions with students and others. Staff members must strive to insure the fair objectives and impartial treatment of all persons with whom they deal.

When handling institutional funds, all staff members must ensure that such funds are managed in accordance with established and responsible accounting procedures.

Staff members must not participate in any form of harassment that demeans persons or creates an intimidating, hostile or offensive campus environment.

International student program staff members must perform their duties within the limits of their training, expertise, and competence. When these limits are exceeded, individuals in need of further assistance must be referred to persons possessing appropriate qualifications.

Staff members must use suitable means to confront and otherwise hold accountable other staff members who exhibit unethical behavior.

Staff members must balance the wants, needs, and requirements of students, institutional policies, laws, and sponsors, having as their ultimate concern the long-term well being of international educational exchange programs and the students participating in them.

International student program staff members must demonstrate cross-cultural sensitivity, treating differences between value systems and cultures in non-judgmental ways. The use of pejorative stereotypical statements must be avoided.

Staff members must maintain the highest principles of ethical behavior in the use of technology.

## Part 13. ASSESSMENT and EVALUATION

International student programs and services must regularly conduct systematic qualitative and quantitative evaluations of program quality to determine whether and to what degree the stated mission and goals are being met. Although methods of assessment vary, programs and services must employ a sufficient range of measures to insure objectivity and comprehensiveness. Data collected must include responses from students and other affected constituencies. Results of these evaluations must be used in revising and improving programs and services and in recognizing staff performance.

# THE ROLE of STUDENT JUDICIAL PROGRAMS
## CAS Standards Contextual Statement

Throughout the history of American higher education, colleges have struggled with how to respond to student misconduct. In his letter to Thomas Cooper on November 2, 1822, Thomas Jefferson described the problem of student discipline as the breakers ahead which he was not sure that American higher education could weather. In recent years, issues related to student discipline, including sexual assault, use and abuse of alcohol and other drugs, and campus safety have come to the forefront.

Traditionally, the courts viewed the administration of student discipline as an internal institutional matter and did not become actively involved in the process through judicial rulings. However, this position changed in 1961, with the landmark case of Dixon v. Alabama State Board of Education, 294 F.2d 150 (5th Cir. 1961), the first of an ever-growing body of case law related to the administration of student discipline. The courts have held under the 14th Amendment to the Constitution that public colleges and universities must afford basic due process rights to students accused of violating student judicial codes. However, it is important to note the rights of due process described in this body of case law differ significantly from those observed in the criminal court system. The limitations placed upon private institutions are also substantially less prescriptive. Although the Constitutional rights afforded to students at public institutions are not generally applicable to private institutions, several authors, including Kaplin (1978, 1990), Kaplin and Lee (1996), and Cerminara and Stoner (1990), have encouraged private institutions to bear in mind the restrictions placed upon public institutions and accord their students the same rights and protections.

In the early American colleges and universities, student discipline was primarily the responsibility of the faculty. As the positions of dean of men and women were established and the field of student affairs evolved, the responsibility for the administration of student discipline shifted. Only in the past twenty years has student discipline emerged as a distinct functional area within student affairs. Prior to this time, the responsibility for student discipline was one of a number of duties which fell to an individual or office such as the dean of students.

In the early 1970s, the American College Personnel Association established Commission XV, Campus Judicial Affairs and Legal Issues, to meet the needs of this emerging profession. In 1988, the Association for Student Judicial Affairs (ASJA) was founded to facilitate the integration of student development concepts with principles of judicial practice in postsecondary education and to promote, encourage, and support student development professionals responsible for judicial affairs. ASJA now has a membership of over 1,000 and has sponsored an annual conference attended by more than 500 people. It has also sponsored a summer training institute for campus judicial affairs since 1993.

The Association for Student Judicial Affairs established three principles for the administration of judicial programs:

- The development and enforcement of standards of conduct for students is an educational endeavor which fosters students personal and social development; students must assume a significant role in developing and enforcing such regulations in order that they might be better prepared for the responsibilities of citizenship.

- Standards of conduct form the basis for behavioral expectations in the academic community; the enforcement of such standards must protect the rights, health, and safety of members of that community in order that they may pursue their educational goals without undue interference.

- Integrity, wisdom, and empathy are among the characteristics most important to the administration of student conduct standards; officials who have such responsibilities must exercise them impartially and fairly.

The primary role of student judicial affairs staff members is that of educator. The *ASJA Statement of Ethical Principles and Standards of Conduct* identifies the maintenance and enhancement of the ethical climate on campus and the promotion of academic integrity as the primary purposes for enforcing standards of student conduct. Clearly articulated and consistently administered standards of conduct form the basis for behavioral expectations within an academic community. These standards of conduct for students should be enforced in such manner as to protect the rights, health, and safety of the entire community. The student judicial programs standards and guidelines that follow represent the fundamental criteria by which programs can assess their quality and effectiveness.

# References, Readings and Resources

Cerminara, K. L., & Stoner, E. N., II. (1990). Harnessing the spirit of insubordination: A model student disciplinary code. *Journal of College and University Law,* 17, 89-121.

Kaplin, W. A. (1978). *The law of higher education.* San Francisco: Jossey-Bass.

Kaplin, W. A. (1990). *The law of higher education* (2nd ed.). San Francisco: Jossey-Bass.

Kaplin, W. A., & Lee, B. (1996). *The law of higher education* (3rd ed.). San Francisco: Jossey-Bass.

American College Personnel Association, Commission XV, Campus Judicial Affairs and Legal Issues. http://www jud-prog.uga.edu/acpaxv.htm

Association for Student Judicial Affairs: http://studlife.tamu. edu/asja/

# JUDICIAL PROGRAMS and SERVICES
## CAS STANDARDS and GUIDELINES

## Part 1. MISSION

The institution and its judicial programs and services must develop, record, disseminate, implement, and regularly review its mission and goals. Mission statements must be consistent with the nature and goals of the institution and with the standards in this document.

The goals of judicial programs and services must address the institution's needs to:

- develop, disseminate, interpret, and enforce campus regulations;
- protect relevant rights of students;
- deal with student behavioral problems in a fair and reasonable manner;
- facilitate and encourage respect for campus governance;
- provide learning experiences for students who are found to be responsible for conduct which is determined to be in violation of institutional standards or who participate in the operations of the judicial system; and
- initiate and encourage educational activities that serve to prevent violations of campus regulations.

Judicial programs should support appropriate individual and group behavior as well as to protect the campus community from disruption and harm. The programs should be conducted in ways that will serve to foster the ethical development and personal integrity of students and the promotion of an environment that is in accord with the overall educational goals of the institution.

## Part 2. PROGRAM

The formal education of students is purposeful, holistic, and consists of the curriculum and the co-curriculum.

Judicial programs must be (a) intentional, (b) coherent, (c) based on theories of knowledge of learning and human development, (d) reflective of developmental and demographic profiles of the student population, and (e) responsive to special needs of individuals.

Judicial programs must promote learning and development in students by encouraging outcomes such as intellectual growth, ability to communicate effectively, realistic self appraisal, enhanced self-esteem, clarification of values, appropriate career choices, leadership development, physical fitness, meaningful interpersonal relations, ability to work independently and collaboratively, social responsibility, satisfying and productive lifestyles, appreciation of aesthetic and cultural diversity, and achievement of personal goals.

Judicial programs must establish the following within the context of its mission and purpose:

1. Authority. A written statement describing the authority, philosophy, jurisdiction and procedures of the campus judicial programs must be developed and disseminated to all members of the campus community.

This statement should address (a) whether student academic or non-academic misconduct are within the programs' jurisdiction, (b) which campus policies and regulations are enforced by these programs, (c) sanctions which may be imposed, (d) a clear description of the relationship between judicial programs and both campus and external law enforcement agencies, including guidelines if law enforcement authorities will be called in, (e) and information regarding the impact, if any, of decisions by the criminal courts on the outcome of corresponding campus judicial proceedings.

2. Components:

Selected components of a judicial system must be described in writing and include:

- hearing officer,
- hearing bodies and their jurisdictions,
- conduct regulations,
- interim suspension,
- pre-hearing procedures,
- investigation procedures,
- hearing procedures,
- disciplinary sanctions,
- appeals procedures,
- confidentiality standards,
- records policy/procedures, and
- statement of rights for accused, accusers and when appropriate, victims.

Generally, the judicial system should involve students on all boards; however, membership on boards need not be limited to students. The system should process complaints in a timely fashion, and yet allow sufficient time for an investigation of all allegations prior to a hearing.

Procedures and processes must ensure timely, substantive, and procedural due process.

Judicial programs should provide students with ample opportunity to receive advice about the process, a general time frame for resolution, and a delineation of individual responsibilities in the process.

Institutional disciplinary action against individual students or recognized student organizations must be administered in the context of a unified and coordinated set of regulations and processes in order to ensure fair and reasonable outcomes. Allegations of improper behavior originating from both instructional and non-instructional components of the institution must be encompassed in a single comprehensive judicial system for students.

The institution should be clear about which body or individual has jurisdiction over which conduct regulations. Students should be assisted in understanding the sources and lines of authority.

The programs should maintain written records to serve as referral materials, to document precedents, and to provide source material for identifying recurring problems or to use for appeals.

The programs should follow up on cases, including enforcement of sanctions, assessing the developmental processes that have been affected, and ensuring that students are directed to appropriate services for assistance.

The institution should be clear about how it defines student status and jurisdiction of the system to include whether students can be held responsible for behavior which takes place off the campus or between academic sessions.

The institution should clearly state the conduct regulations that apply to student organizations, the procedures that will be followed in the hearing of such cases, and the guidelines used to determine if the actions of individual members of an organization constitute action by the organization.

### 3. Information to Campus Community

**The institution must publish information about the campus judicial programs.**

Publications should contain (a) campus policies, such as those concerning legal representation, the maintenance of confidentiality, and the expunging of disciplinary records; (b) campus procedures, such as filing a disciplinary action, gathering information, conducting a hearing, and notifying a student of the hearing/appeal board's decision; (c) the composition, authority, and jurisdiction of all judicial bodies; (d) the types of advice that the complainant and others can receive about the process; (e) the types of disciplinary sanctions, including interim suspension procedures; and (f) a general explanation of how and when non-campus law enforcement officials are used.

Publications should be distributed through processes that reach all students. Students should not have to request such publications. Dissemination mechanisms may include electronic media, the institutional catalog, the orientation program, the student handbook, admissions and registration materials, and campus billing materials.

Published information should include not only descriptions about how the system works, but also the results of the system. By publishing the outcomes of campus judicial cases in a manner which protects the confidentiality of those involved, the institution demonstrates that the system does in fact work and encourages an open discussion of issues related to student conduct.

### 4. Hearing Authority

**In addition to a hearing officer, campus judicial services must include a hearing or appellate body composed of**

representatives of the campus community and responsible for carrying out judicial functions delegated by the administration.

Duties and responsibilities of judicial body members may include (a) reviewing disciplinary referrals and claims; (b) interpreting misconduct allegations and identifying specific charges to be brought against the student(s); (c) conducting preliminary hearings and gathering information pertinent to the charges; (d) advising students on their rights and responsibilities; (e) engaging in substantive discussions with students about relevant ethical issues; (f) scheduling, coordinating, and conducting hearings; (g) reviewing decisions from other hearing bodies, when applicable; (h) notifying the accused in writing about relevant decisions and the board's rationale for such; (i) maintaining accurate written records of the entire proceeding; (j) referring information to an appeal board when applicable; (k) following up on sanctions to ensure they have been implemented; (1) following up with students who have been sanctioned to ensure awareness of available counseling services; (m) establishing and implementing a procedure for maintenance and expunging of disciplinary records; and (n) assessing judicial procedures, policies and outcomes.

A staff judicial officer may be assigned responsibility for training judicial body members, scheduling and facilitating evaluations, and informing faculty, administration, and staff about legal and disciplinary matters.

Judicial body members may participate on campus government committees associated with student conduct, except when a conflict of interest will result.

### 5. Training of Judicial Body Members

**Initial and in-service training of all hearing body members must be provided.**

In order for judicial board members to fulfill their duties, initial training should include (a) an overview of all judicial policies and procedures; (b) an explanation of the operation of the judicial process at all levels including authority and jurisdiction; (c) an overview of the institutions philosophy on student judicial affairs and its role in this process; (d) duties and responsibilities of all judicial bodies and their members; (e) review of constitutional and other relevant legal individual and institutional rights and responsibilities; (f) an explanation of sanctions; (g) an explanation of pertinent ethics, including particularly the importance of confidentiality and the prevention of bias and conflict of interest in the judicial process; (h) a description of available personal counseling programs and referral resources; (i) an outline of conditions and interactions which may involve external enforcement officials, attorneys, witnesses, parents of accused students, and the media; and (j) an overview of developmental and interpersonal issues likely to arise among college students.

In-service training should include participation in relevant workshops, seminars, and conferences. A library containing current resources about the judicial system should be maintained and be accessible to judicial board members.

# Part 3. LEADERSHIP

Effective and ethical leadership is essential to the success of all organizations. The institution must appoint, position, and empower leaders within the administrative structure to accomplish stated missions. Leaders at various levels must be selected on the basis of formal education and training, relevant work experience, personal attributes, and other professional credentials. The institution must determine expectations of accountability for its leaders and fairly assess their performance.

Leaders of judicial programs must exercise authority over resources for which they are responsible to achieve their mission. Leaders must articulate vision for their organization; set goals and objectives; prescribe and practice ethical behavior; recruit, select, supervise, and develop others in the organization; manage, plan, budget, and evaluate; communicate effectively; and marshal cooperative action from colleagues, employees, other institutional constituencies, and persons outside the organization. Judicial program leaders must address individual, organizational, or environmental conditions that inhibit goal achievement. Leaders must improve programs continuously in response to changing needs of students and institutional priorities.

# Part 4. ORGANIZATION and MANAGEMENT

Judicial programs must be structured purposefully and managed effectively to achieve stated goals. Evidence of appropriate structure must include current accessible policies and procedures, written performance expectations for all employees, functional work flow graphics and organizational charts, and service delivery expectations. Evidence of effective management must include clear sources and channels of authority, effective communication practices, decision-making and conflict resolution procedures, responsiveness to changing conditions, accountability systems, and recognition and reward processes. Judicial programs must provide channels within the organization for regular review of administrative policies and procedures

# Part 5. HUMAN RESOURCES

Judicial programs must be staffed adequately by individuals qualified to accomplish its mission and goals. Judicial programs must establish procedures for staff selection, training, and evaluation; set expectations for supervision; and provide appropriate professional development opportunities.

Professional staff members must hold an earned graduate degree in a field relevant to the position description or must possess an appropriate combination of education and experience.

Degree or credential seeking interns or others in training must be qualified by enrollment in an appropriate field of study and relevant experience. These individuals must be trained and supervised adequately by professional staff members.

Student employees and volunteers must be carefully selected, trained, supervised, and evaluated. When their knowledge and skills are not adequate for particular situations, they must refer students in need of assistance to qualified professional staff.

Judicial programs must have secretarial and technical staff adequate to accomplish their mission. Such staff must be technologically proficient and qualified to perform activities including reception duties, office equipment operations, records maintenance, and mail handling.

Salary levels and fringe benefits for staff members must be commensurate with those for comparable positions within the institution, in similar institutions, and in the relevant geographic area. Compensation for paraprofessional staff must be fair and voluntary services recognized adequately.

Judicial programs must intentionally employ a diverse staff to reflect the diversity of the institution's student population, to ensure the existence of readily identifiable role models for students, and to enrich the campus community.

Affirmative action must occur in hiring and promotion practices to ensure diverse staffing profiles as required by institutional policy and local, state/provincial and federal law.

A qualified member of the campus community must be designated as the person responsible for judicial programs.

> The designee should have an educational background in the behavioral sciences (e.g., psychology, sociology, student development including moral and ethical development, higher education administration, counseling, law, criminology, or criminal justice).
>
> The designee and any other professional staff member in the judicial programs should possess (a) a clear understanding of the legal requirements for substantive and procedural due process; (b) legal knowledge sufficient to confer with attorneys involved in student disciplinary proceedings and other aspects of the judicial services system; (c) a general interest in and commitment to the welfare and development of students who participate on boards or who are involved in cases; (d) demonstrated skills in working with decision making processes and conflict resolution; (e) teaching and consulting skills appropriate for the education, advising, and coordination of hearing bodies; (f) the ability to communicate and interact with students regardless of race, sex, disability, sexual orientation, and/or other personal characteristics; (g) understanding of the requirements relative to confidentiality and security of judicial programs files; and (h) the ability to create an atmosphere

where students feel free to ask questions and obtain assistance.

Students from graduate academic programs, particularly in areas such as counseling, student development, higher education administration, or criminology, may assist the judicial programs through practice, internships, and assistantships.

Students who participate on boards may be awarded academic credit for their participation in the system. Clear Teaming objectives and assignments should be outlined to ensure that a student's grade for this participation is in no way influenced by his/her decisions on a particular case.

## Part 6. FINANCIAL RESOURCES

The judicial program must have adequate funding to accomplish its mission and goals. Priorities, whether set periodically or as a result of extraordinary conditions, must be determined within the context of the stated mission, goals, and resources.

## Part 7. FACILITIES, TECHNOLOGY, and EQUIPMENT

The judicial program must have adequate, suitably located facilities, technology, and equipment to support its mission and goals. Facilities, technology, and equipment must be in compliance with relevant federal, state, provincial, and local requirements to provide for access, health, and safety.

Judicial programs must have access to facilities of sufficient size and arrangement to ensure confidentiality of records, meetings, and interviews.

The facilities should include a private office where individual consultations and pre-hearing conferences with those involved in disciplinary actions may be held, hearing room facilities, a meeting room for small groups, a library or resource area, and a secure location for confidential records.

## Part 8. LEGAL RESPONSIBILITIES

The institution must inform staff and students, in a timely and systematic fashion, about extraordinary or changing legal obligations and potential liability.

Staff members must be knowledgeable about and responsive to law and regulations that relate to higher education and judicial programs. Sources for legal obligations and limitations include (a) constitutional, statutory, regulatory, and case law; (b) laws and ordinances emanating from federal, state, provincial, and local governments; and (e) policies of the institution.

Staff members must use reasonable and informed practices to limit the liability exposure of the institution, its offices, employees, and agents. Staff members must be informed about institutional policies regarding personal liability and related insurance coverage options.

The institution must provide access to legal advice for staff members as needed to carry out assigned responsibilities.

Appropriate policies and practices to ensure compliance with regulations should include notification to all constituencies of their rights and responsibilities under the judicial system, a written description of all aspects of the judicial proceeding, accurate record keeping of judicial proceedings, and regular evaluations.

## Part 9. EQUAL OPPORTUNITY, ACCESS, and AFFIRMATIVE ACTION

Staff members must ensure that judicial programs are provided on a fair and equitable basis. Judicial programs must be accessible. Hours of operation must be responsive to the needs of all students. Judicial programs must adhere to the spirit and intent of equal opportunity laws.

Judicial programs must not be discriminatory on the basis of age, ancestry, color, disability, gender, national origin, race, religious creed, sexual orientation, and/or veteran status. Exceptions are appropriate only where provided by relevant law and institutional policy.

Consistent with its mission and goals, judicial programs must take affirmative action to remedy significant imbalances in student participation and staffing patterns.

## Part 10. CAMPUS and COMMUNITY RELATIONS

Judicial programs must establish, maintain, and promote effective relations with relevant campus offices and external agencies.

Representatives of the judicial system should meet regularly with pertinent campus constituencies (e.g., student government, student development agencies, staff, faculty, academic administrators, campus police, legal counsel) in order to exchange information concerning their respective operations and to identify ways to work together to prevent behavioral problems and to correct existing ones. Such collaborative efforts might include educational programs and joint publications.

Representatives should also meet periodically with relevant external agencies to ensure understanding about the judicial programs as well as to continually explore ways to utilize external agencies in dealing with student behavior problems in an effective manner.

## Part 11. DIVERSITY

Within the context of the institution's unique mission, multi-dimensional diversity enriches the community and enhances the collegiate experience for all; therefore, judicial programs must nurture environments where similarities and differences among people are recognized and honored.

109

Judicial programs must promote cultural educational experiences that are characterized by open and continuous communication; that deepen understanding of one's culture and heritage; and that respect and educate about similarities, differences, and histories of cultures.

Judicial programs must address the characteristics and needs of the diverse population when establishing and implementing policies and procedures.

## Part 12. ETHICS

All persons involved in the provision of judicial programs to students must adhere to the highest principles of ethical behavior. Judicial programs staff members must develop and adopt statements of ethical practice addressing their unique issues. These statements must be published, implemented, and reviewed periodically.

Judicial program staff members must ensure that confidentiality is maintained with respect to all communications and records considered confidential unless exempted by law.

Information disclosed in individual counseling sessions must remain confidential, unless written permission to divulge the information is given by the student. However, all staff members must disclose to appropriate authorities information judged to be of an emergency nature, especially when the safety of the individual or others is involved. Information contained in students' educational records must not be disclosed to extra-institutional third parties without appropriate consent, unless classified as "Directory" information or when the information is subpoenaed by law. Judicial programs must apply a similar dedication to privacy and confidentiality to research data concerning individuals.

Staff members must be aware of and comply with the provisions contained in the institution's human subjects research policy and in other relevant institutional policies addressing ethical practices.

Staff members must recognize and avoid personal conflict of interest or appearance thereof in their transactions with students and others. Staff members must strive to ensure the fail objectives and impartial treatment of all persons with whom they deal.

When handling institutional funds, judicial staff members must ensure that such funds are managed in accordance with established and responsible accounting procedures.

Staff members must maintain the highest standards of ethical behavior in the use of technology.

Staff members must not participate in any form of harassment that demeans people or creates an intimidating, hostile, or offensive campus environment.

Staff members must perform their duties within the limits of their training, expertise, and competence. When these limits are exceeded, individuals in need of further assistance must be referred to persons possessing appropriate qualifications.

Staff members must use suitable means to confront and otherwise hold accountable other staff members who exhibit unethical behavior.

Judicial program staff members must maintain the highest principles of ethical behavior in the use of technology.

## Part 13. ASSESSMENT and EVALUATION

Judicial programs must regularly conduct systematic qualitative and quantitative evaluations of program quality to determine whether and to what degree the stated mission and goals are being met. Although methods of assessment vary, judicial programs must employ a sufficient range of measures to ensure objectivity and comprehensiveness. Data collected must include responses from students and other significant constituencies. Results of these evaluations must be used when revising and improving judicial programs and in recognizing staff performance.

Evaluation of judicial programs should include

- performance evaluations of all staff members by their supervisors;
- periodic performance evaluations of individual hearing boards;
- on-going evaluation of training programs and publications; and
- periodic review of applicable state and federal laws and current case law to ensure compliance.

Such an evaluation may include research inquiries into

- whether judicial boards accurately follow the institution's procedural guidelines;
- general impressions of the judicial system according to students, faculty, and staff members;
- developmental effects on students and judicial board members;
- annual trends in case load, rates of recidivism, types of offenses, and efficacy of sanctions;
- effects of programming designed to prevent behavioral problems; and
- unique aspects of special function or special population judicial boards (e.g., traffic court or residence hall board).

# THE ROLE of LEADERSHIP PROGRAMS for STUDENTS
## CAS Standards Contextual Statement

Many college mission statements contain commitments to develop citizen leaders or prepare students for professional and community responsibilities in a global context. Throughout the history of higher education, however, leadership development has primarily been targeted toward students holding leadership positions, such as student government officials, officers in Greek organizations, and resident assistants. Consequently, only a handful of students had a genuine opportunity for focused experience in leadership development.

During the 1970s, many colleges refocused efforts on leadership development when events such as the Watergate scandal caused institutions to ponder how they taught ethics, leadership, and social responsibility. New initiatives such as the women's movement, African-American pride movements, adult reentry programs, increased access to college, and new forms of campus shared governance, coupled with a focus on intentional student development, led to new forms of leadership development through such programs as assertiveness training, emerging leaders' retreats, and leadership targeted toward special populations.

By the late 1970s, professional associations were becoming increasingly interested in broad-based leadership efforts. Several associations, including the American College Personnel Association (ACPA), National Association of Student Personnel Administrators (NASPA), National Association for Campus Activities (NACA), and National Association for Women in Education (NAWE), expanded projects and initiatives with a leadership focus. The publication of Burns *Leadership* (1978) brought new energy with its discussion of transformational leadership grounded in values and moral purpose. Thinking about leadership expanded in the 1980s and 1990s to include such perspectives as cultural influences, service learning, social change, and spirituality.

One college president noted that colleges need to develop not just better, but more leaders, and that efforts should be directed toward the entire student body. Because students experience leadership in many different settings—in and out of the classroom, on and off campus—every student engages in some type of activity that involves the practice of leadership. Regardless of differences in academic discipline,

organizational affiliation, cultural background, or geographical location, students must be better prepared to serve as citizen-leaders in a global community. The role of student affairs professionals in this arena is to help students understand their experiences and to facilitate their learning, so they become effective contributors to their communities. While no specific models target leadership development of college students, the CAS student leadership program standards help professionals provide comprehensive leadership programs and enhance learning opportunities. Leadership for positional leaders will still occur within specific functional areas like student activities or residence life; campuses that seek to develop a comprehensive leadership program will recognize the need to make intentional leadership development opportunities available to all students through coordinated campus-wide efforts.

Leadership is an inherently relational process of working with others to accomplish a goal or to promote change. Most leadership programs seek to empower students to enhance their self efficacy as leaders and understand how they can make a difference, whether as positional leader or active participant in a group or community process. Leadership development involves self-awareness and understanding of others, values and diverse perspectives, organizations, and change. Leadership also requires competence in establishing purpose, working collaboratively, and managing conflict. Institutions can initiate opportunities to study leadership and to experience a range of leadership-related activities designed to intentionally promote desired outcomes of student leadership learning.

The Inter-Association Leadership Project brought student affairs leadership educators together in the early 1980s to create and sustain a leadership agenda. By the end of the decade, higher education's commitment to leadership was clear; over 600 campuses were teaching leadership courses; special leadership centers, including the Jepson School of Leadership Studies at the University of Richmond and the McDonough Leadership Center at Marietta College, had been founded; and special programs, including the National LeaderShape Institute, had been established. In 1992 the National Clearinghouse for Leadership Programs was established at the

University of Maryland-College Park, and a co-sponsored series of symposia encouraged leadership educators to identify a leadership agenda for the 1990s. Projects funded by the Kellogg, Pew, and Lilly Foundations; FIPSE; and the federal Eisenhower Leadership grant program have focused broad-based attention on leadership development in recent years.

# References, Readings and Resources

Roberts, D.C. (1981). *Student leadership programs in higher education.* Carbondale, IL: American College Personnel Association.

Center for Creative Leadership, One Leadership Place, P.O. Box 26300, Greensboro, NC 27438-6300. (910) 288-7210. Publisher of periodic sourcebooks.

*Concepts & connections: A newsletter for leadership educators.* The National Clearinghouse for Leadership Programs, 1135 Stamp Student Union, University of Maryland at College Park, College Park, MD 20742-4631. (301) 314-7174.

*Journal of Leadership Studies.* Baker College of Flint, 1050 W. Bristol Rd., Flint, MI 48507-9987. (313) 766-4105.

*Leadership Quarterly.* JAI Press, 55 Old Post Road, # 2, P.O. Box 1678, Greenwich, CT 06836-1678. (203) 661-7602.

# STUDENT LEADERSHIP PROGRAMS
## CAS STANDARDS and GUIDELINES

## Part 1. MISSION

The student leadership program must develop, record, disseminate, implement and regularly review its mission and goals. The mission statement must be consistent with the mission and goals of the institution and with the standards in this document.

The mission of student leadership programs must be to prepare students for leadership roles and responsibilities. To accomplish this mission, the program must

- provide students with opportunities to develop and enhance a personal philosophy of leadership that includes understanding of self, others, and community, and acceptance of responsibilities inherent in community membership;
- assist students in gaining varied leadership experience;
- use multiple leadership techniques, theories, and models;
- recognize and reward exemplary leadership behavior; and
- be inclusive and accessible.

  Student leadership development should be an integral part of the institution's educational mission.

  The student leadership program should include a commitment to student involvement in the institution's governance activities. Student leadership programs should seek an institution-wide commitment that transcends the boundaries of the units specifically charged with program delivery.

## Part 2. PROGRAM

The formal education of students is purposeful, holistic, and consists of both curricular and co-curricular experiences.

The student leadership program must be (a) intentional, (b) coherent, (c) based on theories and knowledge of learning and human development, (d) reflective of developmental and demographic profiles of the student population, and (e) responsive to special needs of individuals.

The student leadership program must promote learning and development in students by encouraging outcomes such as intellectual growth, ability to communicate effectively, realistic self-appraisal, enhanced self-esteem, clarification of values, appropriate career choices, physical fitness, meaningful interpersonal relations, ability to work independently and collaboratively, social responsibility, satisfying and productive life-

styles, appreciation of aesthetic and cultural diversity, and achievement of personal goals.

The student leadership program must be comprehensive in nature and must include (1) opportunities to develop the competencies required for effective leadership; (2) training, education, and developmental activities; and (3) multiple delivery methods.

1. Competencies.

A comprehensive leadership program must be based on a broad philosophy of leadership upon which subsequent competencies are built. The program must contain components that assist the student in gaining self awareness, the relationship of self to others (differences and commonalties), the uniqueness of the institutional environment within which leadership is practiced, and the relationship to local and global communities. It must advance competencies in the categories of foundations of leadership, individual development, and organizational development.

Competencies should accrue from both cognitive and experiential development in the following areas:

*Foundations of Leadership*

- Historical perspectives and evaluation of leadership theory
- Theoretical, philosophical, and conceptual foundations of leadership of several cultures
- Cultural and gender influences on leadership
- Ethical practices in leadership
- Moral leadership
- Leadership and followership

*Personal Development*

- Awareness and understanding of various leadership styles and approaches
- Exploration and designing of personal leadership approaches
- Human development theories
- The intersections of human development theories, sexual orientation, national origin, and environment
- Personal management issues such as time management, stress reduction, development of relationships, problem solving, goal setting, and ethical decision-making
- Oral and written communication skills
- Critical thinking skills
- Risk taking
- Creativity
- Wellness lifestyle development
- Supervision
- Motivation

*Organizational Development*

- Team building
- Shared leadership
- Group dynamics and development
- Organizational communication
- Group problem-solving and decision making models
- Planning
- Conflict management and resolution
- Methods of assessing and evaluating organizational effectiveness
- Organizational culture, values and principles
- Community development
- Power and empowerment
- Collaboration
- Developing trust
- Organizational politics
- Leadership in diverse organizations

**2. Leadership training, education, and development activities. A comprehensive program must offer activities which represent each element.**

- **Leadership Training**

  Training involves those activities designed to improve performance of the individual in the role presently occupied or that are concretely focused at helping the individual being trained to translate some newly learned skill, or information, to a real and immediate situation. Examples of training include programs for the preparation of residence hall student staff, student government, student judicial board members, community service volunteers, and employment.

- **Leadership Education**

  Education program elements are designed to enhance participants' knowledge and understanding of specific leadership theories, concepts, and models. Education occurs as students gain information in their present roles that serves ultimately to provide generalized theories, principles, and approaches to prepare them for future leadership responsibilities. The student leadership program should explore the processes by which decisions affecting students, faculty, and staff are made. Examples of education include a course on leadership and politics and a seminar on the evolution of leadership theories.

- **Leadership Development**

  Development requires an environment which empowers students to mature and develop toward greater levels of leadership complexity, integration, and proficiency over a period of time. Developmental activities promote positive behavioral, cognitive, and affective outcomes. Examples of developmental activities include peer mentoring and peer leadership consultant programs.

**3. Multiple delivery methods and contexts.**

A comprehensive leadership program must involve a diverse range of faculty, students, and staff members in the delivery of programs and must recognize the diverse contexts of leadership. Regular assessment of the developmental levels and needs of participants must be conducted to implement multiple delivery strategies and contexts.

Examples of delivery methods include internships, panel discussions, movies, lectures, mentor programs, adventure training, and participation in local, regional, and national associations. Examples of contexts for leadership include diverse academic and career fields, campus organizations and committees, employment setting, community involvement, family settings, international settings, and social and religious organizations in both formal and informal positions.

# Part 3. LEADERSHIP

**Effective and ethical leadership is essential for change and to the success of all organizations. Institutions must appoint, position, and empower leaders of student leadership programs within the administrative structure to accomplish stated missions. Administrators at various levels must be selected on the basis of formal education and training, relevant work experience, personal attributes and other professional credentials. Institutions must determine expectations of accountability for program administrators and fairly assess their performance.**

**Student leadership program administrators must exercise authority over resources for which they are responsible to achieve their respective missions. Administrators of the program must articulate a vision for their organization; set goals and objectives; prescribe and practice ethical behavior; recruit, select, supervise, and develop others in the organization; manage, plan, budget, and evaluate; communicate effectively; and encourage collaborative action from colleagues, employees, other institutional constituencies, and persons outside the organization. Program administrators must address individual, organizational, or environmental conditions that inhibit goal achievement. Administrators must improve programs and services continuously in response to changing needs of students and institutional priorities.**

There should be a person or group of persons designated as responsible for the coordination of direction of the leadership program including allocation and maintenance of resources and developing student leadership opportunities.

# Part 4. ORGANIZATION and MANAGEMENT

**The student leadership program must be structured purposefully and managed effectively to achieve stated goals. Evidence of appropriate structure must include current and accessible policies and procedures, written performance expectations for all employees, functional work flow graphics or organizational charts, and service delivery expectations. Evidence of effective management must include clear sources and channels of authority, effective communication practices, decision-**

making and conflict resolution procedures, responsiveness to changing conditions, accountability systems, and recognition and reward processes.

**The student leadership program must provide channels within the organization for regular review of administrative policies and procedures.**

Student leadership programs are typically organized in a variety of offices and departments both in student services and in academic and other administrative areas. An advisory group with representatives from the involved areas should be established for the purpose of communication.

# Part 5. HUMAN RESOURCES

**The student leadership program must be staffed adequately by individuals qualified to accomplish stated mission and goals. The program must establish procedures for staff selection, training, and evaluation; set expectations for supervision; and provide appropriate professional development opportunities.**

**Professional staff members must hold an earned graduate degree in a field relevant to the position description or must possess an appropriate combination of education and experience.**

**Degree or credential seeking interns or others in training must be qualified by enrollment in an appropriate field of study and relevant experience. These individuals must be trained and supervised adequately by professional staff members.**

**Student employees and volunteers must be carefully selected, trained, supervised, and evaluated. When their knowledge and skills are not adequate for particular situations, they must refer students or others in need of assistance to qualified professional staff.**

**The student leadership program must have secretarial and technical staff adequate to accomplish its mission. Such staff must be technologically proficient and qualified to perform activities including reception duties, office equipment operation, records maintenance, and mail handling.**

**Appropriate salary levels and fringe benefits for all staff members must be commensurate with those for comparable positions within the institution, in similar institutions, and in the relevant geographic area.**

The student leadership program must intentionally employ a diverse staff to reflect the diversity of the student population, to ensure the existence of readily identifiable role models for students and to enrich the campus community. Affirmative action must occur in hiring and promotion practices to ensure diverse staffing profiles, and as required by institutional, local, state/provincial, or federal law.

The student leadership program should have adequate and qualified staff or faculty members to implement a comprehensive program.

Program staff should engage in continuous discovery and understanding of emerging leadership models, research, theories, and definitions through disciplined study and professional development activities.

Student organization advisors should be considered as resources to assist both formally and informally in student leadership programs. Advisors can provide information about issues that need to be addressed. The student leadership program staff should assist advisors in conducting leadership training, education, and development for their respective student groups.

Professional staff or faculty involved in leadership programs should possess:

- ability to work with diverse students;
- knowledge of the history and current trends in leadership theories, models, and philosophies;
- leadership experiences;
- followership experiences;
- knowledge of organizational development, group dynamics, strategies for change and principles of community;
- knowledge of diversity issues related to leadership;
- ability to evaluate leadership programs and assess outcomes;
- effective oral and written communication skills;
- ability to effectively organize learning opportunities that are consistent with students' stages of development; and
- ability to use reflection in helping students understand leadership concepts by processing critical incidents with students.

# Part 6. FINANCIAL RESOURCES

**Student leadership programs must have adequate funding to accomplish its mission and goals. Priorities, whether set periodically or as a result of extraordinary conditions, must be determined within the context of the stated mission, goals, and resources.**

Funding for the student leadership program may come from a variety of sources, including institutional funds, grant money, student government funds, fees for services, and government contracts. Where possible, institutional funding should be allocated regularly for the operation of leadership programs.

# Part 7. FACILITIES, TECHNOLOGY and EQUIPMENT

**Student leadership programs must have adequate, suitably located facilities, technology and equipment to support its mission and goals. Facilities and equipment must be in compliance with relevant federal, state, provincial, and local requirements to provide for access, health and safety.**

Leadership program facilities should be conveniently located on campus. Staff, faculty, and student space should be designed to encourage a maximum level of interaction among students, faculty, and staff.

# Part 8. LEGAL RESPONSIBILITIES

Student leadership program staff members must be knowledgeable about and responsive to law and regulations that relate to their respective program or service. Sources for legal obligations and limitations are constitutional, federal, statutory, regulatory, and case law; mandatory laws and orders emanating from federal, state, provincial and local governments; and the institution through its policies.

Student leadership program staff must use reasonable and informed practices to limit the liability exposure of the institution, its officers, employees, and agents. Staff members must be informed about institutional policies regarding personal liability and related insurance coverage options.

The institution must provide access to legal advice for staff members as needed to carry out assigned responsibilities.

The institution must inform staff and students, in a timely and systematic fashion, about extraordinary or changing legal obligations and potential liabilities.

# Part 9. EQUAL OPPORTUNITY, ACCESS, and AFFIRMATIVE ACTION

Staff members must ensure that student leadership programs are provided on a fair and equitable basis. Each program and service must be accessible. Hours of operation must be responsive to the needs of all students.

The student leadership program must adhere to the spirit and intent of equal opportunity laws.

The student leadership program must not be discriminatory on the basis of age, color, disability, gender, national origin, race, religious creed, sexual orientation, and/or veteran status. Exceptions are appropriate only where provided by relevant law and institutional policy.

Consistent with their mission and goals, student leadership program must take affirmative action to remedy significant imbalances in student participation and staffing patterns.

# Part 10. CAMPUS and COMMUNITY RELATIONS

The student leadership program must establish, maintain, and promote effective relations with relevant campus offices and external agencies.

> The student leadership program should maintain positive relations through effective communication and encourage participation with a variety of offices, departments, agencies, and constituencies both on and off campus for leadership involvement opportunities.

# Part 11. DIVERSITY

Within the context of each institution's unique mission, multi-dimensional diversity enriches the community and enhances the collegiate experience for all; therefore, student leadership programs and services must nurture environments where similarities and differences among people are recognized and honored.

Student leadership programs must provide cultural educational experiences that are characterized by open and continuous communication, that deepen understanding of one's own culture and heritage, and that respect and educate about similarities, differences and histories of cultures. The program must explore various cultural perspectives of leadership.

Student leadership programs must address the characteristics and needs of a diverse population when establishing and implementing policies and procedures.

# Part 12. ETHICS

Student leadership program staff members involved in the delivery of programs and services for students must adhere to the highest principles of ethical behavior. The program must develop or adopt and implement statements of ethical practice addressing the issues unique to student leadership development. The program must publish these statements and insure their periodic review by all concerned.

Student leadership program staff members must ensure that confidentiality is maintained with respect to all communications and records considered confidential unless exempted by law.

Information disclosed in individual counseling sessions must remain confidential, unless written permission to divulge the information is given by the student. However, all staff members must disclose to appropriate authorities information judged to be of an emergency nature, especially when the safety of the individual or others is involved. Information contained in students' educational records must not be disclosed to non-institutional third parties without appropriate consent, unless classified as "Directory" information or when the information is subpoenaed by law. The program must apply a similar dedication to privacy and confidentiality to research data concerning individuals. All staff members must be aware of and comply with the provisions contained in the institution's human subjects research policy and in other relevant institutional policies addressing ethical practices.

Student leadership program staff members must recognize and avoid personal conflict of interest or the appearance thereof in their transactions with students and others. In the context of their work, staff members must strive to ensure the impartial treatment of all persons with whom they deal.

When handling institutional funds, student leadership program staff members must ensure that such funds are managed in accordance with established and responsible accounting procedures.

Student leadership program staff members must not participate in any form of harassment that demeans persons or creates an intimidating, hostile, or offensive campus environment.

Student leadership program staff members must perform their duties within the limits of their training, expertise, and competence. When these limits are exceeded, individuals in need of further assistance must be referred to persons possessing appropriate qualifications.

Student leadership program staff members must use suitable means to confront and otherwise hold accountable other staff members who exhibit unethical behavior.

Student leadership program staff members must maintain the highest principles of ethical behavior in the use of technology.

Student leadership program staff members must ensure that facilitators have appropriate training experience and credentials. Expertise, training, and certification are essential in the administration and interpretation of personality, developmental, and leadership assessment instruments.

Where materials and instruments used in student leadership programs are copyrighted, appropriate citations must be made and permission obtained.

## Part 13. ASSESSMENT and EVALUATION

The student leadership program must regularly conduct systematic qualitative and quantitative evaluations of program quality to determine whether and to what degree the stated mission and goals are being met. Although methods of assessment vary, the program must employ a sufficient range of measures to insure objectivity and comprehensiveness. Data collected must include responses from students and other affected constituencies. Results of these evaluations must be used in revising and improving programs and services and in recognizing staff performance.

> Areas to be assessed should include learning outcomes, student satisfaction, goal achievement, and effectiveness of teaching techniques. Particular efforts should be made to conduct longitudinal studies on program evaluations.

© Copyright 1997 Council for the Advancement of Standards in Higher Education (CAS)

# THE ROLE of LEARNING ASSISTANCE PROGRAMS
## CAS Standards Contextual Statement

Learning assistance programs provide student-centered instruction and services for developing skills, strategies, and behaviors that increase the efficiency and effectiveness of the processes that improve learning outcomes. By helping students achieve their learning potential and succeed academically, learning assistance programs significantly influence student retention.

The history of learning assistance programs extends back to 1900, when "how to study books" were first published for underprepared entering freshmen. The reading clinics and study methods laboratories of the 1930s and 1940s and the self-help programs, learning modules, and programmed instruction of the reading and study skills laboratories of the 1950s and 1960s formed part of the historical foundation. By the 1970s, these programs had merged with educational technology and tutoring centers and offered services for the many new nontraditional students. At selective colleges and universities, these services were organized under the auspices of student affairs and typically were open to any student who requested help. At community colleges and institutions with open admissions policies, remedial courses and related services were usually offered under the auspices of either an academic department or a separate developmental education unit.

By the mid-1970s, professionals involved with learning assistance had initiated national organizations. One of these groups, Commission XVI: Learning Centers in Higher Education, was charged by its parent organization, the American College Personnel Association (ACPA), to participate in drafting the CAS Standards and Guidelines for Learning Assistance Programs. Conscious that Commission XVI represented primarily a student affairs-based learning center model, the leadership solicited input and involvement from constituents in other professional organizations to assure broad representation of institutional types and program models. The principle guiding the project was that standards for the profession must address aspects common to all quality programs, but be broad enough to encompass the various models for, and the multi-disciplinary nature of, learning assistance programs. After five years and numerous drafts, the CAS Standards and Guidelines for Learning Assistance Programs were completed and adopted in 1986. This first major document articulating universal concepts, beliefs, and practices for learning assistance practitioners and their programs also confirmed that learning assistance programs had become permanent professional components in higher education.

The initial CAS Standards and Guidelines for Learning Assistance Programs had two major limitations. First, it did not contain a pedagogical component to directly address the teaching function of learning assistance programs. Second, its broad based purpose did not address standards for specific functions and content areas of learning assistance. Recognition of these limitations produced greater interest in standards and the movement gained momentum in professional organizations.

The National Association for Developmental Education (NADE), with help of other learning assistance associations including the College Reading and Learning Association (CRLA), Commission XVI of the American College Personnel Association (ACPA), the Midwest College Learning Center Association (MCLCA), and the New York College Learning Skills Association (NYCLSA), sponsored standards development initiatives that culminated in the 1995 publication of the *NADE Self-Evaluation Guides: Models for Assessing Learning Assistance/Developmental Education Programs*. Using the CAS Standards and Guidelines format as a template, this document applied the CAS process to specific programs, such as tutoring services, adjunct instructional programs, and developmental coursework. To address the profession's pedagogical component, it also included a section on program factors influencing the teaching/learning process. In 1989, CRLA had initiated the Tutor Certification Program to assure that minimum standards for tutor training were being met. As this and subsequent projects satisfy the profession's requirements for content and practice-specific standards, the CAS Standards and Guidelines for Learning Assistance Programs continue to provide a process for conducting a systematic self-study of the essential components of an entire learning assistance program.

In the early 1990s, both NADE and CRLA joined the CAS enterprise and committed to active participation in the revision of the CAS Standards and Guidelines for Learning Assistance Programs. The revision process was conducted over a two-year period and involved input from over 150 professional learning assistance practitioners representing numerous professional bodies. The document that follows is the product of that collaboration and represents professional consensus of the role and importance of learning assistance programs in higher education.

# References, Readings and Resources

Casazza , M. E., & Silverman, S. L. (1996). *Learning assistance and developmental education: A guide for effective practice.* San Francisco: Jossey-Bass.

Hashway, R. M. (Spring 1989). Developmental learning center designs. *Research and Teaching in Developmental Education, 5*(2), 25-38.

Lowenstein, S. (1993). Using advisory boards for learning assistance programs. New York College *Learning Skills Association: Perspectives on practice in Developmental Education.* 93-99.

Maxwell, M. (Ed.) (1994). *From access to success: A book of reading on college developmental education and learning assistance programs.* Clearwater, FL: H&H Publishing Co.

Maxwell, M. (1996). *Evaluating academic skills programs: A sourcebook*—3rd revision. Kensington, MD: MM Associates.

Maxwell, M. (1997). *Improving student learning skills.* (revised ed.) Clearwater, FL: H&H Publishing Co.

National Association for Developmental Education. (1994). *NADE self-evaluation guidelines for adjunct skills programs: Tutoring, developmental courses, and teaching and learning and developmental courses.* Clearwater, FL: H&H Publishing Company.

New York College Learning Skills Association Ethics and Standards Committee. (revised, April 1994). *Statement of ethics and general guidelines for learning assistance programs.* New York: New York College Learning Skills Association.

Robert, E. R. & Thompson, G. (Spring 1994). Learning assistance and the success of underprepared students at Berkeley. *Journal of Developmental Education, 17*(3), 4-15.

Stahl, N. A., Brozo, W. G., & Gordon, B. (1984). The professional preparation of college reading and study-skills specialists. In G. McNinch (Ed.) *Reading teacher education: Yearbook of the 4th Annual conference of the American Reading Forum.* Carrollton, GA: West Georgia College. ERIC #248-761.

White, W. G., Jr., & Schnuth, M. L. (1990). College learning assistance centers: Places for learning. In R.M. Hashway (Ed.), *Handbook of developmental education.* New York: Praeger Press, 157-177.

White, W. G., Jr., Kyzar, B., & Lane, K. E. (1990). College learning assistance centers: Spaces for learning. In R. M. Hashway (Ed.), *Handbook of developmental education.* New York: Praeger Press, 179-195.

Refer to the enclosed Addendum
for Updated Learning Assistance
Programs Standards & Guidelines.
For questions, please call:
1-800-942-9304, ext. 21418

# LEARNING ASSISTANCE PROGRAMS
## CAS STANDARDS and GUIDELINES

## Part 1. MISSION

The learning assistance program must teach the skills and strategies to help students become independent and active learners and to achieve academic success.

The learning assistance program must develop, record, disseminate, implement and regularly review its mission and goals. The learning assistance mission statement must be consistent with the mission and goals of the institution and with the standards of this document. The mission statement must address the purpose of the learning assistance program, the population it serves, the programs and services it provides, and the goals the program is to accomplish.

The learning assistance program must collaborate with faculty, staff, and administrators in addressing the learning needs, academic performance, and retention of students.

> Models of learning assistance programs vary, but should share the following common goals:
> 1. to make students the central focus of the program;
> 2. to assist members of the campus community in achieving their personal potential for learning;
> 3. to provide instruction and services that address the cognitive, affective, and socio-cultural dimensions of learning;
> 4. to introduce students to the expectations of faculty and the culture of higher education;
> 5. to help students develop positive attitudes towards learning and confidence in their ability to learn;
> 6. to foster personal responsibility and accountability for one's own learning;
> 7. to provide a variety of instructional approaches that are appropriate for the level of skills and learning styles of the student population;
> 8. to assist students in transferring skills and strategies they have learned previously to their academic work;
> 9. to provide services and resources to faculty, staff, and administrators that enhance and support classroom instruction and professional development; and
> 10. to support the academic standards and requirements of the institution.

## Part 2. PROGRAM

The formal education of students is purposeful, holistic, and consists of the curriculum and co-curriculum.

The learning assistance program must be (a) intentional; (b) coherent; (c) based on theories and knowledge of learning and human development; (d) reflective of developmental and demographic profiles of the student population; and (e) responsive to the special needs of individuals.

The learning assistance program must promote learning and development in students through assessing and teaching the cognitive and affective skills and strategies necessary for achieving academic and personal learning goals.

The learning assistance program must encourage outcomes such as intellectual growth, ability to communicate effectively, realistic self-appraisal, enhanced self-esteem, learning style awareness, self-monitoring strategies, the ability to work and learn independently and collaboratively, clarification of values, appropriate career choices, leadership development, physical fitness, meaningful interpersonal relations, social responsibility, satisfying and productive lifestyles, appreciation of aesthetic and cultural diversity, and achievement of personal goals. The program must promote, either directly of by referral, the affective skills that influence learning such as stress management, test anxiety reduction, assertiveness, power of concentration, and motivation.

The learning assistance program must refer students to appropriate campus and community resources for assistance with personal problems, severe learning disabilities, financial difficulties and other areas of need that may be outside the purview or beyond the expertise of the learning assistance program.

> The scope of the learning assistance program should be determined by the type and level of skills students require. The format utilized for strengthening academic skills may include mandatory credit-bearing developmental courses or non-credit elective workshops.

> The scope of programs and services should also be determined by the needs of the student populations the learning assistance program is charged to serve. These can range from special populations (such as culturally and ethnically diverse students, international and English-as-a-second-language students, student athletes, returning students, and students with physical and learning disabilities) to the entire student population.

> Formal and informal diagnostic procedures should be conducted to identify skills and strategies that the student should develop to achieve the level of proficiency prescribed or required by the institution or known to be necessary for college learning. Assessment results should be shared with the student to formulate recommendations and a plan of instruction.

The learning assistance program should provide instruction and services for the development of reading, mathematics and quantitative reasoning, writing, critical thinking, problem solving, and study skills. Other programs may include: subject-matter tutoring, adjunct instructional programs and supplemental instruction groups, time management programs, freshman seminars, and preparation for graduate and professional school admissions tests and for professional certification requirements.

Modes of delivering learning assistance programs include individual and group instruction and instructional media such as print, video, audio, computers, and skills laboratories. Instruction and programs may be delivered on-site or through distance learning programs.

The learning assistance program should give systematic feedback to students concerning their progress in reaching cognitive and affective goals, teach self feedback methods utilizing self-monitoring strategies, and give students practice in applying and transferring skills and strategies learned in the program to academic tasks across the curriculum.

The learning assistance program should promote an understanding of the learning needs of the student population. Some of the ways in which learning assistance programs should educate the campus community:

- establishing advisory boards consisting of members from key segments of the campus community;
- holding periodic informational meetings and consulting with staff, faculty, and administrators;
- participating in staff and faculty development and in-service programs on curriculum and instructional approaches that address the development of learning skills, attitudes, and behaviors;
- encouraging the use of learning assistance program resources, materials, instruction and services as integral or adjunct classroom activities;
- conducting in-class workshops that demonstrate the application of learning strategies to the course content;
- disseminating information that describes the programs and services, hours of operation, procedures for registering or scheduling appointments through publications, campus and local media announcements, and informational presentations;
- training and supervising paraprofessionals and preprofessionals to work in such capacities as tutors, peer mentors, and advisors; and
- providing jobs, practica, courses, internships, and assistantships for graduate students interested in learning assistance and related careers.

# Part 3. LEADERSHIP

**Effective and ethical leadership is essential to the success of learning assistance programs. Institutions must appoint, position and empower learning assistance program administrators within the administrative structure to accomplish stated missions.**

**Learning assistance program administrators must be selected on the basis of formal education and training,** relevant work experience, personal attributes and other professional credentials. Institutions must determine expectations of accountability for learning assistance program administrators and fairly assess their performance.

**Learning assistance program administrators must exercise authority over resources for which they are responsible to achieve their respective missions; must articulate a vision for their organization; establish the program mission, policies, and procedures; set goals and objectives; prescribe and practice ethical behavior; recruit, select, supervise and develop others in the learning assistance program; manage, plan, budget and evaluate; communicate effectively; and marshal cooperative action from colleagues, employees, other institutional constituencies, and persons outside the organization. Program administrators must address individual, organizational, or environmental conditions that inhibit goal achievement. Program administrators must improve programs and services continuously in response to changing needs of students and institutional priorities.**

Learning assistance program administrators should

- participate in institutional planning, policy, procedural, and fiscal decisions that affect learning support for students;
- be informed about issues, trends, theories, and methodologies related to student learning and retention;
- represent the learning assistance program on institutional committees;
- collaborate with leaders of academic departments and support services in addressing the learning needs and retention of students;
- be involved in research, publication, presentations, consultation, and the activities of professional organizations; and
- communicate with professional constituents in the learning assistance field and related professions.

# Part 4. ORGANIZATION and MANAGEMENT

**The learning assistance programs must be structured purposefully and managed effectively to achieve stated goals. Evidence of appropriate structure must include current and accessible policies and procedures, written job descriptions and performance expectations for all employees, functional work flow graphics or organizational charts, and service delivery expectations. Evidence of effective management must include clear sources and channels of authority, effective communication practices, decision-making and conflict resolution procedures, responsiveness to changing conditions, accountability systems and recognition and reward processes. Programs must provide channels within the organization for regular review of administrative policies and procedures.**

The mission and goals of the learning assistance program, the needs and demographics of its clients, and its institutional role should determine where the unit is located in the organizational structure of the institution. Learning assistance programs are frequently organized as units in the academic affairs or the student affairs division. Regardless of where the learning assistance program is organized, it should communicate and collaborate with a network of key units across the institution to assure the coordination of related functions, programs, services, policies, procedures, and to expedite client referrals.

The Teaming assistance program should have a broadly constituted advisory board to make suggestions, provide information, and give guidance.

The learning assistance program should provide written goals, objectives, and anticipated outcomes for each program and service. Written procedures should exist for collecting, processing, and reporting student assessment and program data.

Regularly scheduled meetings should be held to share information; to coordinate the planning, scheduling, and delivery of programs and services; to identify and discuss potential and actual problems and concerns; and to collaborate on making decisions and solving problems.

# Part 5. HUMAN RESOURCES

**Each learning assistance program must be staffed adequately by individuals qualified to accomplish its mission and goals. The learning assistance program must establish procedures for staff selection, training, and evaluation; set expectations for supervision, and provide appropriate professional development opportunities.**

**Staff and faculty who hold a joint appointment with the learning assistance program must be committed to the mission, philosophy, goals, and priorities of the program and must possess the necessary expertise for assigned responsibilities.**

**Professional staff members must hold an earned graduate degree in a field relevant to the learning assistance position description or must possess an appropriate combination of education and experience.**

Professional staff should have earned degrees from relevant disciplines such as reading, English, mathematics, student personnel and student development, guidance and counseling, psychology, or education. Learning assistance professionals should be knowledgeable in learning theory and in the instruction, assessment, theory, and the professional standards of practice for their area of specialization and responsibility. In addition, they should understand the unique characteristics and needs of the populations they assist and teach. Learning assistance program professional staff should vary and adjust pedagogical approaches according to the learning needs and styles of their students, to the nature of the learning task, and to content of academic disciplines across the curriculum.

Learning assistance program professional staff should be competent and experienced in:

- teaching, advising, and counseling students at the college level;
- written and oral communication skills;
- working in a culturally and academically diverse environment;
- consulting, collaborating, and negotiating with staff, faculty and administrators of academic and student affairs units;
- designing and implementing instructional strategies and materials and utilizing instructional technologies
- training, supervising, and mentoring paraprofessionals and preprofessionals; and
- identifying and establishing lines of communication for student referral to other institutional and student support units.

**Degree or credential seeking interns or others in training must be qualified by enrollment in an appropriate field of study and relevant experience. These individuals must be trained and supervised adequately by professional staff members.**

The learning assistance program should be informed of the policies and procedures to be followed for internships and practica as required by the students' academic departments. The roles and responsibilities of the learning assistance program and those of the academic department should be clearly defined and understood by all involved.

**Learning assistance program student employees and volunteers must be carefully selected, trained, supervised, and evaluated. When their knowledge and skills are not adequate for particular situations, they must refer students and others in need of assistance to qualified professional staff.**

**The learning assistance program must have secretarial and technical staff adequate to accomplish its mission. Such staff must be technologically proficient to perform activities including reception duties, office equipment operation, records maintenance, and mail handling.**

Secretarial and technical staff should be updated on changes in programs, services, policies and procedures in order to expedite smooth and efficient assistance to clients. Appropriate staff development opportunities should be available.

**Appropriate salary levels and fringe benefits for all staff members must be commensurate with those for comparable positions within the institution, in similar institutions, and in the relevant geographic area.**

**To reflect the diversity of the student population, to ensure the existence of readily identifiable role models for students and to enrich the campus community, the learning assistance program must intentionally employ a diverse staff.**

**Affirmative action must occur in hiring and promotion practices as required to ensure diverse staffing profiles.**

## Part 6. FINANCIAL RESOURCES

The learning assistance program must have adequate funding to accomplish its mission and goals. Priorities, whether set periodically or as a result of extraordinary conditions, must be determined within the context of the stated mission, goals, and resources.

Prior to implementing a new program or service or to significantly expanding an existing program component, a financial analysis should be performed to determine the financial resources required to support the addition or expansion and the appropriate funds made available.

The learning assistance program budget should support its instructional and student support service functions. Adequate funds should be provided for the following budget categories: staff and student salaries, general office functions, student assessment and instructional activities, data management and program evaluation processes, research staff training and professional development activities, instructional materials and media, and instructional and office computing

## Part 7. FACILITIES and EQUIPMENT

The learning assistance program must have adequate, suitably located facilities and equipment to support its mission and goals. Facilities for the learning assistance program must occupy a suitable location that is convenient and accessible to students, faculty, and other clients.

Facilities and equipment must be in compliance with relevant federal, state, provincial, and local requirements to provide for access, health, and safety.

Facilities and equipment should support the instructional, service, and office functions of the learning assistance program. Facility considerations should include flexible space that can be adapted to changes in the delivery of programs, services, and instructional modes; classrooms, labs, resource rooms, media and computer centers, group and one-to-one tutorial space to support instruction; private, sound-proofed areas to support testing, counseling, and other activities that require confidentiality or concentration; adequate and secure storage for equipment, supplies, instructional and testing materials, and confidential records. Attention should be given to environmental conditions that influence learning such as appropriate acoustics, lighting, ventilation, heating and air-conditioning.

## Part 8. LEGAL RESPONSIBILITIES

Learning assistance program staff members must be knowledgeable about and sources for legal obligations and limitations are: constitutional, federal, statutory, regulatory, and case law; mandatory laws and orders emanating from federal, state, provincial and local governments; and the institution through its policies.

Staff members must use reasonable and informed practices to limit the liability exposure of the institution, its officers, employees, and agents. Staff members must be informed about institutional policies regarding personal liability and related insurance coverage options.

The institution must inform learning assistance program staff and students, in a timely and systematic fashion, about extraordinary or changing legal obligations and potential liabilities. The institution must provide access to legal advice for staff members as needed to carry out assigned responsibilities.

Staff development programs should be available to educate learning assistance program staff of these changes.

## Part 9. EQUAL OPPORTUNITY, ACCESS and AFFIRMATIVE ACTION

Learning assistance program staff members must ensure that services and programs are provided on a fair and equitable basis. Each learning assistance program and service must be accessible. Hours of operation must be responsive to the needs of all students.

Each learning assistance program and service must adhere to the spirit and intent of equal opportunity laws.

The learning assistance programs must not be discriminatory on the basis of age, color, disability, gender, national origin, race, religious creed, sexual orientation and/or veteran status. Exceptions are appropriate only where provided by relevant law and institutional policy.

Consistent with their mission and goals, learning assistance programs must take affirmative action to remedy significant imbalances in student participation and staffing patterns.

## Part 10. CAMPUS and COMMUNITY RELATIONS

The learning assistance program must establish, maintain, and promote effective relations with relevant campus offices and external agencies.

The learning assistance program should

- be an integral part of the academic offerings of the institution;
- establish communication with academic and student services units
- to encourage the exchange of ideas, knowledge, and expertise,
- to provide mutual consultation, as needed, on student cases,
- to expedite student referrals to and from the learning assistance program,
- to collaborate on programs and services that efficiently and effectively address the needs of students;
- have representation on institutional committees relevant to the mission and goals of the program such as committees on retention, orientation, basic skills, learning communities, freshmen seminars, probation review, academic

standards and requirements, curriculum design, assessment and placement, and faculty development;

- solicit volunteers from the local community to contribute their skills and talents to the services of the learning assistance program; and

- provide training and consultation to community-based organizations, e.g., literacy associations, corporate training, and school district-based tutorial services.

# Part 11. DIVERSITY

Within the context of each institution's unique mission, multi-dimensional diversity enriches the community and enhances the collegiate experience for all; therefore,

The learning assistance program must nurture environments where similarities and differences among people are recognized and honored.

The learning assistance program must promote cultural educational experiences that are characterized by open and continuous communication, that deepen understanding of one's own culture and heritage, and that respect and educate about similarities, differences and histories of cultures.

The learning assistance program must address the characteristics and needs of a diverse population when establishing and implementing policies and procedures.

The program should facilitate student adjustment to the academic culture of the institution by orienting students to the practices, resources, responsibilities and behaviors that contribute to academic success.

The instructional content, materials, and activities of learning assistance programs should provide opportunities to increase awareness and appreciation of the individual and cultural differences of students.

# Part 12. ETHICS

All persons involved in the delivery of the learning assistance program to students must adhere to the highest standards of ethical behavior. The program must develop or adopt and implement statements of ethical practice addressing the issues unique to each program and service. The program and services must publish these statements and insure their periodic review by all concerned.

All learning assistance program staff members must ensure that confidentiality is maintained with respect to all communications and records considered confidential unless exempted by law. All staff members must receive training in identification of confidential information and proper procedures for obtaining, processing and recording confidential information.

Information disclosed in counseling sessions must remain confidential unless written permission to disclose the information is given by the student. However, all learning assistance program staff members must divulge to the appropriate authorities information judged to be of an emergency nature, especially where the safety of the individual or others is involved. Information contained in students' educational records must not be disclosed to non-institutional third parties without appropriate consent, unless classified as "directory" information or when the information is subpoenaed by law.

The learning assistance program must apply a similar dedication to privacy and confidentiality to research data concerning individuals. All staff members must be aware of and comply with the provisions contained in the institution's human subjects research policy and in other relevant institutional policies addressing ethical practices.

All learning assistance program staff members must recognize and avoid personal conflict of interest or the appearance thereof in their transactions with students and others. Information and training should be made available regarding conflict of interest policies.

Because learning assistance program staff work with students' academic coursework, they must be knowledgeable of policies related to academic integrity, plagiarism, student code of conduct and other similar policies. All staff members must be cognizant of the implications of these policies.

Learning assistance program staff members must strive to insure the fair, objective and impartial treatment of all persons with whom they deal.

Statements or claims made about outcomes that can be achieved from participating in learning assistance programs and services must be truthful and realistic.

Learning assistance program staff members must not participate in any form of harassment that demeans persons or creates an intimidating, hostile or offensive campus environment.

All learning assistance program staff members must perform their duties within the limits of their training, expertise, and competence. When these limits are exceeded, individuals in need of further assistance must be referred to persons possessing appropriate qualifications. All learning assistance program staff members must use suitable means to confront and otherwise hold accountable other staff members who exhibit unethical behavior.

When handling institutional funds, all staff members must ensure that such funds are managed in accordance with established and responsible accounting procedures. Learning assistance program funds acquired through grants and other non-institutional resources must be managed according to the regulations and guidelines of the funding source and the institution.

With the prevalence of student paraprofessional and tutorial staff within learning assistance programs, specific attention should be given to properly orienting and advising student staff about matters of confidentiality. Clear statements should be distributed and reviewed with student staff as to what information is and is not appropriate for student staff to access or to communicate.

# Part 13. ASSESSMENT and EVALUATION

**The learning assistance program must undergo regular and systematic qualitative and quantitative evaluations to determine to what degree the stated mission and goals are being met.**

The learning assistance program should have the ability to collect and analyze data through its own resources and through access to appropriate data generated by the institution.

Periodic evaluations of the learning assistance program and services may be performed by on-campus experts and outside consultants and disseminated to appropriate administrators.

**Although methods of assessment vary, learning assistance programs must employ a sufficient range of qualitative and quantitative measures to insure objectivity and comprehensiveness.**

**Various means of assessment should be conducted for the purpose of identifying the learning needs of the students and guiding them to appropriate programs and services. Assessment results should be communicated to the student confidentially, honestly, and with sensitivity. Students should be advised directed to appropriate, alternative educational opportunities when there is reasonable cause to believe that students will not be able to meet requirements for academic success.**

**Data collected must include responses from students, or other affected constituencies. Results of these evaluations must be used in revising and improving programs and services and in recognizing staff performances.**

Qualitative methods may include standard evaluation forms, questionnaires, interviews, observations, or case studies.

Quantitative measurements range from data on an individual student's performance to the impact on the campus' retention rate. Quantitative methods may include follow-up studies on students' grades in mainstream courses, GPAs, graduation, re-enrollment and retention figures. Comparative data of learning assistance program participants and non-participants is also a measure of program effectiveness. Quantitative measures can include data on the size of the user population, numbers utilizing particular services, number of contact hours, the sources of student referrals to the program, numbers of students who may be on a waiting list or who have requested services not provided by the learning assistance program. Quantitative data should be collected within specific time periods and longitudinally to reveal trends.

Learning assistance programs should conduct periodic self-assessments, utilizing self-study processes endorsed by professional organizations.

The learning assistance program should periodically review and revise its goals and services based on evaluation outcomes and based on changes in institutional goals, priorities, and plans. Data that reveals trends or changes in student demographics, characteristics and needs should be utilized for learning assistance program short- and long-term planning.

# THE ROLE of MINORITY STUDENT PROGRAMS and SERVICES
## CAS Standards Contextual Statement

Minority Student Programs and Services are crucial to the retention and graduation of minority students in higher education. The expansion of the civil rights movement begun in the 1960s promoted increased sensitivity to multicultural backgrounds, expansion of financial aid programs, and awareness of changing ethnic and racial demographics. Consequently, minority enrollments have increased and the need for minority student services has expanded.

Although minority students are enrolling at ever-increasing rates, minority retention continues to be a challenge. The American Association of State Colleges and Universities reported a six-year graduation rate for minority students that ranged from 27 to 57 percent. To retain and graduate minority students requires support above and beyond the traditional student services typically provided college students. Minority students need advocates for changing campus environments and for adapting existing policies and academic curricula to reflect a wide array of cultures. Historically, although minority students have been required to meet institutional expectations, little or no consideration had been given to the deficiencies or shortcomings in their college readiness that may have resulted from their experiences before entering the college.

Although minority student programs and services vary in structure from institution to institution, all provide advocacy for minority students. Some programs organize their services to address specific ethnic populations; others seek to serve all minority students collectively. On campuses where academic departments for ethnic studies exist, the minority student programs usually coordinate services with the programs in these departments. The additional support provided by minority student programs creates a campus climate that allows minority students to function within their unique cultural frameworks, instead of pressuring these students to assimilate into the predominant Eurocentric culture common to most college campuses.

Minority programming often includes academic support services, such as tutoring, study skills training, supplemental instruction, and referral to learning assistance resources; minority student orientation; faculty and peer mentoring programs; minority student organizations; campus-wide programs for awareness and education; programs to prevent racial incidents and for crisis intervention; individualized academic advising and personal counseling; encouragement and mentoring for students entering graduate and professional programs; and advocacy for financial aid and administrative policies that facilitate retention of minority students.

Strong minority student programs and services are essential to the retention and graduation of minority students, and to increasing diversity on college and university campuses. An institution shows its commitment to providing quality education for minority students through the level of support it provides to its minority student programs and services. The CAS Standards and Guidelines for Minority Student Programs and Services provide a relevant and viable model for minority student programs and services.

## References, Readings and Resources

National Council of Educational Opportunity Associations (NCEOA), 1025 Vermont Ave. NW, Suite 1201, Washington, DC 20005. (202) 347-7430; Fax 347-0786. KATIE@HQ.NCEOA.ORG

# MINORITY STUDENT PROGRAMS
## CAS STANDARDS and GUIDELINES

## Part 1. MISSION

Minority student programs and services must develop, record, disseminate, implement and regularly review its mission and goals. Mission statements must be consistent with the mission and goals of the institution and with the standards in this document.

> The provision of minority student programs and services should presuppose a strong campus sense of a common community, serving all its citizens fairly and marked in the main by
> - access to, rather than exclusion from, academic, social, and recreational groups and activities;
> - shared goals;
> - intentional social intercourse, rather than passive social isolation or active social exclusion; and
> - integration rather than segregation.

On those campuses with minority student programs and services, the program must promote the academic and personal growth and development of the various minority students served.

To accomplish this mission, the goals of the program must be to

- assess the needs of minority students in selected areas, set priorities among those needs, and respond to the extent that the number of students, facilities, and resources permit;
- orient minority students to the culture of the institution;
- assist minority students to determine and assess their educational goals and academic skills;
- provide support services to help minority students achieve educational goals and attain or refine academic skills necessary to perform adequately in the classroom;
- promote the intellectual, career, social, and moral development of the students;
- promote and deepen each minority student's understanding of his or her own culture and heritage;
- promote and deepen majority students' understanding of their unique cultures and heritages;
- provide training in leadership skills and other personal and social skills for minority students and those seeking to assist them; and
- offer or identify appropriate minority mentors and role models.

In addition, the program must provide educational efforts for both majority and minority students that focus on

- awareness of cultural differences;
- self-assessment of cultural awareness and possible prejudices; and
- changing prejudicial attitudes or behaviors.

> The program can include efforts supplementary to other institutional functional areas such as recruitment, placement, academic advising, counseling, and alumni relations.

> Staff members in minority programs and services should coordinate their efforts with academic units and other student affairs areas.

> It is important not to look upon minority student programs and services as the only organized agency to meet the needs of minority students. All institutional units should be responsible for meeting the needs of minority students in their areas of responsibility.

> Coordinated efforts to promote multicultural sensitivity and the elimination of prejudicial behaviors should be made at every institution by all functional areas.

## Part 2. PROGRAM

The formal education of students is purposeful, holistic, and consists of the curriculum and the co-curriculum.

Minority student programs and services must be (a) intentional, (b) coherent, (c) based on theories and knowledge of learning and human development, (d) reflective of developmental and demographic profiles of the student population, and (e) responsive to special needs of individuals.

Minority student programs and services must promote learning and development in students by encouraging outcomes such as intellectual growth, ability to communicate effectively, realistic self-appraisal, enhanced self-esteem, clarification of values, appropriate career choices, leadership development, physical fitness, meaningful interpersonal relations, ability to work independently and collaboratively, social responsibility, satisfying and productive lifestyles, appreciation of aesthetic and cultural diversity, and achievement of personal goals.

Minority student program components must include

- Assessment of the educational goals, academic skills, personal developmental levels, and social, recreational, and cultural needs of minority students;

> Assessments may be carried out in many ways. Survey instruments, interviews, behavioral tests, observations, or some combination of these methods may be appropriate in a given institution.

- **Educational programs to enhance the knowledge, understanding, and skills necessary for academic success;**

  Educational programming should complement students' academic interests and be based upon assessment of students and demands of the institution's educational programs. It may be provided in collaboration with efforts by academic units and other support service offices.

- **Educational programs to enhance the knowledge, understanding, and skills necessary for personal development;**

  Activities that attempt to promote student's career, social, recreational, and moral development should be based upon assessments and should reflect unique dimensions of the minority student experience.

  Social and recreational programs should enhance the knowledge, understanding, and skills necessary for social success, the productive use of leisure time, and the development of satisfying interpersonal relationships.

  Recreational programs should be designed to promote physical health, leisure time enjoyment, and psychological well-being of students.

  For both social skills and recreational programs, proper emphasis should be placed on any unique needs or cultural expressions of social relationships and recreational activities.

- **Educational programs to enhance the knowledge, understanding, and skills necessary for the exercise of leadership;**

  Leadership programs should be designed to help individuals understand the components and styles of leadership.

- **Supplemental orientation programming to enhance knowledge and understanding of the purposes of the institution, its values, and predictable ways of behaving;**

  This program should help students assess the degree of congruence between their educational goals and skills and the culture of the institution. It also should emphasize institutional programs and services available to help students achieve the knowledge, understanding, and skills necessary to perform adequately, both in and out of the classroom.

- **Programming to enhance the knowledge and understanding of individual student's unique culture and heritage;**

  These programs should explore both the heritage and current expressions of the student's culture.

  Various dimensions of the student's culture, such as history, philosophy, world view, literature, and various forms of artistic expression, should be explored.

- **Human relations programming to explore awareness of cultural differences, self-assessment of possible prejudices, and the facilitation of desired behavioral changes;**

  Human relations programs should be designed to assist both majority and minority students, faculty, and staff to develop more tolerance, understanding, and ability to relate to others.

- **Advocacy within the institution for minority student life experiences and organizations;**

  Tacit or overt prejudices or discriminations against minority students should be challenged.

  Sometimes institutions espouse one point of view but practice knowingly or unknowingly another. If the practical effects of policies are prejudicial, then staff members should bring these facts to the attention of the proper authorities in the institution.

  Impediments to the growth and development of minority students or full participation of minorities within the institution should be identified and addressed.

- **Advising of groups and individual students;**

  Advising services may include but are not limited to

  - monitoring scholastic standing of groups and individual students and recommending programs for improvement;
  - providing workshops, programs, retreats, and seminars on relevant topics and encouraging attendance at activities and services sponsored by other campus offices;
  - encouraging attendance at conferences, meetings, and programs;
  - advising formal groups such as editorial staffs of minority publications, fraternal groups, preprofessional clubs, and program councils;
  - providing assistance and advice in planning of minority student celebrations (e.g., Hispanic Week or Black History Month);
  - assisting minority student groups or individuals in identifying and gaining access, where appropriate, to institutional services such as printing, bulk mailing, and computer services;
  - providing a directory of minority faculty and staff; and
  - publishing a newsletter focusing on current events, leadership opportunities, and other relevant information.

# Part 3. LEADERSHIP

**Effective and ethical leadership is essential to the success of all organizations. Institutions must appoint, position and empower leaders within the administrative structure to accomplish stated missions. Minority student program leaders must be selected on the basis of formal education and training, relevant work experience, personal attributes, and other professional credentials. Institutions must determine expectations of accountability for leaders and fairly assess their performance.**

**Leaders of minority student programs and services must exercise authority over resources for which they are responsible to achieve their respective missions. Leaders must articulate a vision for their organization; set goals and objectives; prescribe and practice ethical behavior; recruit, select, supervise, and develop others in the organization; manage, plan, budget, and evaluate; communicate effectively; and marshal cooperative action from colleagues, employees, other institutional constituencies, and persons outside the organization. Program leaders must address individual, organiza-**

tional, or environmental conditions that inhibit goal achievement. Leaders must improve programs and services continuously in response to changing needs of students and institutional priorities.

## Part 4. ORGANIZATION and MANAGEMENT

Minority student programs and services must be structured purposefully and managed effectively to achieve stated goals. Evidence of appropriate structure must include current and accessible policies and procedures, written performance expectations for all employees, functional work flow graphics or organizational charts, and service delivery expectations. Evidence of effective management must include clear sources and channels of authority, effective communication practices, decision-making and conflict resolution procedures, responsiveness to changing conditions, accountability systems, and recognition and reward processes.

Minority student programs must provide channels within the organization for regular review of administrative policies and procedures.

> Many models exist for organizing minority student programs and services. The size and philosophy of the institution usually determine its organization. Generally, however, it is recommended that minority student programs be organized within the division of student affairs.

## Part 5. HUMAN RESOURCES

Minority student programs and services must be staffed adequately by individuals qualified to accomplish its mission and goals. Minority student programs must establish procedures for staff selection, training, and evaluation; set expectations for supervision; and provide appropriate professional development opportunities.

Professional staff members must hold an earned graduate degree in a field relevant to the position description or must possess an appropriate combination of education and experience.

Degree or credential seeking interns or others in training must be qualified by enrollment in an appropriate field of study and relevant experience. These individuals must be trained and supervised adequately by professional staff members.

Student employees and volunteers must be carefully selected, trained, supervised, and evaluated. When their knowledge and skills are not adequate for particular situations, they must refer students or others in need of assistance to qualified professional staff

Minority student programs and services must have secretarial and technical staff adequate to accomplish its mission. Such staff must be technologically proficient and qualified to perform activities including reception duties, office equipment operation, records maintenance, and mail handling.

Appropriate salary levels and fringe benefits for all staff members must be commensurate with those for comparable positions within the institution, in similar institutions, and in the relevant geographic area.

Minority student programs and services must intentionally employ a diverse staff to reflect the diversity of the institution's student population, to ensure the existence of readily identifiable role models for students, and to enrich the campus community.

Affirmative action must occur in hiring and promotion practices to ensure diverse staffing profiles as required by institutional, local, state/provisional, and federal law.

Minority student programs and services must have a regular system of staff selection and evaluation, and must provide continuing professional development opportunities for staff including inservice training, participation in professional conferences, workshops, and other continuing education activities.

> It is important that representatives of the various cultures involved be included on the professional staff.
>
> Professional staff should be competent in career planning and development, group facilitation, leadership training and development, workshop design, social-interpersonal development, and individual and group counseling. Generally, these competencies are found in persons who graduate from graduate level college student affairs, higher education administration, or counseling programs.
>
> Specific coursework in organizational development, counseling theory and practice, group dynamics, leadership development, human development, and research and evaluation is desirable.
>
> The use of graduate assistants and interns should be encouraged. Such assistants expand staff abilities, provide peer role models, and give valuable preprofessional experience. Particular attention should be given to preparing all preprofessional assistants to be especially sensitive to cultural differences and the special needs of minority students.
>
> Student employees and volunteers from minority groups should be utilized and assigned responsibilities that are within their scope of competence. These paraprofessional helpers should be selected carefully, trained to do their assigned jobs, and regularly supervised by the professional staff members.

## Part 6. FINANCIAL RESOURCES

Minority student programs and services must have adequate funding to accomplish its mission and goals. Priorities, whether set periodically or as a result of extraordinary conditions, must be determined within the context of the stated mission, goals, and resources.

> It is common in many institutions for some of the activities offered by minority student programs and services to be

funded by grant resources. In these cases, the institution should make appropriate efforts to transfer funding from grants to the regular institutional budget when the programs have demonstrated effectiveness and efficiency, and are judged to be valuable.

## Part 7. FACILITIES, TECHNOLOGY, and EQUIPMENT

Minority student programs and services must have adequate, suitably located facilities, technology, and equipment to support its mission and goals. Facilities, technology, and equipment must be in compliance with relevant federal, state, provincial, and local requirements to provide for access, health and safety.

> Adequate space should be provided for a resource library, private individual consultations, group workshops, and work areas for support staff. Many of the activities offered by minority student programs and services require the same level of privacy as individual and group counseling. It is important, therefore, that the physical facilities be adequate for these purposes.

## Part 8. LEGAL RESPONSIBILITIES

Minority student program staff members must be knowledgeable about and responsive to laws and regulations that relate to their respective responsibilities. Sources for legal obligations and limitations include constitutional, statutory, regulatory, and case law; mandatory laws and orders emanating from federal, state/provincial and local governments; and the institution through its policies.

Minority student program staff members must use reasonable and informed practices to limit the liability exposure of the institution, its officers, employees, and agents. Staff members must be informed about institutional policies regarding personal liability and related insurance coverage options.

The institution must provide access to legal advice for staff members as needed to carry out assigned responsibilities.

The institution must inform staff and students, in a timely and systematic fashion, about extraordinary or changing legal obligations and potential liabilities.

## Part 9. EQUAL OPPORTUNITY, ACCESS, AND AFFIRMATIVE ACTION

Minority student program staff members must ensure that services and programs are provided on a fair and equitable basis. Each program and service must be accessible and hours of operation must be responsive to the needs of all students. The minority student program must adhere to the spirit and intent of equal opportunity laws.

Minority student programs and services must not be discriminatory on the basis of age, color, disability, gender, national origin, race, religious creed, sexual orientation, and/or veteran status. Exceptions are appropriate only where provided by relevant law and institutional policy.

Consistent with its mission and goals, minority student programs must take affirmative action to remedy significant imbalances in student participation and staffing patterns.

## Part 10. CAMPUS and COMMUNITY RELATIONS

Minority student programs and services must establish, maintain, and promote effective relations with relevant campus offices and external agencies.

Professional staff members must coordinate, or where appropriate, collaborate with faculty and other staff in providing services and programs for minority students.

> Coordination and collaboration are important in order to minimize isolation of the minority student program and maximize the use of faculty and other staff resources in meeting the needs of minority students.

## Part 11. DIVERSITY

Within the context of each institution's unique mission, multi-dimensional diversity enriches the community and enhances the collegiate experience for all; therefore, minority student programs must nurture environments where similarities and differences among people are recognized and honored.

Minority student programs must promote cultural educational experiences that are characterized by open and continuous communication, that deepen understanding of one's own culture and heritage, and that respect and educate about similarities, differences and histories of cultures.

Minority student programs must address the characteristics and needs of a diverse population when establishing and implementing policies and procedures.

## Part 12. ETHICS

All persons involved in the delivery of minority student programs must adhere to the highest principles of ethical behavior. Minority student programs and services must develop or adopt and implement statements of ethical practice addressing the issues unique to its functions. Minority student programs and services must publish these statements and insure their periodic review by all concerned.

Staff members must ensure that confidentiality is maintained with respect to all communications and records considered confidential unless exempted by law.

Information disclosed in individual counseling sessions must remain confidential, unless written permission to divulge the information is given by the student. However, all staff members must disclose to appropriate authorities information judged to be of an emergency nature, especially when the safety of the individual or others is involved. Information contained in students' educational records must not be disclosed to non-institutional third parties without appropriate consent, unless classified as "Directory" information or when the information is subpoenaed by law. Minority student programs and services must apply a similar dedication to privacy and confidentiality to research data concerning individuals. All staff members must be aware of and comply with the provisions contained in the institution's human subjects research policy and in other relevant institutional policies addressing ethical practices.

Staff members must recognize and avoid personal conflict of interest or appearance thereof in their transactions with students and others. Staff members must strive to insure the fair, objective, and impartial treatment of all persons with whom they deal.

When handling institutional funds, minority student program staff members must ensure that such funds are managed in accordance with established and responsible accounting procedures.

Staff members must not participate in any form of harassment that demeans persons or creates an intimidating, hostile, or offensive campus environment.

Staff members must perform their duties within the limits of their training, expertise, and competence. When these limits are exceeded, individuals in need of further assistance must be referred to persons possessing appropriate qualifications.

Staff members must use suitable means to confront and otherwise hold accountable other staff members who exhibit unethical behavior.

Staff members must maintain the highest principles of ethical behavior in the use of technology.

The professional staff must be knowledgeable about the research and practice in areas appropriate to their programming with minority students.

Professional staff must respond in some manner to formal requests by students for personal recommendations.

Recommendations made by minority student program staff members should reflect only the professional contacts and observations they have personally experienced with the students.

The use of pejorative stereotypical statements should be carefully avoided.

Professional staff members should not initiate formal employment recommendations without the knowledge and consent of the student involved.

Professional staff members should inform students if they cannot make positive recommendations.

## Part 13. ASSESSMENT and EVALUATION

Minority student programs must regularly conduct systematic qualitative and quantitative evaluations of program quality to determine whether and to what degree the stated mission and goals are being met. Although methods of assessment vary, programs and services must employ a sufficient range of measures to insure objectivity and comprehensiveness. Data collected must include responses from students and other affected constituencies. Results of these evaluations must be used in revising and improving programs and services and in recognizing staff performance.

Periodic evaluation should be implemented for both developing and established programs.

Formative and summative evaluations are especially important when the development or operation of a program or service is funded by grants or other "soft" moneys. Accountability to granting agencies and data generated to support transfer of programs to the general budget both require careful evaluation.

General evaluation of the minority student programs and services should be conducted on a regularly scheduled basis. Evaluation data should be solicited from current minority students and alumni who have used the programs or services.

© Copyright 1997 Council for the Advancement of Standards in Higher Education (CAS)

# THE ROLE of STUDENT ORIENTATION PROGRAMS and SERVICES
## CAS Standards Contextual Statement

To understand current trends in student orientation it is helpful to view today's practice within an historical context. The history of orientation programs in the United States is virtually as old as the history of the country's higher education. Harvard College was the first to formalize a system by which experienced students assisted new students in their transition to the institution. In addition to a personalized support system, students also experienced certain rites of passage which, from today's perspective, would likely be considered hazing. Clearly the system was flawed, but it was the beginning of the formalization of orientation as a process that includes support of students as they make the transition to higher education.

Later in the 19th century, Harvard institutionalized faculty-student contact by assigning faculty members educational and administrative responsibilities outside the classroom. One of these responsibilities was the orientation of new students. Soon other colleges were taking an interest in those problems specific to freshman students.

Increases in the number and diversity of college students in the mid-1900s posed issues that many institutions had not previously considered. Today's orientation programs have responded to these demographics, recognizing that women, people of color, and nontraditional students have clearly changed institutional agendas across the nation. These programs have evolved from simply providing individualized faculty attention to focusing on a multitude of important issues while responding to the needs of an increasingly diverse student population.

Today, most orientation programs seek to provide a clear and cogent introduction to an institution's academic community. Orientation is viewed by most as an important tool for improving student retention. Many institutions have included academic advising in their orientation programs as an impetus for active participation. Many institutions are implementing continuing orientation programs via a freshman orientation course. Because of such changes, colleges and universities are taking steps to encourage student and parent attendance by formalizing and marketing orientation programs from a clearly academic perspective.

What trends will guide future approaches to student orientation? It is clear that retention will continue to be a major force in the development of orientation programs. Likewise, attempts to foster an environment responsive to the individual needs of students will also continue to have a profound effect on orientation programming. Very likely, funding for orientation programs will continue to be an issue of concern. Demographic changes in institutions of higher education and in the society at large will require institutional and programmatic accommodations. Simply maintaining current orientation programs by reacting to change will satisfy neither students, parents, or other constituents nor institutional leaders and the public in the years to come. New and creative programs must be assessed, planned, and ultimately implemented if the personal and educational needs of new and transfer students and their families are to be met.

The CAS Student Orientation Programs and Services Standards and Guidelines that follow have utility for institutions of all types and size and provide criteria to judge the quality and appropriateness of student orientation programs.

## References, Readings and Resources

National Orientation Directors Association (NODA). Orientation Coordinator, Wayne State University. University Advising Center. HNJ Student Services, 2 East, Detroit, MI 48302. (313) 577-4544; Fax (313) 577-5020. CECOOK@ CMS.CC.WAYNE.EDU; http//www.umich.edu/~ noda

# STUDENT ORIENTATION
## CAS STANDARDS and GUIDELINES

## Part 1: MISSION

The student orientation program must develop, record, disseminate, implement, and regularly review its mission and goals. Mission statements must be consistent with the mission and goals of the institution and with the standards in this document.

The mission of the student orientation program must include:

- facilitating the transition of new students into the institution;
- preparing new students for the institution's educational opportunities; and
- initiating the integration of new students into the intellectual, cultural, and social climate of the institution.

## Part 2. PROGRAM

Orientation is a ongoing process that begins when a student decides to attend a particular institution. The process should aid students in understanding the nature and purpose of the institution, their membership in the academic community, and their relationship to the intellectual, cultural, and social climate of the institution. The orientation process should include pre-enrollment, entry, and post-matriculation activities. Components may include credit and non-credit courses, comprehensive mailings, electronic communications, and campus visitations and may be administered through multiple institutional offices.

The formal education of students is purposeful, holistic, and consists of the curriculum and the co-curriculum. Student orientation programs must be (a) intentional, (b) coherent, (c) based on theories and knowledge of learning and human development, (d) reflective of developmental and demographic profiles of the student population, and (e) responsive to special needs of individuals.

Student orientation programs must promote learning and development in students by encouraging outcomes such as intellectual growth, ability to communicate effectively, realistic self-appraisal, enhanced self-esteem, clarification of values, appropriate career choices, leadership development, health and physical fitness, meaningful interpersonal relations, ability to work independently and collaboratively, social responsibility, satisfying and productive lifestyles, appreciation of aesthetic and cultural diversity, and achievement of personal goals.

The student orientation program must
- be based on stated goals and objectives.

A comprehensive orientation program should be based on clearly defined and delineated goals and objectives that include service to both the student and the institution.

- be coordinated with the relevant programs and activities of other institutional units.

- be available to all students new to the institution.

First-year, transfer, and entering graduate students should be served as distinct population groups with specific attention given to the special needs of sub-groups (e.g., students with disabilities, athletes, adult learners, traditionally underrepresented students, honor students, and international students).

- assist new students in understanding the purposes of higher education and the mission of the institution.

New students should have a clear understanding of the overall purpose of higher education and how this general purpose translates to the institution they are attending. The roles, responsibilities, and expectations of faculty, staff, and students should be included.

- assist new students in understanding their responsibilities within the educational setting.

The student orientation program should set forth the institution's expectations of students (e.g., scholarship, integrity, conduct, financial obligations, ethical use of technology) and should provide information that clearly identifies relevant administrative policies and procedures.

- provide new students with information about academic policies, procedures, requirements, and programs sufficient to make well-reasoned and well-informed choices.

Class scheduling and registration processes should be explained and assistance should be provided by qualified faculty, staff, or peer academic advisors for developing educational plans.

- inform new students about the availability of services and programs.

The student orientation program should identify appropriate referral resources (e.g., counselors and advisors) and provide information about relevant services and programs.

- assist new students in becoming familiar with the campus and local environment.

The student orientation program should provide information about the physical layout of the campus, including the location and purposes of academic facilities, support services, co-curricular venues, and administrative offices. Information about personal health, safety and security should also be included.

- **provide intentional opportunities for new students to interact with faculty, staff, and continuing students.**

  The student orientation program should design and facilitate opportunities for new students to discuss their expectations and perceptions of the campus and to clarify their educational goals.

- **provide new students with information and opportunities for self-assessment.**

  Assist students in the selection of appropriate courses and course levels making use of placement examinations, career interest inventories, and study skills evaluations.

- **provide relevant orientation information and activities to the new students' primary support groups (e.g., parents, guardians, spouses, children).**

# Part 3. LEADERSHIP

Effective and ethical leadership is essential to the success of all organizations. The institution must appoint, position, and empower leaders within the administrative structure to accomplish stated missions. Leaders at various levels must be selected on the basis of formal education and training, relevant work experience, personal attributes, and other professional credentials. The institution must determine expectations of accountability for its leaders and fairly assess their performance.

Leaders of student orientation programs must exercise authority over resources for which they are responsible to achieve their respective missions. Leaders must articulate vision for their organization; set goals and objectives; prescribe and practice ethical behavior; recruit, select, supervise, and develop others in the organization; manage, plan, budget, and evaluate; communicate effectively; and marshal cooperative action from colleagues, employees, other institutional constituencies, and persons outside the organization. Leaders must address individual, organizational, or environmental conditions that inhibit goal achievement. Leaders must improve programs and services continuously in response to changing needs of students and institutional priorities

# Part 4. ORGANIZATION and MANAGEMENT

The student orientation program must be structured purposefully and managed effectively to achieve stated goals. Evidence of appropriate structure must include current and accessible policies and procedures, written performance expectations for all employees, functional work flow graphics and organizational charts, and service delivery expectations. Evidence of effective management must include clear sources and channels of authority, effective communication practices, decision-making and conflict resolution procedures,

responsiveness to changing conditions, accountability systems, and recognition and reward processes.

The student orientation program must provide channels for regular review of administrative policies and procedures.

There must be written policies and procedures regarding program delivery that are reviewed regularly.

All institutional offices involved in program delivery should be involved in the review.

Coordination of the student orientation program should occur even though a number of offices may be involved in the delivery of structured activities. The size, nature, and complexity of the institution should guide the administrative scope and structure of the orientation program.

# Part 5. HUMAN RESOURCES

The student orientation program must be staffed adequately by individuals qualified to accomplish its mission and goals. The student orientation program must establish procedures for staff selection, training, and evaluation; set expectations for supervision; and provide appropriate professional development opportunities.

Professional staff members must hold an earned graduate degree in a field relevant to the position description or must possess an appropriate combination of education and experience.

Degree or credential seeking interns or others in training must be qualified by enrollment in an appropriate field of study and relevant experience. These individuals must be trained and supervised adequately by professional staff members.

Student employees and volunteers must be carefully trained, supervised, and evaluated. When their knowledge and skills are not adequate for particular situations, they must refer students in need of assistance to qualified professional staff.

The student orientation program must have secretarial and technical staff adequate to accomplish its mission. Such staff must be technologically proficient, skilled in human relations and qualified to perform activities including reception duties, office equipment operation, records maintenance, and mail handling.

Salary levels and fringe benefits for staff members must be commensurate with those for comparable positions within the institution, in similar institutions, and in the relevant geographic area. Compensation for paraprofessional staff must be fair and voluntary services recognized adequately.

The student orientation program must intentionally employ a diverse staff to reflect the diversity of the institution's student population, to ensure the existence of readily identifiable role models for students and to enrich the campus community. Affirmative action must occur in hiring and promotion practices to ensure diverse staffing profiles as required by institutional policies and local, state/provincial, and federal law.

Faculty involvement in the development and delivery of the student orientation program is essential to its success. Faculty should be included as part of the overall staffing pattern.

# Part 6. FINANCIAL RESOURCES

The student orientation program must have adequate funding to accomplish its mission and goals. Priorities, whether set periodically or as a result of extraordinary conditions, must be determined within the context of the stated mission, goals, and resources.

Money to underwrite expenses for the student orientation program should be allocated on a permanent basis. In additional to institutional funding through general funds, other funding sources may be considered, including state appropriations, student fees, user fees, donations, contributions, fines, concession and store sales, rentals, and dues.

Overnight programs may require students and their families to stay on campus. Although recovering room and board costs directly from participants is an acceptable practice, the student orientation program should be designed so as to impose as little financial burden on students and their families as possible.

# Part 7. FACILITIES, TECHNOLOGY, and EQUIPMENT

The student orientation program must have adequate, suitably located facilities and equipment to support its mission and goals. Facilities, technology, and equipment must be in compliance with relevant federal, state, provincial, and local requirements to provide for access, health and safety.

Cooperation from within the campus community is necessary to provide appropriate facilities. Whenever possible, a single office location to house personnel and provide adequate work space should be conveniently located and suitable for its high interaction with the public.

# Part 8. LEGAL RESPONSIBILITIES

Staff members must be knowledgeable about and responsive to law and regulations that relate to their respective program or service. Sources for legal obligations and limitations include constitutional, statutory, regulatory, and case law; mandatory laws and orders emanating from federal, state, provincial and local governments; and the institution through its policies.

Staff members must use reasonable and informed practices to limit the liability exposure of the institution, its officers, employees, and agents. Staff members must be informed about institutional policies regarding personal liability and related insurance coverage options.

The institution must provide access to legal advice for staff members as needed to carry out assigned responsibilities.

The institution must inform staff and students, in a timely and systematic fashion, about extraordinary or changing legal obligations and potential liabilities.

# Part 9: EQUAL OPPORTUNITY, ACCESS, and AFFIRMATIVE ACTION

Staff members must ensure that the student orientation program is provided on a fair and equitable basis. The student orientation program must be accessible. Hours of operation must be responsive to the needs of all students.

The student orientation program must adhere to the spirit and intent of equal opportunity laws.

The student orientation program must not be discriminatory on the basis of age, ancestry, color, disability, gender, national origin, race, religious creed, sexual orientation, and/or veteran status. Exceptions are appropriate only where provided by relevant law and institutional policy.

Consistent with its mission and goals, the student orientation program must take affirmative action to remedy significant imbalances in student participation and staffing patterns.

# Part 10. CAMPUS and COMMUNITY RELATIONS

The student orientation program must establish, maintain, and promote effective relations with relevant campus offices and external agencies.

The student orientation program should be an institution-wide process that systematically involves student affairs, academic affairs, and other administrative units, such as campus police, physical plant, and the business office.

The student orientation program should disseminate information relating to other programs and services on campus. These services should, in turn, provide the media and human resources necessary to accomplish the transmission of information.

# Part 11. DIVERSITY

Within the context of the institution's unique mission, multi-dimensional diversity enriches the community and enhances the collegiate experience for all; therefore, the student orientation program must nurture environments where similarities and differences among people are recognized and honored.

The student orientation program must promote cultural educational experiences that are characterized by open and continuous communication; that deepen understanding of one's culture and heritage; and that respect and educate about similarities, differences, and histories of cultures.

The student orientation program must address the characteristics and needs of a diverse population when establishing and implementing policies and procedures.

## Part 12. ETHICS

All persons involved in the delivery of the student orientation program must adhere to the highest principles of ethical behavior. The student orientation program must develop or adopt statements of ethical practice to address their unique issues. These statements must be published, implemented, and reviewed periodically.

> Ethical standards of relevant professional associations should be considered.

Orientation staff members must ensure that confidentiality is maintained with respect to all communications and records considered confidential unless exempted by law.

Information disclosed in individual counseling sessions must remain confidential, unless written permission to divulge the information is given by the student. However, all staff members must disclose to appropriate authorities information judged to be of an emergency nature, especially when the safety of the individual or others is involved. Information contained in students' educational records must not be disclosed to non-institutional third parties without appropriate consent unless classified as "Directory" information or when the information is subpoenaed by law. The student orientation program must apply a similar dedication to privacy and confidentiality to research data concerning individuals.

Staff members must be aware of and comply with the provisions contained in the institution's human subjects research policy and in other relevant institutional policies addressing ethical practices.

Orientation staff members must recognize and avoid personal conflict of interest or appearance thereof in their transactions with students and others. Staff members must strive to ensure the fair objectives and impartial treatment of all persons with whom they deal.

When handling institutional funds, staff members must ensure that such funds are managed in accordance with established and responsible accounting procedures.

Staff members must maintain the highest standards of ethical behavior in the use of technology.

Staff members must not participate in any form of harassment that demeans people or creates an intimidating, hostile, or offensive campus environment.

Orientation staff members must perform their duties within the limits of their training, expertise, and competence. When these limits are exceeded, individuals in need of further assistance must be referred to persons possessing appropriate qualifications.

Staff members must use suitable means to confront and otherwise hold accountable other staff members who exhibit unethical behavior.

Staff members must maintain the highest principles of ethical behavior in the use of technology.

## Part 13. ASSESSMENT and EVALUATION

The student orientation program must regularly conduct systematic qualitative and quantitative evaluations of program quality to determine whether and to what degree the stated mission and goals are being met. Although methods of assessment vary, the student orientation program must employ a sufficient range of measures to ensure objectivity and comprehensiveness. Data collected must include responses from students and other significant constituencies. Results of these evaluations must be considered when revising and improving the student orientation program and in recognizing staff performance.

> Evaluation of student and institutional needs, goals, objectives, and the effectiveness of the student orientation program should occur on a periodic basis. A representative cross-section of appropriate people from the campus community should be involved in reviews of the student orientation program.

# OUTCOMES ASSESSMENT and PROGRAM EVALUATION
## CAS Standards Contextual Statement

As early as 1899, William Rainey Harper, visionary President of the University of Chicago, called on colleges and universities to adopt a program of research with the college student as the subject. "In order that the student may receive the assistance so essential to his highest success, another step in the onward evolution will take place. This step will be the scientific study of the student himself; . . . provision must be made, either by the regular instructors or by those appointed for the purpose, to study in detail the men and women to whom instruction is offered" (quoted in Rentz, 1996, p. 38). The original Student Personnel Point of View (SPPV, 1937/1994), which responded to Harper's challenge, called for "studies designed to evaluate and improve . . . [the] functions and services" (p. 70) of the student affairs division. Later in the document, four specific kinds of studies were called for: student out-of-class life and its importance to the educational mission, faculty-student out-of-class relationships, financial aid to students, and follow-up study of college students to ascertain the effects of college on careers and personal adjustment.

The 1949 revision of the SPPV again stated that an adequate student affairs program *should* include "a continuing program of evaluation of student personnel services and of the educational program to insure the achievement by students of the objectives for which this program is designed" (SPPV, 1949/1994, p. 118). Wrenn (1951) in one of the pioneering texts in the field, proposed a guide for evaluating the effectiveness of student affairs programs. One of the "standards" in his evaluation reads: "carrying on research designed to evaluate and improve personnel functions and services" (p. 557).

These fundamental documents clearly mandate that institutions, primarily through student affairs divisions, have responsibility for systematic, continuing outcomes assessment and program evaluation. Yet, as Williamson and Biggs (1975) noted, while most agree about the importance of conducting research on students and programs, few student affairs divisions have considered it a vital part of their operations. A prominent exception to this caveat was Williamson's creation of the Student Life Studies Bureau, under the leadership of Ralph Berdie, in 1965, at the University of Minnesota.

Upcraft and Schuh (1996) identified five reasons why student affairs divisions can no longer ignore the necessity to assess student needs and evaluate programs and services. *First,* there is a widespread impression among important publics that higher education is not delivering on its promise to produce "educated persons." Consequently, there is an increased demand for accountability by governing boards, tax payers, parents, and legislative bodies. *Second,* there is rising dissatisfaction with steady increases in the cost of higher education. *Third,* there are questions about the quality of education, including instruction and programs and services available to students. *Fourth,* there is a discrepancy between the success rates of traditionally underrepresented groups and those of middle-class white students. Members of underrepresented groups want to know why. Finally, regional accrediting agencies now require institutions to provide evidence that they are achieving the goals and objectives to which they aspire.

Adequate assessment programs should employ both qualitative and quantitative research methods and should include the following elements:

- Tracking of student use of services, programs, and facilities and determining their satisfaction with what is provided
- Assessing student needs and wants
- Assessing environments and their influences on student behavior
- Assessing student cultures and their influences on behavior
- Assessing individual and collective outcomes of programs and services
- Assessing developmental impact of individual programs and the total collegiate experience

Student affairs divisions currently beginning to implement programs to assess student outcomes and evaluate effects of programs should not be discouraged because of the enormity of the undertaking. The important thing is to begin, to be systematic, to use sound research methods, and to expand and improve operations incrementally. The standards and guidelines that follow provide a basis for such action.

# References, Readings and Resources

Beeler, K. J., & Hunter, D. E. (Eds.). (1991). *Puzzles and pieces in wonderland: The promise and practice of student affairs research.* Washington, DC: National Association of Student Personnel Administrators.

Erwin, T. D. (1991). *Assessing student learning and development.* San Francisco: Jossey-Bass.

Erwin, T. D., Scott, R. L., & Menard, A. J. (1991). Student outcome assessment in student affairs. In T. K. Miller & R. B. Winston, Jr. (Eds.), *Administration and leadership in student affairs: Actualizing student development in higher education* (2nd ed., pp. 741-763). Muncie, IN: Accelerated Development.

Pascarella, E. T., & Terenzini, P. T. (1991). *How college affects students: Findings and insights from twenty years of research.* San Francisco: Jossey-Bass.

Rentz, A. L. (1996). A history of student affairs. In A. L. Rentz (Ed.), *Student affairs practice in higher education* (2nd ed., pp. 28-55). Springfield, IL: Thomas.

Stage, F. K. (Ed.). (1992). *Diverse methods for research and assessment of college students.* Washington, DC: American College Personnel Association.

*Student Personnel Point of View.* (1937/1994). In A. L. Rentz (Ed.), Student affairs: A profession's heritage (2nd ed., pp. 66-78). Washington, DC: American College Personnel Association.

*Student Personnel Point of View.* (1949/1994). In A. L. Rentz (Ed.), Student affairs: A profession's heritage (2nd ed., pp. 108-123). Washington, DC: American College Personnel Association.

Upcraft, M. L. , & Schuh, J. H. (1996). *Assessment in student affairs: A guide for practitioners.* San Francisco: Jossey-Bass.

Williamson, E. G., & Biggs, D. A. (1975). *Student personnel work: A program of developmental relationships.* New York: John Wiley & Sons.

Winston, R. B., Jr., & Miller, T. K. (1994). A model for assessing developmental outcomes related to student affairs programs and services. *NASPA Journal, 32,* 2-19.

Wrenn, C. G. (1951). *Student personnel work in college.* New York: Ronald Press.

# OUTCOMES ASSESSMENT and PROGRAM EVALUATION
## CAS STANDARDS and GUIDELINES

## Part 1.  MISSION

Those responsible for outcomes assessment and program evaluation in higher education must develop, record, disseminate, implement and regularly review the program's mission and goals. Mission statements must be consistent with the mission and goals of the institution and with the standards in this document.

Outcomes assessment and program evaluation efforts must strive to improve student services and development programs, to expand the knowledge base about student development and student services work in general, and to assess the organizational effectiveness of student services. Most institutions do not have a separate student affairs assessment agency. In such institutions the chief student affairs officer must be the advocate for student affairs assessment and program evaluation and must collaborate with, and otherwise provide support to, the institutional assessment efforts so as to accomplish the program. More specifically, the outcomes assessment and program evaluation effort must:

- describe students in terms of demographics, developmental characteristics, and personal behavior;

- conduct periodic needs assessments for use in the design of programs;

- study, or use available information about developmental changes of college students;

- assess whether student services programs are consistent with and achieve their stated objectives;

- assess in terms of behavior changes in students; and

- study the extent to which students are satisfied with their educational experiences.

Student services professionals are responsible for translating a diverse set of service functions into an integrated series of programs and activities designed to encourage students' growth and development. The degree to which these programs and activities are necessary and successful should be measured through periodic assessment of both programs and students. Equally important is the responsibility for continually expanding the knowledge base about the relationship between student development theory and student services practices. The outcomes assessment and program evaluation function should seek to provide assessment and evaluation support for all institutional student support service programs. Further, the assessment and evaluation program should strive to increase the institution's knowledge base about its student clientele.

## Part 2. PROGRAM

The formal education of students is purposeful, holistic, and consists of the curriculum and the co-curriculum.

Outcomes assessment and program evaluation services must be (a) intentional, (b) coherent, (c) based on theories and knowledge of learning and human development, (d) reflective of developmental and demographic profiles of the student population, and (e) responsive to special needs of individuals.

Assessment and evaluation findings must promote learning and development in students by encouraging outcomes such as intellectual growth, ability to communicate effectively, realistic self-appraisal, enhanced self-esteem, clarification of values, appropriate career choices, leadership development, physical fitness, meaningful interpersonal relations, ability to work independently and collaboratively, social responsibility, satisfying and productive lifestyles, appreciation of aesthetic and cultural diversity, and achievement of personal goals.

However organized, the assessment and evaluation effort must include studies of students and their development and studies of student services program effectiveness. Furthermore, results of these studies must be disseminated throughout the institution.

Activities of the outcomes assessment and program evaluation effort should include:

- collecting and analyzing student data beginning with pre-enrollment characteristics of first year students and continuing through follow-up studies of former students;

- planning, coordinating or conducting periodic studies of the characteristics of students and various student sub-groups;

- students may be described in terms of their intellectual, emotional, social, moral, spiritual, and physical development and behavior; such data should be continually collected, updated, and disseminated;

- regularly coordinating or conducting student needs assessments to guide program development;

- analyzing data indicating trends in student behavior satisfaction retention, and attitudes in terms of the institution's purposes and interpreting the implications of these trends for institutional policies and practices;

- assisting in collaborative assessments and planning of programs, activities, and services in the student services/development division;

- collecting and analyzing data to be used for making decisions about the continuation, modification, or termination of student services programs;

- assessing on a systematic basis the professional contributions of staff members and providing feedback appropriate to professional development;

- coordinating, conducting, or collaborating in accountability and cost effectiveness studies of student services/ development programs;

- acting as a resource to faculty and staff regarding assessment and evaluation efforts;

- regularly disseminating information about assessment and evaluation findings to concerned members of the campus community; and

- where appropriate, guiding and evaluating research efforts conducted by students.

# Part 3. LEADERSHIP

Effective and ethical leadership is essential to the success of all organizations. Institutions must appoint, position and empower leaders within the administrative structure to accomplish stated missions. Leaders at various levels must be selected on the basis of formal education and training, relevant work experience, personal attributes, and other professional credentials. Institutions must determine expectations of accountability for leaders and fairly assess their performance.

Leaders of assessment and evaluation functions must exercise authority over resources for which they are responsible to achieve their respective missions. Leaders must articulate a vision for their organization; set goals and objectives; prescribe and practice ethical behavior; recruit, select, supervise, and develop others in the organization; manage, plan, budget, and evaluate; communicate effectively; and marshal cooperative action from colleagues, employees, other institutional constituencies, and persons outside the organization. Leaders must address individual, organizational, or environmental conditions that inhibit goal achievement. Leaders must improve programs and services continuously in response to changing needs of students and institutional priorities.

# Part 4. ORGANIZATION and MANAGEMENT

Assessment and evaluation programs must be structured purposefully and managed effectively to achieve stated goals. Evidence of appropriate structure must include current and accessible policies and procedures, written performance expectations for all employees, functional work flow graphics or organizational charts, and service delivery expectations. Evidence of effective management must include clear sources and channels of authority, effective communication practices, decision-making and conflict resolution procedures, responsiveness to changing conditions, accountability systems, and recognition and reward processes.

The assessment and evaluation program must provide channels within the organization for regular review of administrative policies and procedures.

Because outcomes assessment and program evaluation efforts are conducted on most campuses in cooperation with other institutional research and evaluation efforts, the chief student affairs officer must be central to the establishment of specific objectives for student services research and evaluation.

Assessment and evaluation objectives should result from a collaborative effort between the chief student affairs officer, those responsible for the various student services programs and others responsible for institutional research evaluation efforts.

# Part 5. HUMAN RESOURCES

The assessment and evaluation program must be staffed adequately by individuals qualified to accomplish its mission and goals. Programs and services must establish procedures for staff selection, training, and evaluation; set expectations for supervision, and provide appropriate professional development opportunities.

Professional staff members must hold an earned graduate degree in a field relevant to the position description or must possess an appropriate combination of education and experience.

Degree or credential seeking interns or others in training must be qualified by enrollment in an appropriate field of study and relevant experience. These individuals must be trained and supervised adequately by professional staff members.

Student employees and volunteers must be carefully selected, trained, supervised, and evaluated. When their knowledge and skills are not adequate for particular situations, they must refer students or others in need of assistance to qualified professional staff

The assessment and evaluation program must have secretarial and technical staff adequate to accomplish its mission. Such staff must be technologically proficient and qualified to perform activities including reception duties, office equipment operation, records maintenance, and mail handling.

Appropriate salary levels and fringe benefits for all staff members must be commensurate with those for comparable positions within the institution, in similar institutions, and in the relevant geographic area.

The assessment and evaluation program must intentionally employ a diverse staff to reflect the diversity of the institution's student population, to ensure the existence of readily identifiable role models for students, and to enrich the campus community.

Affirmative action must occur in hiring and promotion practices to ensure diverse staffing profiles as required by institutional, local, state/provincial, and federal law.

Within the institution, a qualified professional staff person must be designated to coordinate the outcomes assessment and program evaluation efforts and must work closely with or be responsible to the chief student affairs or academic affairs officer.

> The number of staff members assigned to the assessment and evaluation effort will be a function of the size, complexity and purpose of the institution. Institutions unable to assign a full-time professional staff member should devote a portion of their research and evaluation program's resources to this effort.
>
> Staff assigned responsibility for the assessment and evaluation effort should possess effective communication and consultation skills and have an appropriate combination of coursework, training, and experience in the following areas: statistics, research design, assessment, computer literacy, program planning and implementation strategies, human development theory, student subgroup cultures, and student affairs programs. When research staff lack adequate knowledge in any of these critical areas, they should seek expertise from appropriate campus officials.

## Part 6. FINANCIAL RESOURCES

Outcomes assessment and program evaluation services must have adequate funding to accomplish its mission and goals. Priorities, whether set periodically or as a result of extraordinary conditions, must be determined within the context of the stated mission, goals, and resources.

## Part 7. FACILITIES, TECHNOLOGY, and EQUIPMENT

The assessment and evaluation program must have adequate, suitably located facilities, technology, and equipment to support its mission and goals. Facilities, technology, and equipment must be in compliance with relevant federal, state, provincial, and local requirements to provide for access, health and safety.

> It is important that the outcomes assessment and program evaluation effort have secure storage facilities, computer support, sufficient work space, and ready access to appropriate institutional records. Financial resources should be sufficient to support research mailings and data collection, data entry and analysis and printing and distribution of research findings.

## Part 8. LEGAL RESPONSIBILITIES

Outcomes assessment and program evaluation staff members must be knowledgeable about and responsive to law and regulations that relate to their respective program or service. Sources for legal obligations and limitations include constitutional, federal, statutory, regulatory, and case law; mandatory laws and orders emanating from, state/provincial and local governments; and the institution through its policies.

Staff members must use reasonable and informed practices to limit the liability exposure of the institution, its officers, employees, and agents. Staff members must be informed about institutional policies regarding personal liability and related insurance coverage options.

The institution must provide access to legal advice by professional staff members as needed to carry out assigned responsibilities.

The institution must inform staff and students, in a timely and systematic fashion, about extraordinary or changing legal obligations and potential liabilities.

## Part 9. EQUAL OPPORTUNITY, ACCESS, and AFFIRMATIVE ACTION

Assessment and evaluation staff members must ensure that services and programs are provided on a fair and equitable basis. Outcomes assessment and program evaluation findings must be accessible. Hours of operation must be responsive to the needs of students and staff members. The program must adhere to the spirit and intent of equal opportunity laws.

Assessment and evaluation programs must not be discriminatory on the basis of age, color, disability, gender, national origin, race, religious creed, sexual orientation, and/or veteran status. Exceptions are appropriate only where provided by relevant law and institutional policy.

Consistent with their mission and goals, assessment and evaluation programs must take affirmative action to remedy significant imbalances in student participation and staffing patterns.

## Part 10. CAMPUS and COMMUNITY RELATIONS

Outcomes assessment and program evaluation programs must establish, maintain, and promote effective relations with relevant campus offices and external agencies.

> Regular and effective communication systems for the dissemination of results and procuring expertise are particularly important among the full range of academic and administrative offices, institutional governance bodies, and other appropriate constituencies.

## Part 11. DIVERSITY

Within the context of each institution's unique mission, multi-dimensional diversity enriches the community and enhances the collegiate experience for all; therefore, assessment and evaluation programs and services must nurture environments where similarities and differences among people are recognized and honored.

The outcomes assessment and program evaluation effort must promote cultural educational experiences that are characterized by open and continuous communication, that deepen understanding of one's own culture and heritage, and that respect and educate about similarities, differences and histories of cultures.

Assessment and evaluation programs and services must address the characteristics and needs of a diverse population when establishing and implementing policies and procedures.

# Part 12. ETHICS

All persons involved in the delivery of outcomes assessment and program evaluation efforts must adhere to the highest principles of ethical behavior. The evaluation program must develop or adopt and implement statements of ethical practice addressing the issues unique to each program and service. The program must publish these statements and insure their periodic review by all concerned.

Staff members must ensure that confidentiality is maintained with respect to all communications and records considered confidential unless exempted by law.

Information disclosed in individual counseling and data interpretation sessions must remain confidential, unless written permission to divulge the information is given by the student. However, all staff members must disclose to appropriate authorities information judged to be of an emergency nature, especially when the safety of the individual or others is involved. Information contained in students' educational records must not be disclosed to non-institutional third parties without appropriate consent, unless classified as "Directory" information or when the information is subpoenaed by law. Programs and services must apply a similar dedication to privacy and confidentiality to research data concerning individuals. All staff members must be aware of and comply with the provisions contained in the institution's human subjects research policy and in other relevant institutional policies addressing ethical practices.

Assessment and evaluation staff members must recognize and avoid personal conflict of interest or appearance thereof in their transactions with students and others. Staff members must strive to insure the fair, objective, and impartial treatment of all persons with whom they deal.

When handling institutional funds, all staff members must ensure that such funds are managed in accordance with established and responsible accounting procedures.

Outcomes assessment and program evaluation staff members must not participate in any form of harassment that demeans persons or creates an intimidating, hostile, or offensive campus environment.

Staff members must perform their duties within the limits of their training, expertise, and competence. When these limits are exceeded, individuals in need of further assistance must be referred to persons possessing appropriate qualifications.

Staff members must use suitable means to confront and otherwise hold accountable other staff members who exhibit unethical behavior.

Staff members must maintain the highest principles of ethical behavior in the use of technology.

The privacy of study subjects and the confidential nature of data must not be breached. Institutional research policies concerning human subjects must be followed.

Information on individuals should be purged regularly to protect the privacy of current and former students and other subjects.

# Part 13. ASSESSMENT and EVALUATION

The outcomes assessment and program evaluation staff must regularly conduct systematic qualitative and quantitative evaluations of program quality to determine whether and to what degree the stated mission and goals are being met. Although methods of assessment vary, programs and services must employ a sufficient range of measures to insure objectivity and comprehensiveness. Data collected must include responses from students and other affected constituencies. Results of these evaluations must be used in revising and improving programs and services and in recognizing staff performance.

© Copyright 1997 Council for the Advancement of Standards in Higher Education

# THE ROLE of RECREATIONAL SPORTS
## CAS Standards Contextual Statement

Recreational sports are viewed as an essential component of higher education, supplementing the educational process through enhancement of students' physical and mental development. Students who participate in recreational sports tend to develop positive self-images, awareness of their strengths, increased tolerance and self-control, stronger social interaction skills and maturity—all gleaned from their recreational sports experiences. The field of recreational sports has grown into a dynamic, organized presence providing quality co-curricular opportunities for the majority of the student body.

The term "intramural" is derived from the Latin words "intr", meaning "within", and "muralis", meaning walls. Intramurals began in US colleges and universities during the 19th century as students developed leisure time sporting events. Throughout the century, intramural sports were almost exclusively the only form of athletic competition for college males. Originating from intramurals, interest in varsity athletics increased in popularity and the institutions assumed responsibility for organizing athletic events.

Until late in the 1800's, intramural sports were perceived by most to be of little instructional or educational value. Near the end of the century, however, colleges and universities began to administer intramural sports for men. In 1913 the first professional staff members were employed to direct intramural programs. Intramurals continued to grow in strength and gain support, until by the 1950's there was a general realization by institutional leaders of the intrinsic educational value of sports. Programs expanded and additional facilities were constructed in response to student-led initiatives, and campus facilities were established exclusively for recreational sports activities.

Over time, intramural programs diversified and participation increased. The rise in popularity of aerobic exercise produced an influx of women into recreational sports, resulting in even higher levels of interest and participation. Consequently, the late 1980's witnessed a second period of rapid growth in programs and the advent of new and better campus facilities for physical activities.

As they evolved, recreational sports programs experienced changing perceptions about their institutional roles and the standards appropriate for their administration. The wide range of programming currently organized and managed by recreational sports personnel has resulted in a multiplicity of administrative structures. At a majority of institutions, recreational sports programs are administratively placed under the auspices of a division of student affairs. The National Intramural-Recreational Sports Association (NIRSA, 1996) suggests that while organizational designs vary from institution to institution, the full realization for the contribution of recreational sports to any campus depends on institutional commitment to that endeavor.

The NIRSA has delineated five primary goals of recreational sports programs:

- To provide participation in a variety of recreational sports activities which satisfy the diverse needs of students, faculty and staff, and where appropriate, guests, alumni and public participants.

- To coordinate the use of campus recreation facilities in cooperation with other user units, such as athletics, physical education, and student activities.

- To provide extracurricular education opportunities through participation in recreational sports and the provision of relevant leadership positions.

- To contribute positively to institutional relations through significant and high-quality recreational sports programming.

- To cooperate with academic units, focusing on the development of a recreational sports curricula and accompanying laboratory experiences.

Recreational sports programming significantly impacts student life, development and learning, as well as recruitment and retention. Hossler and Bean (1990), in *The Strategic Management of College Enrollment,* write that "recreational sports (i.e., informal leisure time relaxation, games, intramurals) have been endorsed by institutions for their value in helping students maintain good physical health, enhancing their mental health by providing a respite from rigorous academic work and teaching recreational skills with a carryover for leisure time exercise throughout life." Through participation in recreational sports, students are encouraged to develop critical thinking skills, create new problem-solving strategies, hone decision-making skills, enhance creativity, and more effectively synthesize and integrate this information into all aspects of their lives. In this way, students both perform more effectively in an academic environment and flourish throughout all phases of the co-curricular experience.

# References, Readings, and Resources

Hossler, D., Bean, P., & Associates. (1990). *The strategic management of college enrollment.* San Francisco: Jossey-Bass.

Mull, R. F., Bayless, K. G., & Ross, C. M. (1987). *Recreational sports programming.* North Palm Beach, FL: The Athletic Institute.

National Intramural-Recreational Sports Association (1996). *General and specialty Standards for collegiate recreational sports.* Corvallis, OR: Author


National Intramural-Recreational Sports Association (NIRSA). 850 S.W. 15th Street, Corvallis, OR 97333-4145. (503) 737-2088; Fax (503) 727-2026. holsbeerw@ucs. orst.edu

# RECREATIONAL SPORTS
## CAS STANDARDS and GUIDELINES

## Part 1: MISSION

The Recreational Sports program must develop, record, disseminate, implement, and regularly review its mission and goals. The mission statement must be consistent with the mission and goals of the institution and with the standards in this document.

The mission of recreational sports is to enhance students' fitness and wellness, knowledge, personal skills, and enjoyment by providing:

- opportunities for a variety of activities that may contribute to individual physical fitness and wellness;
- opportunities for cooperative and competitive play activity in the game form;
- a medium through which students can learn and practice leadership, management, program planning and interpersonal skills; and
- access to quality facilities, equipment and programs.

To accomplish this mission recreational sports programs should:

- provide a variety of opportunities including informal programs (self-directed), intramural sports (structured), sports clubs (interest groups), instructional programs, special events, outdoor programs, fitness and wellness programs, extramural programs, family and youth programs and programs for people with disabilities;
- coordinate effectively the scheduling of events and maintenance of campus sport facilities with other campus units:
- provide extracurricular opportunities through participation and leadership roles designed to enhance social, psychological, and physiological development;
- contribute positively to public relations efforts of the institution, including the recruitment and retention of students;
- when appropriate, work in collaboration with academic units to help teach courses and facilitate laboratory experiences; and
- assist with the socialization of students into the campus environment.

## Part 2. PROGRAM

The formal education of students is purposeful, holistic, and consists of the curriculum and the co-curriculum. The campus recreational sports program must be (a) intentional, (b) coherent, (c) based on theories and knowledge of learning and human development, (d) reflective of developmental and demographic profiles of the student population, and (e) responsive to special needs of individuals.

The campus recreational sports program must promote learning and development in students by encouraging outcomes such as intellectual growth, ability; to communicate effectively, realistic self-appraisal, enhanced self-esteem, clarification of values, appropriate career choices, leadership development, physical fitness, meaningful interpersonal relations, ability to work independently and collaboratively, social responsibility, satisfying and productive lifestyles, appreciation of aesthetic and cultural diversity, and achievement of personal goals.

Recreational sports programs must reflect the needs and interests of students, faculty, staff, and other members of the campus community. Programs must satisfy the particular needs of the campus by balancing team, dual, individual meet, and special event sport experiences.

The overall recreational sports program should include:

- Informal programs to provide for self-directed, individualized approach to participation. This program area accommodates the desire to participate in sport for fitness and enjoyment.
- Intramural sports to provide structured contests, meets, tournaments, and leagues limiting participation to the individuals within the institution. A variety of forms of tournaments should be available, including elimination, challenge, league, and meets. Equitable participation opportunities should be provided for men and women, and when appropriate, co-recreational activity should be offered. Opportunities to participate at various levels of ability should be made available to students (e.g., beginner, intermediate, and advanced).
- Sport clubs to provide opportunities for individuals to organize around a common interest. Opportunities should be available for a variety of interest focused on a sport within or outside the institution. Self-administered and self-regulated groups are normally coordinated and assisted by staff in such areas as governance, facilities, scheduling, safety, budgeting, and fund-raising through sport club coordination. Formation of clubs should be accomplished through appropriate and established channels.
- Instructional programs to provide learning opportunities, knowledge, and skills through lessons, clinics, and workshops. Depending on type, size, resources, and setting of the institution, the program may include extramural sports, outdoor recreation, fitness and wellness, and special events.
- Special events to introduce new sport or related activities that are unique in approach or nature from traditional programs. These events may be held within or outside the institution.

- Outdoor programs and activities to provide participants with opportunities to enjoy natural environments and experience new challenges.

- Fitness programs to provide opportunities and assistance in personal exercise programs. This voluntary program should motivate individuals to assess their levels of fitness and maintain a positive fitness lifestyle. Individual assessment should be available for participant feedback.

- Recreation and aquatic programs.

- Wellness programs to encourage achievement of one's full health potential. These programs should provide an opportunity to work cooperatively with professionals in health services including counselors and physicians and may be accomplished in concert with others who are similarly oriented.

- Extramural sports to provide structured tournaments, contests and meets among participants from other institutions. Champions from intramural sports are frequently chosen to represent the institution.

- Family and youth programs for members of the campus community. These activities may include special events, sports, games, instructional programs, fitness and wellness, and outdoor programs.

- Programs for people with disabilities to engage in activities designed to have a positive impact on mobility, socialization, independence, fitness, and community integration.

Program planning and implementation should include consideration of:

- proper facility coordination and scheduling;

- rules and regulations that address participant safety;

- an environment that minimizes the chance of injuries;

- advice to groups and organizations;

- accurate interpretation of institutional policies and procedures to program participants;

- conflict management issues;

- proper supervision of recreational sports activities;

- inventory, maintenance, and procedures for participant use of equipment;

- participant involvement in program content and procedures through committee structures;

- recognition system for participants, employees, and volunteers;

- cultural diversity issues;

- accurate and adequate publicity and promotion; and

- volunteerism.

# Part 3. LEADERSHIP

Effective and ethical leadership is essential to the success of all organizations. The institution must appoint, position, and empower leaders within the administrative structure to accomplish stated missions. Administrators at various levels must be selected on the basis of formal education and training, relevant work experience, personal attributes, and other professional credentials. The institution must determine expectations of accountability for its program administrators and fairly assess their performance.

Administrators of campus recreational sports programs must exercise authority over resources for which they are responsible to achieve their respective missions. Administrators must articulate vision for their organization; set goals and objectives; prescribe and practice ethical behavior; recruit, select, supervise, and develop others in the organization; manage, plan, budget, and evaluate; communicate effectively; and marshal cooperate action from colleagues, employees, other institutional constituencies, and persons outside the organization. Recreational sports program leaders must address individual, organizational, or environmental conditions that inhibit goal achievement. Administrators must improve programs and services continuously in response to changing needs of students and institutional priorities.

# Part 4. ORGANIZATION and MANAGEMENT

The campus recreational sports program must be structured purposefully and managed effectively to achieve stated goals. Evidence of appropriate structure must include current and accessible policies and procedures, written performance expectations for all employees, functional work flow graphics and organizational charts, and service delivery expectations. Evidence of effective management must include clear sources and channels of authority, effective communication practices, decision-making and conflict resolution procedures, responsiveness to changing conditions, accountability systems, and recognition and reward processes.

The campus recreational sports program must provide channels for regular review of administrative policies and procedures.

There must be written policies and procedures regarding program delivery that are reviewed regularly.

Institutional leaders should recognize the significant differences in mission among intercollegiate athletics, physical education and recreation academic units, and the recreational sports programs, and act accordingly. The organizational placement of recreational sports within the institution should ensure the accomplishment of the program's mission.

Members of the campus community should be involved in the selection, design, governance, and administration of programs and facilities. Students, faculty and staff and members, and the public, when appropriate, may be involved through committees, councils, and boards.

# Part 5. HUMAN RESOURCES

The recreational sports program must be staffed adequately by individuals qualified to accomplish its mission and goals. The recreational sports program must establish procedures for staff selection, training, and evaluation; set expectations for supervision; and provide appropriate professional development opportunities.

Professional staff members must hold an earned graduate degree in a field relevant to the position description or must possess an appropriate combination of education and experience.

Degree or credential seeking interns or others in training must be qualified by enrollment in an appropriate field of study and relevant experience. These individuals must be trained and supervised adequately by professional staff members.

Student employees and volunteers must be carefully selected, trained, supervised, and evaluated. When their knowledge and skills are not adequate for particular situations, they must refer students or others in need of assistance to qualified professional staff.

The recreational sports program must have secretarial and technical staff adequate to accomplish its mission. Such staff must be technologically proficient and qualified to perform activities including reception duties, office equipment operation, records maintenance, and mail handling.

Salary levels and fringe benefits for all staff members must be commensurate with those for comparable positions within the institution, in similar institutions, and in the relevant geographic area. Compensation for paraprofessional staff, when provided, must be fair and voluntary services must be recognized adequately.

The recreational sports program must intentionally employ a diverse staff to reflect the diversity of the student population, to ensure the existence of readily identifiable role models for students, and to enrich the campus community. Affirmative action must occur in hiring and promotion practices as required to ensure diverse staffing profiles, and as required by institutional, local, state/provincial or federal law.

# Part 6: FINANCIAL RESOURCES

The recreational sports program must have adequate funding to accomplish its mission and goals. Priorities, whether set periodically or as a result of extraordinary conditions, must be determined within the context of the stated mission, goals, and resources.

Institutional funds for the recreational sports program should be allocated on a permanent basis. In addition to institutional funding, other sources may be considered, including state appropriations, student fees, user fees, donations, contributions, fines, concession and store sales, rentals, and dues.

# Part 7. FACILITIES, TECHNOLOGY and EQUIPMENT

The recreational sports program must have adequate, suitably located facilities and equipment to support its mission and goals. Facilities, technology and equipment must be in compliance with relevant federal, state, provincial, and local requirements to provide for access, health, and safety.

The institution must provide adequate indoor and outdoor facilities, technology and equipment with prioritized blocks of time, for recreational sports programs to accommodate the diverse needs and interest of the campus community.

As a general rule, the larger the population and the more geographically isolated the institution, the greater the need for quality and diversity of facilities. Consideration should be given to a balance of facilities that would provide participation opportunities in team, dual, individual, and meet sports, as well as in fitness and conditioning. Examples of such facilities include swimming pools, gymnasiums, weight rooms and fitness facilities, and general use playing fields.

# Part 8. LEGAL RESPONSIBILITIES

Recreational sports program staff members must be knowledgeable about and responsive to law and regulations that relate to higher education and recreational sports programs. Sources for legal obligations and limitations are (a) constitutional, statutory, regulatory, and case law; (b) mandatory laws and orders emanating from federal, state/ provincial, and local governments; and (c) policies of the institution.

Recreational sports program staff members must use reasonable and informed practices to limit the liability exposure of the institution, its officers, employees, and agents. Staff members must be informed about institutional policies regarding personal liability and related insurance coverage options.

The institution must provide access to legal advice for staff members as needed to carry out assigned responsibilities.

The institution must inform staff and students, in a timely and systematic fashion, about extraordinary or changing legal obligations and potential liabilities.

Recreational sports professionals should be fully aware of and understand legal areas such as due process, employment procedures, equal opportunity, and civil rights and liberties.

Although participation in recreational sports is a voluntary action, liability of wrongful or negligent acts should be a continuing concern.

Reasonable efforts must be made to insure a safe environment, properly maintained equipment, proper instruction, and adequate supervision.

# Part 9. EQUAL OPPORTUNITY, ACCESS, and AFFIRMATIVE ACTION

Staff members must ensure that the recreational sports program is provided on a fair and equitable basis. The recreational sports program must be accessible. Hours of operation must be responsive to the needs of students.

The recreational sports program must not be discriminatory on the basis of age, ancestry, color, disability, gender, national origin, race, religious creed, sexual orientation, and/or veteran status. Exceptions are appropriate only where provided by relevant law and institutional policy.

Consistent with its mission and goals, the recreational sports program must take affirmative action to remedy significant imbalances in student participation and staffing patterns.

# Part 10. CAMPUS and COMMUNITY RELATIONS

The recreational sports program must establish, maintain, and promote effective relations with relevant campus offices and external agencies.

The recreational sports program should be an institution-wide process that systematically involves student affairs, academic affairs, and other administrative units, such as campus police, physical plant, and the business office.

The recreational sports program should collaborate campus-wide to disseminate information abut their own and other programs and services on campus.

The program staff should serve as a resource to the community, providing expert advice on recreational issues and activities.

# Part 11. DIVERSITY

Within the context of the institution's unique mission, multi-dimensional diversity enriches the community and enhances the collegiate experience for all; therefore, the recreational sports program must nurture environments where similarities and differences among people are recognized and honored.

The recreational sports program must promote cultural educational experiences that are characterized by open and continuous communication; that deepen understanding of one's own culture and heritage; and that respect and educate about similarities, differences, and histories of cultures.

The recreational sports program must address the characteristics and needs of a diverse population when establishing and implementing policies and procedures.

# Part 12. ETHICS

All persons involved in the delivery of the recreational sports program must adhere to the highest principles of ethical behavior. The recreational sports program must develop or adopt statements of ethical practice to address their unique issues. These statements must be published, implemented, and reviewed periodically.

Ethical standards of relevant professional associations should be considered.

All staff members must ensure that confidentiality is maintained with respect to all communications and records considered confidential unless exempted by law.

Information disclosed in individual counseling sessions must remain confidential, unless written permission to divulge the information is given by the student. However, staff members must disclose to appropriate authorities information judged to be of an emergency nature, especially when the safety of the individual or others is involved. Information contained in students' educational records must not be disclosed to non-institutional third parties without appropriate consent, unless classified as "Directory" information or when the information is subpoenaed by law. The recreational sports program must apply a similar dedication to privacy and confidentiality to research data concerning individuals.

Staff members must be aware of and comply with the provisions contained in the institution's human subjects research policy and in other relevant institutional policies addressing ethical practices.

Staff members must recognize and avoid personal conflict of interest or appearance thereof in their transactions with students and others. Staff members must strive to ensure the fair objectives and impartial treatment of all persons with whom they deal.

When handling institutional funds, staff members must ensure that such funds are managed in accordance with established and responsible account procedures.

Staff members must maintain the highest principles of ethical behavior in the use of technology.

Staff members must not participate in any form of harassment that demeans people or creates an intimidating, hostile, or offensive campus environment.

Staff members must perform their duties within the limits of their training, expertise, and competence. When these limits are exceeded, individuals in need of further assistance must be referred to persons possessing appropriate qualifications.

Staff members must use suitable means to confront and otherwise hold accountable other staff members who exhibit unethical behavior.

## Part 13. ASSESSMENT and EVALUATION

The recreational sports program must regularly conduct systematic qualitative and quantitative evaluations of program quality to determine whether and to what degree the stated mission and goals are being met. Although methods of assessment vary, the recreational sports program must employ a sufficient range of measures to ensure objectivity and comprehensiveness. Data collected must include responses from students and other significant constituencies. Results of these evaluations must be considered when revising and improving the recreational sports program and in recognizing staff performance.

Evaluation of student and institutional needs, goals, objectives, and the effectiveness of the recreational sports program should occur on a periodic basis. A representative cross-section of appropriate people from the campus community should be involved in reviews of the recreational sports program.

© Copyright 1997 Council for the Advancement of Standards in Higher Education (CAS)

# THE ROLE of the REGISTRAR
## CAS Standards Contextual Statement

The position of registrar evolved from the position of "Bedel" in Europe, which appeared in the 12th century. As the position developed and the office changed, the "registrar" emerged in the 15th century. With the founding of Harvard, the position of registrar became an integral part of American higher education. In 1910, 15 registrars met in Detroit to discuss the need to share information and develop common practices, a meeting marked the birth of the American Association of Collegiate Registrars (AACR). That group added admission officers in 1949 and changed its name to the American Association of Collegiate Registrars and Admissions Officers (AACRAO) (Quann, 1979). Over the years AACR and AACRAO and their more than 30 state and regional associations have provided linkages among registrars nationally and internationally, for the exchange of ideas and information that has led to a set of generally accepted policies and practices.

As the role of registrar evolved, it shifted from being essentially the number-two leadership position responsible for handling many aspects of administration, to filling a role more narrowly focused but vital to the life of all institutions of higher learning. Today's registrar usually reports to the vice president for academic affairs, student affairs, or enrollment management, and manages a staff that may vary from a few members to more than 100, depending on institution size. The registrar determines the organizational structure for the office; ensures the availability of adequate facilities, equipment, supplies, and services; develops position descriptions for and employs, trains, and supervises office staff; and oversees day-to-day activities.

The office of the registrar is a primary point of contact for students on the college campus. Through the registrars office, students obtain schedules of classes, register for courses, drop/add/withdraw, obtain grade reports and transcripts, and receive diplomas. Therefore, providing fast and efficient service to students and continuous quality improvement are major objectives for the registrar.

The registrar's office is also a primary point of contact for faculty members for the scheduling of classes and assignment of classroom and laboratory space. In support of faculty members, who often assist in the advising and registration processes, the registrar's office provides class rosters and grade rolls, receives and processes grades, and produces grade reports and transcripts. Maintaining a close working relationship with faculty members, department heads, and academic deans is therefore an important role of the registrar.

While duties and responsibilities vary from institution to institution, the registrar is typically responsible for working with academic departments and faculty to determine which courses and sections are offered each term, assigning classroom facilities, and producing the catalog and schedule of classes students use to select courses.

The registrar oversees the registration process by which students select classes each academic term. When less sophisticated technological support was available, registration was usually conducted in an arena setting where students registered in person. Today, registration may be conducted on line, by touch-tone telephone, and on the world wide web and students may register from campus or off-campus residences, workplaces, or elsewhere, as long as they have access to a telephone or on-line computer.

The registrar also is responsible for the maintenance of student records. While records are still maintained in paper or on microfilm, most institutions now store student records in electronic data bases. Imaging systems also are used increasingly to store former paper records in electronic form.

Other duties of most registrars include the production of class rosters, grade rosters, and grade reports; clearance of students for graduation, preparation of diplomas, and organization of graduation ceremonies; and publication of the college catalog. Registrars also play a vital role in developing and implementing policies and procedures, services, and systems to facilitate student enrollment, maintenance of student records, transfer of records to other institutions, and acceptance of transfer credit.

In addition, the registrar is the individual responsible for assuring that the Family Education Rights and Privacy Act (FERPA) requirements are met throughout the institution. Likewise, as student information systems increasingly are being implemented, responsibility for oversight of these technologies has gained greater importance as well.

Often, registrars are at the forefront of implementing new technologies on campus. Initially, student information systems were manual in design, but since mid-century they have involved increased levels of automation. Many, institutions now maintain student information systems that include on-line and/or touchtone registration, on-line records, imaging systems, electronic interchange of records and data among institutions, and desktop publishing of class schedules and catalogs. Currently, increased levels of information are available through such on-line technology as the world wide web; once again, registrars are at the forefront by providing class schedules and other relevant information and making student registration available through the web.

The pace of change in higher education will increasingly affect the registrar's functions. The standards that follow, in addition to providing basic functional guidelines, are designed to help institutions address such challenges as distance learning; virtual universities; proficiency-based education; assessment; learning opportunities that are not constrained by time, location, or duration; and continuous rapid change in technology.

# References, Readings, and Resources

Aucoin, P., & Associates (1996). *Academic record and transcript guide.* Washington, DC: American Association of Collegiate Registrars and Admissions Officers.

Bell, M. M. (1993). *Touchtone telephone/voice response registration: A guide for successful implementation.* Washington, DC: American Association of Collegiate Registrars and Admissions Officers.

Bilger, T. A., & Associates (1987). *Professional development guidelines for registrars: A self-audit.* Washington, DC: American Association of Collegiate Registrars and Admissions Officers.

Lonabocker, L., & Gwinn, D. (1996). *Breakthrough systems: Student access and registration.* Washington, DC: American Association of Collegiate Registrars and Admissions Officers.

Ockerman, E. & Legere, J. (1989). *The role of the registrar.* Washington, DC: American Association of Collegiate Registrars and Admissions Officers (AACRAO).

Perkins, H. L. (1996). *Electronic imaging in admissions, records and financial aid offices.* Washington, DC: American Association of Collegiate Registrars and Admissions Officers.

Peterson, E. D., & Associates (1987). *Retention of records: A guide for retention and disposal of student records.* Washington, DC: American Association of Collegiate Registrars and Admissions Officers.

Quann, C. J., & Associates (1979). *Admissions, academic records, and registrar services: A handbook of policies and procedures.* San Francisco: Jossey-Bass.

Rainsberger, R. A., & Associates. (1995). *Guidelines for postsecondary institutions for implementation of the Family Educational Rights and Privacy Act of 1974 as amended.* Washington, DC: American Association of Collegiate Registrars and Admissions Officers.

# REGISTRAR PROGRAMS AND SERVICES
## CAS STANDARDS and GUIDELINES

## Part 1. MISSION

Registrar programs and services in higher education must develop, record, disseminate, implement and regularly review the stated mission and goals. Registrar mission statements must be consistent with the mission and goals of the institution and with the standards in this document.

In support of the overall mission of the institution, and when responsibility is assigned, the mission of the Registrar programs and services must be to:

- develop institutional publications to provide information about courses, programs, policies, and procedures;
- develop course schedules to provide information on courses and sections being offered in any given term with their day, time, and location;
- schedule appropriate space for all classes;
- provide information on regulations, policies and procedures;
- develop forms and procedures as required;
- provide a registration process for enrolling students in classes each term, which may include the assessment of tuition and fees;
- certify student enrollment as required (e.g., veterans services, rehabilitation services, student loans, athletic eligibility);
- provide reports as required (e.g., class rosters, grade rosters, grade reports, transcripts);
- record properly evaluated transfer credit;
- administer academic eligibility policies (e.g., graduation, honors, academic probation or dismissal);
- prepare and distribute diplomas;
- maintain student record data base and archival files;
- ensure that the security and confidentiality of student record data are maintained throughout the university/college;
- prepare statistical reports (e.g., enrollment projections, retention, attrition, and graduation rates);

  The registrar may also coordinate the arrangements for commencement and provide administrative support to the faculty senate or other governance bodies.

## Part 2. PROGRAM

The formal education of students is purposeful, holistic, and consists of the curriculum and the co-curriculum.

Registrar programs and services must be (a) intentional, (b) coherent, (c) based on theories and knowledge of learning and human development, (d) reflective of developmental and demographic profiles of the student population, and (e) responsive to special needs of individuals.

Registrar programs and services must support the overall learning and development in students by encouraging outcomes such as intellectual growth, ability to communicate effectively, realistic self-appraisal, enhanced self-esteem, clarification of values, appropriate career choices, leadership development, physical fitness, meaningful interpersonal relations, ability to work independently and collaboratively, social responsibility, satisfying and productive lifestyles, appreciation of aesthetic and cultural diversity, and achievement of personal goals.

The registrar must

- have the authority to operate effectively in the academic community;
- ensure that relevant policies and procedures are communicated widely;
- ensure the accuracy and reliability of the data collected and distributed;
- provide for the maintenance, upkeep, security, integrity and proper dissemination of academic records;

  The Registrar should assist in institutional efforts to establish and maintain co-curricular transcripts or other records as appropriate;

- develop a workable disaster recovery plan that will allow the registrar to function in the event of catastrophic circumstances; and
- educate the institutional community with regard to the security and release of student data.

## Part 3. LEADERSHIP

Effective and ethical leadership is essential to the success of all organizations. Institutions must appoint, position and empower leaders within the administrative structure to accomplish stated missions. Leaders at various levels must be selected on the basis of formal education and training, relevant work experience, personal attributes, and other professional credentials. Institutions determine expectations of accountability for leaders and fairly assess their performance.

Registrars must exercise authority over resources for which they are responsible to achieve their respective missions. The registrar must articulate a vision for their organization; set goals and objectives, prescribe and practice ethical behavior; recruit, select, supervise, and develop others in the organization; manage, plan, budget, and evaluate; communicate effectively; and marshal cooperative action from colleagues, employees, other constituencies, and persons outside the organization. The registrar must address individual, organizational, or environmental conditions that inhibit goal achievement. The registrar must improve programs and services continuously in response to changing needs of students, institutional priorities, and technological advances.

The registrar's office should

- develop, advocate, and implement a statement of the mission, goals, and objectives for the unit that is congruent with and complementary to the institutional mission;

- be responsible for implementing services congruent with institutional mission, goals, and objectives;

- provide accurate information and timely service to all constituencies;

- be at the forefront of technological advancement;

- be able to justify investment in hardware, by identifying time and cost efficiencies that will accrue to the institution;

- be sensitive to the special needs of all students including evening students, commuting students, married students, single parents, students with disabilities, adult learners and students of various ethnic and cultural groups;

- assess decision-making and problem-solving models and select those most appropriate to the institutional milieu; and

- serve as a catalyst in team building because the activities of the registrar impinge on most other institutional units.

# Part 4. ORGANIZATION and MANAGEMENT

Registrar programs and services must be structured purposefully and managed effectively to achieve stated goals. Evidence of appropriate structure must include current and accessible policies and procedures, written performance expectations for all employees, functional work flow graphics or organizational charts, and service delivery expectations. Evidence of effective management must include clear sources and channels of authority, effective communication practices, decision-making and conflict resolution procedures, responsiveness to changing conditions, accountability systems, and recognition and reward processes.

Registrar programs and services must provide channels within the organization for regular review of administrative policies and procedures and document such policies, practices, and procedures in a manual.

The registrar should:

- Develop an organizational chart that describes the reporting lines within the office and identifies cooperative interrelationships with other institutional units;

- Coordinate programs and services with other institutional personnel, offices, functions, and activities;

- Develop operational policies and procedures that include the detailed descriptions of responsibilities for each staff member;

- Ensure that staff responsibilities are consonant with the abilities of designated personnel;

- Provide for periodic review of policies, procedures, organizational structures, and currency of the office manual;

- Develop and maintain the office budget;

- Develop clear and concise criteria for decision making and establish primary responsibility when more than one unit is involved;

- Assume responsibility for establishing, updating, and evaluating staff training and professional development programs that also include skill improvement, interpersonal, organizational, and tine management components.

- Identify and be responsive to external constraints and requirements that impact on unit operation (e.g., implications of local, state, and federal regulations, union agreements, accreditation, professional, and athletic conference requirements); foster communication among the staff by scheduling regular staff meetings;

- Encourage staff members to participate in state, regional, and national professional activities; and

- Expend significant effort for long-range planning for changes in technology, policy, procedure, and customer service.

There should be an office manual that includes:

- Organizational charts showing accountability and reporting lines; interrelationships with other institutional units; applicable operating policies, practices and procedures; unit-specific policies, practices and procedures; external constraints (union, state and federal requirements); ethical standards statements; grievance/appeal procedures; job descriptions and expectations; personnel policies; task and job evaluation forms; and procedures in case of an emergency, natural disaster, or school closure.

# Part 5. HUMAN RESOURCES

Registrar programs and services must be staffed adequately by individuals qualified to accomplish their mission and goals. Registrar programs and services must establish procedures for staff selection, training, and evaluation; set expectations for supervision; and provide appropriate professional development opportunities.

Staff members should be aware of the criteria on which they are to be evaluated at the beginning of each evaluation period. They should be properly trained and their performance monitored so that the evaluation at the end of the period does not contain judgment of criteria that have not been previously discussed.

Professional staff members must hold an earned graduate degree in a field relevant to the position description or must possess an appropriate combination of education and experience.

The chief administrator of the office should have the capacity to motivate, inspire, and help staff members develop a team atmosphere in the office. Attention should be paid to recognizing and rewarding the efforts of those who have accomplished expected and exceptional work.

Since the registrar works with all sectors of the institution, many of whom have terminal degrees, it would be advantageous if the registrar had a terminal degree as well. Other professional registrar staff may not require a terminal degree, but a master's or bachelor's degree is appropriate. Most degree programs do not specifically prepare individuals to become registrars. Courses of study relevant to the registrar area include: administration, education, business, counseling, curriculum, personnel, sociology, and psychology. Often professional staff are employed in the area after prior teaching or administrative experience. A demonstrated service-oriented philosophy is important since the office will be serving the entire campus population.

The registrar should possess an array of budget management skills: developing budgets, writing proposals for special projects, performing cost benefit analyses, amortizing the cost of major equipment purchases, and preparing analyses of future needs. Additionally, the registrar should be aware of the institution's personnel policies that could affect the budget, of accounting reports that track expenditures, and of policies governing unused funds.

The selection criteria for the registrar's position should include consideration of the match between a candidate's educational, personal, and experiential qualifications and the institution's mission, goals, and objectives. Staff member's selection should attempt to ensure the responsibilities are consonant with abilities.

Typically, the registrar reports to a vice president of academic affairs, student affairs, enrollment management, or comparable senior officer. Specific titles and reporting structures will necessarily reflect institutional mission, goals, and objectives.

**Degree or credential-seeking interns or others in training must be qualifies by enrollment in an appropriate field of study and relevant experience. These individuals must be trained and supervised adequately by professional staff members.**

**Student employees and volunteers must be carefully selected, trained, supervised, and evaluated. When their knowledge and skills are nor adequate for particular situations, they must refer students or others in need of assistance to qualified professional staff.**

**The registrar must have secretarial and technical staff adequate to accomplish the program's mission. Such a staff must be technologically proficient and qualified to perform activities including reception duties, office equipment operation, records maintenance, and mail handling.**

The support staff should be skilled in interpersonal communications, public relations, and the dissemination of information. Personnel should be adept in handling complex and detailed activities and responsibilities. Accuracy is essential because the office is recording the academic history of students.

Development for the support staff should include adequate initial training to be able to represent the institution in their office function in a competent and professional manner. Ongoing training and staff development should be designed to enhance and broaden understanding of roles and responsibilities within the office and the institution.

**Appropriate salary levels and fringe benefits for all staff members must be commensurate with those for comparable positions within the institution, in similar institutions, and in the relevant geographic area.**

**Registrar programs must intentionally employ a diverse staff to reflect the diversity of the institution's student population, to ensure the existence of readily identifiable role models for students, and to enrich the campus community.**

**Affirmative action must occur in hiring and promotion practices to ensure diverse staffing profiles as required by institutional, local, state/provincial, and federal law.**

Because the office often involves routine and repetitive work, special attention should be given to the accuracy of all work.

# Part 6. FINANCIAL RESOURCES

**Registrar programs and services must have adequate funding to accomplish its mission and goals. Priorities, whether set periodically or as a result of extraordinary conditions, must be determined within the context of the stated mission, goals, and resources.**

The registrar should have a clear understanding of the office's mission, sources of funding, and the budgeting process used by the institution.

Funds should be provided for salaries and benefits of staff and temporary or part time workers; professional development and staff training; office furnishings; communications and data processing equipment and software; postage, printing, and office supplies; subscriptions to professional and technical publications; membership in appropriate professional organizations; attendance at professional meetings, conferences, and workshops; special projects; and unexpected emergencies.

# Part 7. FACILITIES, TECHNOLOGY, and EQUIPMENT

**The registrar program must have adequate, suitably located facilities, technology, and equipment to support its mission and goals. Facilities, technology, and equipment must be in compliance with relevant federal, state, provincial, and local requirements to provide for access, health, and safety.**

**The design of the office must guarantee the security of the records and ensure the confidentiality of all sensitive information. The location and layout of the office must be sensitive to the special needs of students with disabilities as well as the needs of the general student population.**

Facilities which produce a comfortable, functional, and pleasant work environment encourage staff members to be more productive. The administrative staff members should have private space in which to conduct their business. The offices should be equipped and furnished to support activities. All other employees should have work stations which are well equipped, adequate in size, as private as possible, and appropriately designed for their work.

Offices should be well lighted, properly ventilated, and heated or cooled to acceptable standards. Adequate space should be allocated for the secure storage of student records and supplies. Space should be provided for meetings with students, conferring with staff, and completing special projects. Ideally a comfortable area within the office or nearby should be available for staff breaks and lunches.

**When the Registrar is responsible for determining facilities usage outside the immediate office, policies and procedures must be developed and disseminated with respect to the assignment of such space.**

**Backup copies of important documentation such as transcripts and the student data base must be stored off site in the event of a natural disaster or damage to the records.**

## Part 8. LEGAL RESPONSIBILITIES

**Registrar staff members must be knowledgeable about and responsive to law and regulations that relate to their respective responsibilities. Sources for legal obligations and limitations include constitutional, federal, statutory, regulatory, and case law; mandatory laws and orders emanating from state/provincial and local governments; and the institution through its policies.**

**Staff members must use reasonable and informed practices to limit the liability exposure of the institution, its officers, employees, and agents. Staff members must be informed about institutional policies regarding personal liability and related insurance coverage options.**

**The institution must provide access to legal advice for staff members as needed to carry out assigned responsibilities.**

**The institution must inform staff and students, in a timely and systematic fashion, about extraordinary or changing legal obligations and potential liabilities.**

**The registrar must ensure that the institution has written policies on all office transactions which may have legal implications.**

**The registrar must have procedures to keep staff members informed of all requirements related to the maintenance of academic records. Forms used to implement regulations must be developed and reviewed to assure fulfillment of all institutional requirements.**

The registrar should meet with the institution's legal counsel periodically to review all relevant documents for clarity and to determine that current regulations are being followed. Some of the relevant areas that should be reviewed include affirmative action policies; certification of diplomas, degrees, and dates of attendance; court orders; academic and disciplinary dismissals; degree requirements; tuition, fees, and refund policies; fraudulent records; name changes; personnel issues; record keeping practices; residency status determination; requests for information from law enforcement agencies; security procedures; social security number usage; and subpoenas.

**The registrar's office must protect students' rights to privacy and access as defined in the legislative statute entitled Family Educational Rights and Privacy Act of 1974 (FERPA).**

FERPA commonly known as the Buckley Amendment, protects the privacy of student records by requiring

- institutions to limit the disclosure of information from student records to third persons;

- notification to students or their parents, if dependency has been established, of their right to review student educational records; and

- institutions to inform students of their right to seek correction of information contained in their educational records.

## Part 9. EQUAL OPPORTUNITY, ACCESS, and AFFIRMATIVE ACTION

**Registrar's office staff members must ensure that services and programs are provided on a fair and equitable basis and be accessible to all eligible individuals. Hours of operation must be responsive to the needs of all students.**

**Registrar programs and services must adhere to the spirit and intent of equal opportunity laws and must not be discriminatory on the basis of age, color, disability, gender, national origin, race, religious creed, sexual orientation, and/or veteran status. Exceptions are appropriate only where provided by relevant law and institutional policy.**

**Consistent with the mission and goals, the registrar programs and services must take affirmative action to remedy significant imbalances in student participation and staffing patterns.**

## Part 10. CAMPUS and COMMUNITY RELATIONS

**Registrar programs and services must establish, maintain, and promote effective relations with relevant campus offices and external agencies. Staff members must relate effectively with administrators, faculty, students, alumni, and the public.**

# Part 11. DIVERSITY

Within the context of the institution's unique mission, multi-dimensional diversity enriches the community and enhances the collegiate experience for all; therefore, registrar programs and services must nurture environments where similarities and differences among people are recognized and honored.

Registrar programs and services must promote cultural educational experiences that are characterized by open and continuous communication; that deepen understanding of one's own culture and heritage; and that respect and educate about similarities, differences, and histories of cultures.

Registrar programs and services must address the characteristics and needs of a diverse population when establishing and implementing policies and procedures.

# Part 12. ETHICS

All persons involved in the delivery of registrar programs and services for students must adhere to the highest principles of ethical behavior. The registrar programs and services must develop or adopt and implement statements of ethical practice addressing the issues unique to it existence. These statements must be published and reviewed periodically by all concerned.

Standards of ethical practice that address the unique problems of managing the day to day maintenance of records and registration processes must be published. These standards must be made a part of the orientation program for each new employee and be routinely reviewed and updated.

> Ethical standards statements previously used by the profession at large or relevant professional associations should be reviewed in the formulation of institutional standards.

All staff members must ensure that confidentiality is maintained with respect to all communications and records considered confidential unless exempted by law.

> The institutional responsibilities of the registrar and records personnel in keeping and releasing student information demands conduct that consistently reflects fairness, common sense, honesty, and respect for the dignity of all persons.

Information disclosed in individual counseling sessions must remain confidential, unless written permission to divulge the information is given by the student. However, all staff members must disclose to appropriate authorities information judged to be of an emergency nature, especially when the safety of the individual or others is involved. Information contained in students' educational records must not be disclosed to non-institutional third parties without appropriate consent unless classified as "Directory" information or when the information is subpoenaed be law. Registrar programs and services must apply a similar dedication to privacy and confidentiality to research data concerning individuals. Program staff members must be aware of and comply with the provisions contained in the institution's human subjects research policy and in other relevant institutional policies addressing ethical practices.

The registrar must ensure the institution has a written policy and published statement regarding confidentiality of records and procedures for access, release, and challenge of educational records. The same basic principles of confidentiality must govern electronic data as well as paper documents.

Staff members must recognize and avoid personal conflict of interest or appearance thereof in their transactions with students and others. Staff members must strive to ensure that fair objectives and impartial treatment of all persons with whom they deal.

When handling institutional funds, all staff members must ensure that such funds are managed in accordance with established and responsible accounting procedures.

Staff members must not participate in any form of harassment that demeans persons or creates an intimidating, hostile, or offensive campus environment.

Staff members must perform their duties within the limits of their training, expertise, and competence. When these limits are exceeded, individuals in need of further assistance must be referred to persons possessing appropriate qualifications.

Staff members must use suitable means to confront and otherwise hold accountable other staff members who exhibit unethical behavior.

> The registrar should promote ethical awareness in the academic community as well as within the registrar's office. This can best be accomplished by developing a broad conceptual understanding of higher education, acquiring knowledge of the philosophy and values in the design and application of policies and practices, and implementing the philosophy and values developed for the registrar's office.

Staff members must maintain the highest principles of ethical behavior in the use of technology.

# Part 13. ASSESSMENT and EVALUATION

Registrar programs and services must regularly conduct systematic qualitative and quantitative evaluations of program quality to determine whether and to what degree that stated mission and goals are being met. Although methods of assessment vary, programs and

**services must employ a sufficient range of measures to ensure objectivity and comprehensiveness. Data collected must include responses from students and other affected constituencies. Results of these evaluations must be used in revising and improving programs and services and in recognizing staff performance.**

The evaluation of the operations of the registrar's office may be external or internal. In either case, the registrar's office should have a mechanism in effect that systematically reviews all of its activities and policies. As technology, laws, and regulations change, new activities or policies may need to be implemented. When developing new programs or activities, an evaluation should be a part of the plan to ensure effectiveness, efficiency, and/or appropriateness for future use.

Periodically, the entire office should undertake an extensive self-audit to determine if current activities and policies follow the standards in the profession. The registrar should continuously evaluate the activities of the office to determine if the services meet the needs of its constituents and continue to parallel the mission of the institution.

© Copyright 1997 Council for the Advancement of Standards in Higher Education (CAS)

# THE ROLE OF RELIGIOUS PROGRAMS AND SERVICES
## CAS Standards Contextual Statement

The history of higher education in the United States and that of religious programs and services go hand in hand. Early colleges and universities were all established by some religious denomination, and education of the clergy was their primary goal. Religion permeated the entire campus, not only within the curriculum but also through all aspects of student life.

In the mid-1850s, the role of religion in higher education changed to "seek a broader public good through an increase in the number of professions for which students would be trained, more precision in the disciplines, less control by religion, and a democratic society" (Butler, 1989, p. 5). This trend continued with the passage of the Morrill Land-Grant Act of 1862 and the Morrill Act of 1890, which made public education more widely available. More areas of study became available outside of religious training and access to higher education generally was eased. Consequently, the numbers of citizens seeking advanced levels of education increased significantly.

With more students attending the new public institutions, various religious denominations began to establish student organizations to function on these campuses as student support services. Religious groups such as the Methodist Wesley Foundation, the Jewish Hillel programs, and the Catholic Newman Apostolate provided both religious support and social support for students. Subsequently, numerous independent religious organizations were established on college campuses, many of which are ecumenical in nature and not tied to any particular denomination (e.g., the Campus Crusade for Christ and the Fellowship of Christian Athletes).

Moving toward a more collaborative approach to providing campus religious programs and services was viewed as an important trend; however, as Butler (1989) pointed out, "major problems in level of funding, program direction and accountability, quality of professional training and placement, and the nature of relationships exist in practically every state" (p. 11). Through all of this, various faiths have sought to maintain their unique characteristics and traditions. Today, several ecumenical organizations exist to increase cooperation among religious groups on campus including the National Campus Ministries Association, National Association of College and University Chaplains, and Campus Ministry Women.

Today, religious groups on campus play an important role in the spiritual development of college students; they also provide safe havens for discussing personal issues and problems. Many campus clergy members provide personal and spiritual counseling. In addition, involvement with religiously affiliated student organizations or clubs can provide an avenue for students to develop leadership and interpersonal skills. Religious programs and services often provide significant out-of-classroom developmental opportunities for college students.

## References, Readings, and Resources

Butler, J. (1989). An overview of religion on campus. In J. Butler (ed.). Religion on campus. *New Directions for Student Services,* No. 46. San Francisco: Jossey-Bass.

Barker, V. L., & Voorhis, R. V. (1994). *An index for higher education programs and resources.* Charlotte, NC: United Ministries in Higher Education.

United Ministries in Education (1996). *Directory of ministries in higher education.* Charlotte, NC: Author.

The Resource Center (serving higher education campus ministries). Council for Higher Education Ministries/United Ministries in Higher Education. 7407 Steele Creek Road, Charlotte, NC 28217. (704) 588-2182. <linda_freeman@cunet.org>

# RELIGIOUS PROGRAMS
## CAS STANDARDS and GUIDELINES

## Part 1. MISSION

The institution and its religious programs must develop, record, disseminate, implement and regularly review its mission and goals. Mission statements must be consistent with the mission and goals of the institution and with the standards in this document.

> A private or church-related institution may state its preference for a particular faith or church and may directly use its own resources for this purpose.

Public institutions must offer or provide access to programs that enable interested students to pursue full spiritual growth and development, and foster a campus atmosphere in which interested members of the college community may freely express their religion and faith.

> In this document "religion" is defined by function rather than substance. The courts have held that the First Amendment provides protection to religious believers and non-believers, and that the state shall be neutral in its relations with persons who profess a belief or disbelief in any religion. Everson v. Board of Education, 330 US 1 (1977).

> A clear distinction should be made between two separate but related functions of an educational institution: providing for the academic study of religions, and for programs that promote the spiritual and moral development of its students.

> A distinction should also be made between accommodation and promotion of religions and faiths by public institutions. The court has mandated an even-handed accommodation of religious beliefs, whereas it has prohibited the promotion of a particular religious belief. Illinois ex rel. McCollum v. Board of Education, 333 US 203, S. Ct.; Zorach v. Causon, 343 US 306 (1952).

According to the courts, any public institution's program must meet the following conditions to avoid violating the "establishment" clause of the US Constitution:

- It must have a secular purpose.
- Its principal or primary effect must be one that neither advances nor inhibits religion.

It must not foster an excessive entanglement of the public institution with religion. Lemon v. Kurtzman, 403 US 602, 91 SC 2105, 29 L. Ed. 2d 745 (1071); Widmar v. Vincent, 454 US 263, Tol Ed. 2d 440, 102 S. Ct. 2 (1981).

Public institutions are prohibited from giving any preferential treatment to a particular religion or faith, to all religions or faiths, or to prefer one religion or faith over another. School District of Abington Township v. Schernpp, 374 US 203, (1963). The First Amendment mandates neutrality among religions, and between religion and non-religion. Epperson v. Arkansas, 393 US 97, (1968). The Constitution forbids the preference of a religious doctrine and the prohibition of a theory antagonistic to an individual dogma. Epperson v. Arkansas, 393 US 97, (1968). Public institutions should make provisions for religious programs indirectly, that is, through cooperation with off-campus agencies which provide religious services and programs.

> The goals of any organized religious program or service should include:
> - assisting interested students to achieve the religious development they seek through:
> - the articulation of a personal philosophy of life;
> - the acquisition of skills and knowledge needed to address issues of values, ethics, and morality in life;
> - an understanding of the interaction of faith, intellectual inquiry, and social responsibility as bases for finding and affirming meaning and satisfaction in life;
> - providing a forum for dialogue between and among representatives of the religious and the secular; and
> - providing interested members of the campus community with reasonable opportunity to express their faith(s).

## Part 2. PROGRAM

The formal education of students is purposeful, holistic, and consists of the curriculum and the co-curriculum.

Religious programs must be (a) intentional, (b) coherent, (c) based on theories and knowledge of learning and human development, (d) reflective of developmental and demographic profiles of the student population, and (e) responsive to special needs of individuals.

Religious programs and services must promote learning and development in students by encouraging outcomes such as intellectual growth, ability to communicate effectively, realistic self-appraisal, enhanced self-esteem, clarification of values, appropriate career choices, leadership development, physical fitness, meaningful interpersonal relations, ability to work independently and collaboratively, social responsibility, satisfying and productive lifestyles, appreciation of aesthetic and cultural diversity, and achievement of personal goals.

Religious programs and services will vary depending on the requirements and beliefs of specific denominations and faiths, as well as the needs and traditions of the particular institution.

To the extent either required or prohibited by constitutional, statutory, or regulatory provisions, institutions must provide reasonable opportunities for students to:

- question, explore, understand, affiliate with or avoid, and express or reject various religious faiths;
- seek individual counseling and/or group associations for the examination and application of spiritual values and beliefs;
- worship communally; and
- pray and meditate.

In public institutions, staff members coordinate programs, while adjunct personnel associated with there religious groups provide the direct ministry.

In church-related and private colleges, religious ministry and religious programs may be provided directly by staff members of the institution.

The types of religious programs and activities that may be offered are:

- religious studies;
- opportunities for religious nurturance;
- service opportunities;
- where appropriate by law or regulation, opportunity to propagate specific faiths;
- advocacy for particular ethical or moral policies in public life; and
- opportunities to relate religious beliefs to academic and professional programs through a variety of informational and experiential activities.

In addition, institutions may provide counseling services to promote spiritual or religious growth. Cocurricular programs (e.g., lectures, discussions, or service projects) which are designed to help students understand their faiths and the faiths of others may also be offered.

## Part 3. LEADERSHIP

Effective and ethical leadership is essential to the success of all organizations. Institutions must appoint, position and empower leaders within the administrative structure to accomplish stated missions. Leaders at various levels must be selected on the basis of formal education and training, relevant work experience, personal attributes, and other professional credentials. Institutions must determine expectations of accountability for leaders and fairly assess their performance.

Leaders of religious programs must exercise authority over resources for which they are responsible to achieve their respective missions. Leaders must articulate a vision for their organization; set goals and objectives; prescribe and practice ethical behavior; recruit, select, supervise, and develop others in the organization; manage, plan, budget, and evaluate; communicate effectively; and marshal cooperative action from colleagues, employees, other institutional constituencies, and persons outside the organization. Religious program leaders must address individual, organizational, or environmental conditions that inhibit goal achievement. Leaders must improve programs and services continuously in response to changing needs of students and institutional priorities.

## Part 4. ORGANIZATION and MANAGEMENT

Religious programs must be structured purposefully and managed effectively to achieve stated goals. Evidence of appropriate structure must include current and accessible policies and procedures, written performance expectations for all employees, functional work flow graphics or organizational charts, and service delivery expectations. Evidence of effective management must include clear sources and channels of authority, effective communication practices, decision-making and conflict resolution procedures, responsiveness to changing conditions, accountability systems, and recognition and reward processes.

Religious programs must provide channels within the organization for regular review of administrative policies and procedures.

The organization and administration of any campus religious program must be designed to be responsive to the needs of faculty and staff members as well as students in the institution served.

The religious program must have established written policies and procedures regarding the professional responsibilities, selection, and evaluation of staff members.

Program activities, policies, and procedures should be scrutinized regularly in light of the growing body of constitutional law in the area of religion and higher education.

## Part 5. HUMAN RESOURCES

The religious program must be staffed adequately by individuals qualified to accomplish its mission and goals. Programs and services must establish procedures for staff selection, training, and evaluation; set expectations for supervision; and provide appropriate professional development opportunities.

Professional staff members must hold an earned graduate degree in a field relevant to the position description or must possess an appropriate combination of education and experience.

Degree or credential seeking interns or others in training must be qualified by enrollment in an appropriate field of study and relevant experience. These individuals must be trained and supervised adequately by professional staff members.

Student employees and volunteers must be carefully selected, trained, supervised, and evaluated. When their knowledge and skills are not adequate for particular situations, they must refer students or others in need of assistance to qualified professional staff.

The religious program must have secretarial and technical staff adequate to accomplish its mission. Such staff must be technologically proficient and qualified to perform activities including reception duties, office equipment operation, records maintenance, and mail handling.

Appropriate salary levels and fringe benefits for all staff members must be commensurate with those for comparable positions within the institution, in similar institutions, and in the relevant geographic area.

Religious programs must intentionally employ a diverse staff to reflect the diversity of the institution's student population to ensure the existence of readily identifiable role models for students and to enrich the campus community.

Affirmative action must occur in hiring and promotion practices to ensure diverse staffing profiles as required by institutional policies and local, state/provincial, and federal law.

At public institutions, the title "director or "coordinator" of religious programs is more appropriate because of the predominantly educational and liaison functions of the position.

At public institutions, religious programs may be coordinated by a professional person and/or a committee. Adjunct professional or volunteer persons named (and paid) by the religious groups represented on the campus may carry out their respective religious activities.

Preferred titles for the chief coordinator at private institutions are "chaplain," "campus minister," or "director of religious life."

At private institutions, campus religious programs are typically coordinated by a professional person. Additional staff members may be employed by the institution. Religious groups may also provide additional staff for the institution. Church related institutions should permit on campus programs of religions other than those espoused by the institution.

Any director or coordinator of religious programs should have an appropriate combination of graduate coursework, formal training, and experience. The director or coordinator of religious programs may have a doctoral graduate theological degree, such as a Th.D. or Ph.D., and course work in theology, Bible, church history, religion in higher education, and pastoral counseling.

Any director or coordinator should have:
• an understanding of and a commitment to spiritual and religious development as a part of a student's human growth, and
• the ability to treat fairly all varieties of campus religious experience and personal faith.

Depending upon the legal constraints of the institution, the responsibilities of the director or coordinator for religious programs may include:
• the development and communication of policies relating to religious programs which are educationally sound and legally acceptable;
• the development of procedures whereby students may organize for religious or moral purposes and participate in programs and activities aimed at their spiritual and religious growth;

• the provision of access to campus facilities for those responsible for religious programs; and the provision of opportunities for counseling in relation to students' religious needs.

On a campus that is not church-related, any employee responsible for coordinating the religious program should be paid by the institution. This official should be unbiased and neutral in his/her relationships to all agencies participating in the program.

Professional staff members should have a graduate theological degree such as a Th.D., a Ph.D., or a Master of Divinity or its equivalent and coursework in theology, church history, religion in higher education, and pastoral counseling.

Affiliation with appropriate professional organizations is encouraged.

Adjunct staff members should possess qualifications consistent with the particular religious body they represent and appropriate for a higher education setting.

## Part 6. FINANCIAL RESOURCES

The religious program must have adequate funding to accomplish its mission and goals. Priorities, whether set periodically or as a result of extraordinary conditions, must be determined within the context of the stated mission, goals, and resources.

The institution must provide funds for all personnel, facilities, and programs for which it assumes direct responsibility.

At a minimum the institution should provide sufficient funding for any institutional staff member(s) and the operational costs related to its religious programs. If this assignment accounts for only a part of an individual staff member's work-load, the budget should clearly indicate the portion that is available for religious programs.

Funding for personnel and programs of adjunct agencies (i.e., not directly provided by the institution) must be assumed by the sponsors of the adjunct agency.

## Part 7. FACILITIES, TECHNOLOGY, and EQUIPMENT

Each program and service must have adequate, suitably located facilities, technology, and equipment to support its mission and goals. Facilities, technology, and equipment must be in compliance with relevant federal, state/provincial, and local requirements to provide for access, health, and safety.

Opportunity must be provided for all student religious groups to utilize campus facilities on the same basis as other student organizations.

In public institutions, whenever space is made permanently and/or exclusively available for specific religious personnel of adjunct agencies, arrangements should be made whereby the institution is appropriately reimbursed for expenses.

Public institutions should provide fair and equitable arrangements and facilities for specific religious groups' programming.

Private institutions may provide facilities specifically designed to suit the purpose of a preferred religious group.

Wherever possible, but especially in residential units, suitable areas for individual meditation and small group spiritual interaction are desirable.

## Part 8. LEGAL RESPONSIBILITIES

Religious program staff members must be knowledgeable about and responsive to law and regulations that relate to their respective program or service. Sources for legal obligations and limitations include constitutional, statutory, regulatory, and case law; mandatory laws and orders emanating from federal, state, provincial and local governments; and the institution through its policies.

Staff members must use reasonable and informed practices to limit the liability exposure of the institution, its officers, employees, and agents. Staff members must be informed about institutional policies regarding personal liability and related insurance coverage options.

The institution must provide access to legal advice for religious program staff members as needed to carry out assigned responsibilities.

The institution must inform staff and students, in a timely and systematic fashion, about extraordinary or changing legal obligations and potential liabilities.

## Part 9. EQUAL OPPORTUNITY, ACCESS, and AFFIRMATIVE ACTION

Religious program staff members must ensure that services and programs are provided on a fair and equitable basis. The religious program must be accessible. Hours of operation must be responsive to the needs of all students. The religious program must adhere to the spirit and intent of equal opportunity laws.

Religious programs and services must not be discriminatory on the basis of age, color, disability, gender, national origin, race, religious creed, sexual orientation, and/or veteran status. Exceptions are appropriate only where provided by relevant law and institutional policy.

Consistent with their mission and goals, the religious program must take affirmative action to remedy significant imbalances in student participation and staffing patterns.

## Part 10. CAMPUS and COMMUNITY RELATIONS

The religious program must establish, maintain, and promote effective relations with relevant campus offices and external agencies.

Because religion and spirituality may be concerns of many academic disciplines and may have an important impact on some aspects of student development activity, staff assigned to religious programs should consult with and coordinate their programs with interested colleagues.

The director/coordinator or chaplain may interact will faculty and staff formally through advisory councils or through informal contacts.

Continuing attention should be given to developing and improving relationships with both on-campus and off campus publics. Specific programs and action projects may arise from many sources (e.g., academic departments, on-campus groups such as residence halls and college students unions, and off-campus organizations, whether local, regional, and/or national).

Institutional staff should meet with adjunct personnel from religious groups on a periodic basis.

## Part 11. DIVERSITY

Within the context of each institution's unique mission, multi-dimensional diversity enriches the community and enhances the collegiate experience for all; therefore, religious programs and services must nurture environments where similarities and differences among people are recognized and honored.

The religious program must promote cultural educational experiences that are characterized by open and continuous communication, that deepen understanding of one's own culture and heritage, and that respect and educate about similarities, differences and histories of cultures.

Religious programs and services must address the characteristics and needs of a diverse population when establishing and implementing policies and procedures.

## Part 12. ETHICS

All persons involved in the delivery of religious programs and services must adhere to the highest principles of ethical behavior. The religious programs must develop or adopt and implement statements of ethical practice addressing the issues unique to each program and service. The religious program must publish these statements and insure their periodic review by all concerned.

Religious program staff members must ensure that confidentiality is maintained with respect to all communications and records considered confidential unless exempted by law. Information disclosed in individual counseling sessions must remain confidential, unless written permission to divulge the information is given by the student. However, all staff members must disclose to appropriate authorities information judged to be of an emergency nature, especially when the safety of the individual or others is involved. Information contained in students' educational records must not be disclosed to non-institutional third parties without appropriate consent, unless classified as "Directory" information or when the information is subpoenaed by law. Programs and services must apply a similar dedication to privacy and confidentiality to research data concerning individuals. All staff members must be aware of and comply with the provisions contained in the institution's human subjects research policy and in other relevant institutional policies addressing ethical practices.

Staff members must recognize and avoid personal conflict of interest or appearance thereof in their transactions with students and others. Staff members must strive to insure the fair, objective, and impartial treatment of all persons with whom they deal.

When handling institutional funds, religious program staff members must ensure that such funds are managed in accordance with established and responsible accounting procedures.

Staff members must not participate in any form of harassment that demeans persons or creates an intimidating, hostile, or offensive campus environment.

Staff members must perform their duties within the limits of their training, expertise, and competence. When these limits are exceeded, individuals in need of further assistance must be referred to persons possessing appropriate qualifications.

Staff members must use suitable means to confront and otherwise hold accountable other staff members who exhibit unethical behavior.

Staff members must maintain the highest principles of ethical behavior in the use of technology.

The Constitutional rights of students and faculty and staff members of all religious beliefs must be respected.

Public institutions must avoid any policies or actions which favor one particular faith over another.

Private institutions which sponsor or require particular religious activities must clearly state so in their pre-admission literature, thus permitting a potential student to exercise free choice in this regard before admission. Staff members must work to provide reasonable access for all groups and points-of-view to any public forums sponsored by the institution.

Membership requirements for on-campus religious groups must be consistent with their stated purposes. No group can be required to participate in any extraor-

dinary institutional arrangement or program that would violate a principle or tenet of their faith.

All religious groups must be accorded the same rights and privileges and be held accountable in the same manner as any other campus organization.

Staff members must attempt to protect students, through policy and practice, from undue influence or harassment from persons advocating particular religious positions or activities.

As the institution carries out its academic program, fair and reasonable consideration should be given to the need of campus members to participate in the basic activities of their faiths. Institutional policies and practices should be reviewed regularly so as to avoid undue interference with the free exercise of religion.

Accommodation may be made in institutional class schedules so that students and staff from religious minorities may carry out the essential practices of their religion. Administrators should proceed with caution in such matters, however, due to the inevitable conflict of competing religious practices within any campus community.

## Part 13. ASSESSMENT and EVALUATION

The religious program must regularly conduct systematic qualitative and quantitative evaluations of its quality to determine whether and to what degree its stated mission and goals are being met. Although methods of assessment vary, religious programs and services must employ a sufficient range of measures to insure objectivity and comprehensiveness. Data collected must include responses from students and other affected constituencies. Results of these evaluations must be used in revising and improving the religious program and in recognizing staff performance.

Each institution should require evaluation of its religious program to determine the achievement of goals, the public being reached and its overall effectiveness.

This evaluation may be made in concert with the periodic examination of the diverse needs and interests of students and other members of the campus community.

In the case of church-related institutions, policies and practices should be assessed to ensure consistency with theological and moral standards of sponsoring bodies.

Data should be collected from officers and advisors of campus religious organizations to determine the effectiveness of policies affecting religious activity.

# WOMEN STUDENT PROGRAMS and SERVICES
## CAS Standards Contextual Statement

With the appointment of the first Dean of Women, Alice Freeman Palmer, at the University of Chicago in 1892, female college students began to receive more systematic institutional attention. In comparison to their male counterparts, however, women were not as highly valued nor did deans of women have much authority. Consequently, it was no surprise when the women deans caucused soon after their positions came into being and the National Association for Deans of Women (NADW) was established. This organization actually preceded the establishment of its counterpart for deans of men, the National Association for Deans of Men (NADM) by two years, in 1916. Even with the existence of these professional associations, it took half a century for institution and association politics to evolve to a point where equality and integration of men and women in the academic community became a reality.

The American College Personnel Association (ACPA), established in 1924, was from the outset open to both men and women. Although it initially joined forces with NADW under the auspices of the National Education Association (NEA), immediately following WW2, ACPA chose to become Division I of the American Personnel and Guidance Association (APGA), while NADW remained autonomous. NADM became the National Association of Student Personnel Administrators (NASPA), which women joined in large numbers after they were accepted for membership. NADW evolved into the National Association for Women in Education (NAWE) and, although open to male members, it has remained an overwhelmingly female association committed to the advancement of both women students and professionals. Its members and leaders have been highly involved in the development of programs and services for women students during the past two decades.

Women students currently represent over 50 percent of all college and university students and an increasing number of women are returning to campus after years in the workforce or at home raising families. With the passage of Title IX of the Education Amendments of 1972, which prohibits discrimination on the basis of gender, women programs and services were established for women to better assure institutional access by removing barriers that had developed over the years. These programs also provide support for women students who need help in achieving their personal and educational goals, many of which are unclear after a hiatus of several years from higher education.

Women student programs and services typically include personal and career counseling, developmental workshops and classes, small weekly programs, and large campus events. These support services provide both individual and comprehensive campus-wide advocacy for women, often centering on empowerment, violence, and safety issues. Programs also focus on political and personal issues that assist women students in decision-making in accordance with their values and beliefs. Provision of these support activities is designed to help women students achieve success in their chosen careers and better understand the changing roles of women in society.

Because women student programs and services are an essential and integral part of any comprehensive institution of higher learning, there is a continuing need for creating and maintaining well-managed and adequately financed programs designed to meet the special educational and developmental needs of women students. The CAS Standards and Guidelines for Women Student Programs and Services have been created to enhance this important educational need.

## References, Readings, and Resources

Aburdene, P., & Naisbitt, J., (1992). *Megatrends for women.* New York: Villard Books.

Astin, H. S., & Leland, C.(1991). *Women of influence, women of vision: A cross-generational study of leaders and social change.* San Francisco: Jossey-Bass.

Pearson, C. S., Shavlik, D. L. & Touchton, J. G. (1989). *Educating the majority: Women challenge tradition in higher education.* New York: American Council on Education, Macmillan.

Sagaria, M. A., (Ed.). (1989). *Empowering women: Leadership development strategies on campus.* New Directions for Student Services, No. 44. San Francisco: Jossey-Bass.

*About Women On Campus,* published quarterly by the National Association for Women in Education.

*Initiatives.* Published quarterly by the National Association for Women in Education (NAWE).

National Association for Women in Education (NAWE). Suite 210, 1325 Eighteenth St., NW, Washington, DC 20036-6511. (202) 659-9330; <nawe@clark.net>

# WOMEN STUDENT PROGRAMS AND SERVICES
## CAS STANDARDS and GUIDELINES

## Part 1.  MISSION

The institution's women student programs and services must develop, record, disseminate, implement and regularly review its mission and goals. Mission statements must be consistent with the mission and goals of the institution and with the standards in this document.

The mission of women student programs and services is to promote unrestricted access and full involvement of women students in all aspects of the college or university experience. Women student programs and services must consider and respond to the diverse needs of women students and must help these students benefit from the institution's total educational process.

To accomplish this mission, the goals of women student programs and services must be to:

- **assist women in achieving full potential in education, personal lives and work through personal empowerment, expansion of opportunities, and professional development;**

- **provide programs, services and facilities to meet educational, personal, physical, and safety needs of women students;**

- **ensure that the institution provides women students equal access to educational opportunities, services, and facilities;**

- **encourage the development of self-awareness, self esteem, and self-confidence of women students and promote leadership opportunities for them;**

- **recognize and plan for diversity among the women student population, e.g., ethnicity, race, religion, disability, sexual orientation, age, and socioeconomic status;**

- **act as an advocate for women students;**

- **serve as a catalyst for change to enhance the education of women on campus; and**

- **offer or identify appropriate mentors and role models for women students.**

Women students in any institution of higher education arc entitled to the full benefits of the curricular and co-curricular programs and services offered. Each woman student is entitled to fair and reasonable access to institutional resources and full administrative support.

Women student services and programs should address:

- needs of women students that are special in such areas as health services, child care, safety, and protection from sexual harassment;

- developmental opportunities, such as tutoring for reentry women students, assessment of prior experience, social programs, and support groups for those experiencing major life transitions;

- provision of demographic data to the campus community such as: head of household status, dependents, marital status, age, employment status, and financial aid;

- dissemination of information to the campus community regarding societal trends and conditions that affect socialization patterns, cultural expectations, stereotypic behaviors, various lifestyle characteristics, "chilly climate," institutional sexism, and sexual harassment; and

- provision of adequate financial aid.

To respond to the woman student and her special needs, many colleges and universities create a separate women 's center or women students' area within the institution or on campus. When no specific office is identified for women students, then all areas of the institution should be evaluated to ensure that women students have equal access to quality programs and services.

## Part 2. PROGRAM

The formal education of students is purposeful, holistic, and consists of the curriculum and the co-curriculum.

Women student programs and services must be (a) intentional, (b) coherent, (c) based on theories and knowledge of learning and human development, (d) reflective of developmental and demographic profiles of the student population, and (e) responsive to special needs of individuals.

Women student programs and services must promote learning and development in students by encouraging outcomes such as intellectual growth, ability to communicate effectively, realistic self-appraisal, enhanced self-esteem, clarification of values, appropriate career choices, leadership development, physical fitness, meaningful interpersonal relations, ability to work independently and collaboratively, social responsibility, satisfying and productive lifestyles, appreciation of aesthetic and cultural diversity, and achievement of personal goals.

Women student programs and services must assist students in overcoming specific personal, physical, or educational problems or skill deficiencies.

Women student programs and services must identify environmental conditions that may negatively influence welfare and propose interventions that may neutralize such conditions.

The educational experience of students consists of both academic efforts in the classroom and developmental opportunities through student services and development programs. Institutions must define the relative importance of these processes.

Women student programs and services staff must address the needs of all undergraduate and graduate women students regardless of ethnicity, race, religion, disability, sexual orientation, age, socioeconomic status, degree and enrollment status.

Women student programs and services must include the following elements:

- **promotion of an institutional commitment for understanding and addressing the concerns of women students on campus;**
- **services to women students to assure equitable access to and involvement in all educational programs;**

  Women student programs and services should address the provision of:

  - adequate, accessible, affordable, and flexible-time child care;
  - flexible scheduling of classes, academic support, and extra-curricular activities;
  - psychological counseling and career services both for groups and individuals that are sensitive to special needs of women students; and
  - referral for individual women students who need expertise on a specific issue.

- **creation and nurturance of a campus environment which dominates barriers, diminishes prejudice and bigotry, and extends a hospitable climate to all women students;**

  Awareness of cultural differences and prejudices or discrimination against racial or ethnic groups or other minority women students should be identified and addressed.

  Women student programs and services should monitor campus-based publications and publicity and encourage strategies to increase the visibility of women students on campus, with particular attention to how publications affect the recruitment and retention of women students.

- **research and assessment of the status of women students with regard to educational programs and services, financial aid and awards such as fellowships and athletic scholarships, and lack of enrollment or over enrollment of women in particular disciplines;**
- **advocacy for assessment of the campus environment for the presence of gender bias in the areas of employment, educational opportunities, classroom climate, and other issues facing women students;**
- **monitoring of the campus climate for women students in areas of sexual harassment and sexual**

violence, and creating systematic procedures to institutionalize appropriate policies, education, and programs to work toward the elimination of violence against women;

- **publicizing of services, events, and issues of concern to women students on campus;**
- **sponsorship of events which address women students' needs and issues, and maintenance of contact with the campus and community to increase awareness of the status of women students on campus;**

  Women student programs and services should seek to enhance awareness of the roles of women students in the multiple aspects of campus life, appreciating the positive and seeking to improve upon the negative.

- **encouragement of support systems and communication networks for women students on campus;**

  Women student programs and services should provide opportunities for women on campus to:

  - participate in campus activities which provide an opportunity for women students to meet appropriate role models;
  - publicize services, events, and issues of concern to women students on campus;
  - sponsor events which address women's needs and issues;
  - maintain contact with the community to enrich the flow of communication to and from the campus; and
  - organize activities around specific issues and needs.

- **development of structures which encourage liaisons between women's organizations in the state and nation and the campus based women student programs and services, to focus campus attention on emerging critical issues outside the institution;**
- **identification of role models by the sharing and publicizing of the accomplishments of women faculty, staff, and students;**

  Women student programs and services should create liaisons with campus offices and organizations which have an impact on women.

- **education of women students and the campus community at large when institutional decisions affect or have the potential to affect the status and/or achievement of women students;**

  Women student programs and services should Particularly focus attention on those institutional policies which result in an inequitable impact on women as students or employees, or on a particular subgroup of women students.

- **promotion of new scholarship and research on women through a women studies program if available or through traditional departments if no program exists; and**

- education of women students through understanding and practical experiences to use campus organizational systems, political influences, and other sources of power effectively to contribute productively to the construction and maintenance of a campus climate that is responsive to their needs.

## Part 3. LEADERSHIP

Effective and ethical leadership is essential to the success of all organizations. Institutions must appoint, position and empower leaders within the administrative structure to accomplish stated missions. Leaders at various levels must be selected on the basis of formal education and training, relevant work experience, personal attributes, and other professional credentials. Institutions must determine expectations of accountability for leaders and fairly assess their performance.

Leaders of women student programs and services must exercise authority over resources for which they are responsible to achieve their respective missions. Leaders must articulate a vision for their organization; set goals and objectives; prescribe and practice ethical behavior; recruit, select, supervise, and develop others in the organization; manage, plan, budget, and evaluate; communicate effectively; and marshal cooperative action from colleagues, employees, other institutional constituencies, and persons outside the organization. Leaders must address individual, organizational, or environmental conditions that inhibit goal achievement. Leaders must improve programs and services continuously in response to changing needs of students and institutional priorities.

## Part 4. ORGANIZATION and MANAGEMENT

Women student programs and services must be structured purposefully and managed effectively to achieve stated goals. Evidence of appropriate structure must include current and accessible policies and procedures, written performance expectations for all employees, functional work flow graphics or organizational charts, and service delivery expectations. Evidence of effective management must include clear sources and channels of authority, effective communication practices, decision-making and conflict resolution procedures, responsiveness to changing conditions, accountability systems, and recognition and reward processes.

Programs and services must provide channels within the organization for regular review of administrative policies and procedures.

Women student programs and services should play a principal role in implementing institutional programs developed in response to the assessed needs of women students. Access to the policy makers of the institution should be readily avail-

able. The administrative organization of women student programs and services should be governed by the size, nature, and mission of the institution. Women student programs and services may function as autonomous units or may be housed as components of other units on campus. In either instance, women student programs and services should be organized and administered in a manner that permits the stated mission to be fulfilled.

Many models for organizing women student programs and services exist in higher education. Individual units should be afforded the opportunity to organize in a manner that is efficient and best promotes equity concerns on campus. Emphasis should be placed on achieving an organizational placement so that activities of women student programs and services are not limited to a specific group of women students (e.g., solely undergraduate women) or specific service (e.g., solely counseling services).

## Part 5. HUMAN RESOURCES

Women student programs and services must be staffed adequately by individuals qualified to accomplish its mission and goals. Programs and services must establish procedures for staff selection, training, and evaluation; set expectations for supervision; and provide appropriate professional development opportunities.

Professional staff members must hold an earned graduate degree in a field relevant to the position description or must possess an appropriate combination of education and experience.

Degree or credential seeking interns or others in training must be qualified by enrollment in an appropriate field of study and relevant experience. These individuals must be trained and supervised adequately by professional staff members.

Student employees and volunteers must be carefully selected, trained, supervised, and evaluated. When their knowledge and skills are not adequate for particular situations, they must refer students or others in need of assistance to qualified professional staff

Each women student programs and services organizational unit must have secretarial and technical staff adequate to accomplish its mission. Such staff must be technologically proficient and qualified to perform activities including reception duties, office equipment operation, records maintenance, and mail handling.

Appropriate salary levels and fringe benefits for all staff members must be commensurate with those for comparable positions within the institution, in similar institutions, and in the relevant geographic area.

Women student programs and services must intentionally employ a diverse staff to reflect the diversity of the institution's student population, to ensure the existence of readily identifiable role models for students and to enrich the campus community,

Affirmative action must occur in hiring and promotion practices to ensure diverse staffing profiles as required by institutional policies and local, state/provincial, and federal law.

> Leadership of the program by persons with the credentials and ability to forge gender equity on campus is important to promoting the integrity of the unit. Professionals working within the program should represent the diversity of women students on the campus. It is important that the leadership position be evaluated and scaled within the administration of the institution on a level commensurate with its institution-wide mission.

> The professional staff should possess the academic preparation, experience, abilities, professional interests, and competencies essential for the efficient operation of the office as charged, as well as the ability to identify additional areas of concern about the female student population. Specific coursework in organizational development, counseling (theory and practice), group dynamics, leadership development, human development, and research and evaluation may be desirable. It is important that the leadership have knowledge of and preferably experience with gender issues and their impact on development. Coursework in and/or a relationship with women studies courses and/or a program is desirable.

> Professional staff should: (a) develop and implement programs and services; (b) conduct assessment, research, and evaluation; (c) advocate for the improvement of the quality of life for women as students; and (d) perform developmental educational functions.

> Technical and support staff should be sufficient to per form office and administrative functions, including reception, information-giving, problem identification, and referral. In the selection and training of technical and support staff members, special emphasis should be placed on skills in the areas of public relations, information dissemination, problem identification, and referral. A thorough knowledge of the institution and its various offices is important.

> Where student staff members are employed, they should be provided with clear and precise job descriptions, preservice training which including an understanding of gender issues, and adequate supervision.

> Women working within women student programs and services should be afforded the same professional opportunities and institutional commitment to advancement as other employees of the institution. The use of appropriate professional support staff and professional consultant staff is to be encouraged. The use of paid and supervised graduate and undergraduate student interns may be encouraged. Paraprofessionals and volunteers should be trained in the mission of the program and should be assigned duties commensurate with their abilities. Supervision by the professional staff is essential to their role.

> Staff development is an essential activity if staff members are to remain current and effective in an educational setting. Additional credit courses, seminars, professional conferences, and access to published research and opinion and relevant other media are examples of staff development activities.

> Preprofessional, practicum, or intern student staff members may come from academic programs in a variety of disciplines.

# Part 6. FINANCIAL RESOURCES

Each program and service must have adequate funding to accomplish its mission and goals. Priorities, whether set periodically or as a result of extraordinary conditions, must be determined within the context of the stated mission, goals, and resources.

> Funding for women student programs and services may come from a composite of institutional funds, grant money, student government funds, fees for services, and government contracts. It is important that permanent institutional funding be allocated for the operation of women student programs and services.

# Part 7. FACILITIES, TECHNOLOGY, and EQUIPMENT

Women student programs and services must have adequate, suitably located facilities and equipment to support its mission and goals. Facilities, technology, and equipment must be in compliance with relevant federal, state, provincial, and local requirements to provide for access, health and safety.

Facilities must be located in an area determined to be easily accessible by women students.

> The location of facilities should give special accommodation to safety factors and the diversity of women students as such relates to scheduling, availability, and use of facilities.

# Part 8. LEGAL RESPONSIBILITIES

Women student programs staff members must be knowledgeable about and responsive to law and regulations that relate to their respective program or service. Sources for legal obligations and limitations include constitutional, statutory, regulatory, and case law; mandatory laws and orders emanating from federal, state, provincial and local governments; and the institution through its policies.

Staff members must use reasonable and informed practices to limit the liability exposure of the institution, its officers, employees, and agents. Staff members must be informed about institutional policies regarding personal liability and related insurance coverage options.

The institution must provide access to legal advice for women student program staff members as needed to carry out assigned responsibilities.

The institution must inform women student program staff and students, in a timely and systematic fashion, about extraordinary or changing legal obligations and potential liabilities.

> Women student programs and services should play a major role in seeing that the institution, as a whole, is knowledgeable about and in compliance with legal requirements of Title IX of The Education Amendments of 1972.

## Part 9. EQUAL OPPORTUNITY, ACCESS, and AFFIRMATIVE ACTION

Women student programs and services staff members must ensure that services and programs are provided on a fair and equitable basis. Each program and service must be accessible. Hours of operation must be responsive to the needs of all students. Each program and service must adhere to the spirit and intent of equal opportunity laws.

Women student programs and services must not be discriminatory on the basis of age, color, disability, gender, national origin, race, religious creed, sexual orientation, and/or veteran status. Exceptions are appropriate only where provided by relevant law and institutional policy.

Consistent with their mission and goals, women student programs must take affirmative action to remedy significant imbalances in student participation and staffing patterns.

## Part 10. CAMPUS and COMMUNITY RELATIONS

Women student programs and services must establish, maintain, and promote effective relations with relevant campus offices and external agencies.

Women student programs and services should maintain good working relationships with such agencies as counseling, financial aid, health services, recreational sports and athletics, residential life, and campus security. Women student programs and services should maintain a high degree of visibility with academic units through direct promotion and delivery of services, through involvement with co-curricular programs, and through staff efforts to increase understanding of the needs of women students.

Program staff should be an integral part of appropriate campus networks in order to effectively participate in the establishment of institution-wide policy and practices, and to effectively collaborate with other staff and faculty in providing services. In addition, women student programs and services should provide effective liaisons between the community and the institution to assist each group in articulation of common concerns and in using each other as resources.

## Part 11. DIVERSITY

Within the context of the institution's unique mission, multi-dimensional diversity enriches the community and enhances the collegiate experience for all; therefore, women student programs and services must nurture environments where similarities and differences among people are recognized and honored.

Women student programs and services must promote cultural educational experiences that are characterized by open and continuous communication, that deepen understanding of one's own culture and heritage, and

that respect and educate about similarities, differences and histories of cultures.

Women student programs must address the characteristics and needs of a diverse population when establishing and implementing policies and procedures.

## Part 12. ETHICS

All persons involved in the delivery of women student programs and services must adhere to the highest principles of ethical behavior. Women student programs and services must develop or adopt and implement statements of ethical practice addressing the issues unique to each program and service. Women student programs must publish these statements and insure their periodic review by all concerned.

Staff members must ensure that confidentiality is maintained with respect to all communications and records considered confidential unless exempted by law.

Information disclosed in individual counseling sessions must remain confidential, unless written permission to divulge the information is given by the student. However, all staff members must disclose to appropriate authorities information judged to be of an emergency nature, especially when the safety of the individual or others is involved. Information contained in students' educational records must not be disclosed to non-institutional third parties without appropriate consent, unless classified as "Directory" information or when the information is subpoenaed by law. Programs and services must apply a similar dedication to privacy and confidentiality to research data concerning individuals. All staff members must be aware of and comply with the provisions contained in the institution's human subjects research policy and in other relevant institutional policies addressing ethical practices.

Women student program staff members must recognize and avoid personal conflict of interest or appearance thereof in their transactions with students and others. Staff members must strive to insure the fair, objective, and impartial treatment of all persons with whom they deal.

When handling institutional funds, all staff members must ensure that such funds are managed in accordance with established and responsible accounting procedures.

Women student program staff members must not participate in any form of harassment that demeans persons or creates an intimidating, hostile, or offensive campus environment.

Staff members must perform their duties within the limits of their training, expertise, and competence. When these limits are exceeded, individuals in need of further assistance must be referred to persons possessing appropriate qualifications.

Staff members must use suitable means to confront and otherwise hold accountable other staff members who exhibit unethical behavior.

Staff members must maintain the highest principles of ethical behavior in the use of technology.

# Part 13. ASSESSMENT and EVALUATION

Women student programs and services must regularly conduct systematic qualitative and quantitative evaluations of program quality to determine whether and to what degree the stated mission and goals are being met. Although methods of assessment vary, programs and services must employ a sufficient range of measures to insure objectivity and comprehensiveness. Data collected must include responses from students and other affected constituencies. Results of these evaluations must be used in revising and improving programs and services and in recognizing staff performance.

A comprehensive evaluation of the ongoing program should be carried out in accordance with the general practice of program review for other units of the institution. To assist staff in planning and program formation, an ongoing evaluation process of women student programs and services should be established.

# THE ROLE of PROFESSIONAL STUDENT AFFAIRS PREPARATION
## CAS Standards Contextual Statement

Historically, standards for the professional education of student affairs practitioners are of relatively recent vintage, having largely been developed during the past two decades. Although the philosophical foundations of formal student affairs practice have been and continue to be of interest (NASPA, 1987; Whitt et al., 1990), documents that identify and postulate basic principles of student affairs practice are not adequate to the task of guiding the academic preparation of student affairs practitioners. In 1964 the Council of Student Personnel Associations in Higher Education (COSPA) drafted "A Proposal for Professional Preparation in College Student Personnel Work," which subsequently evolved into a statement drafted by COSPA in collaboration with the Inter-divisional Committee of the American Personnel and Guidance Association, entitled "Guidelines for Graduate Programs in the Preparation of Student Personnel Workers in Higher Education," dated March 5, 1967. The change in title from "proposal for" in the 1964 version to "guidelines for" in this fourth draft revision exemplifies the movement from a rather tentative statement of what professional preparation should entail to one asserting specific guidelines that should be followed in graduate education programs. A final statement, popularly recognized as the COSPA Report, was actually published some time after the dissolution of the Council (1975).

During this period, others concerned with the graduate education of counselors and other professional helpers were busy developing counselor education standards and exploring the possibilities for accrediting graduate academic programs. A moving force in this effort was the Association of Counselor Educators and Supervisors (ACES), a division of the American Personnel and Guidance Association (APGA), now the American Counseling Association (ACA). In 1978, ACES published a set of professional standards to be used to accredit counseling and personnel services education programs. APGA had recognized ACES as its official counselor education accrediting body and moved to establish an interassociation committee to guide counselor education program accreditation activity and the review and revision

of the ACES/APGA preparation standards. In response to this initiative, the American College Personnel Association (ACPA) established an ad hoc Preparation Standards Drafting Committee to develop a set of preparation standards designed to focus on the special concerns of student affairs graduate education. At its March 1979 meetings, the ACPA Executive Council adopted the committee's statement entitled "Standards for the Preparation of Counselors and College Student Affairs Specialists at the Master's Degree Level" as the official ACPA preparation standards. ACPA then initiated a two-pronged effort in the area of professional standards. One was a collaborative effort with NASPA to establish a profession-wide program of standards development and the other was a concerted effort to work under the then-APGA organizational umbrella to establish an agency for the accreditation of counseling and student affairs preparation programs. The former initiative resulted in the creation of the Council for the Advancement of Standards in Higher Education (CAS) and the latter in the establishment of the Council for the Accreditation of Counseling and Other Related Educational Programs (CACREP), an academic program accrediting agency. Both the CAS and CACREP preparation standards reflected the influence of the ACPA standards for student affairs preparation.

The history presented above was prelude to the CAS Preparation Standards and Guidelines at the Master's Degree Level for Student Affairs Professionals in Higher Education, which follow immediately. A major value of preparation standards is that they provide criteria by which academic programs of professional preparation can be judged. Whether used for accreditation or program development purposes, standards allow faculty, staff, administrators, and students alike to measure a particular program's characteristics against a set of well-conceived criteria which, if complied with, provide quality assurance and educational effectiveness to the profession.

One may ask, "Why should student affairs preparation faculty members be concerned about using preparation standards in their academic programs?" Although it goes without saying that an academic program reflects the quality of its faculty, curriculum, learning environment, students, and support systems, that fact alone is not sufficient to assure educational quality. Probably the single best way to assure that an academic program is accomplishing its educational objectives substantially is to document with reasonable evidence that the program merits recognition as being of academic worth and social value. That is the primary value of the CAS preparation standards.

# References, Readings, and Resources

Association of Counselor Educators and Supervisors (ACES). (1978). Standards for the preparation of counselors and other personnel services specialists at the master's degree level. Washington, DC: Author.

Bryant, W. A., Winston, R. B. Jr., & Miller, T. K. (Eds.) (1991). *Using professional standards in student affairs,* No. 53. New Directions for Student Affairs. San Francisco: Jossey-Bass.

Council of Student Personnel Associations (COSPA). (1964). A proposal for professional preparation in college student personnel work. Unpublished manuscript, Indianapolis: Author.

Council of Student Personnel Associations (COSPA). (March, 1967). Guidelines for graduate programs in the preparation of student personnel workers in higher education. Unpublished manuscript, Washington, DC: Author.

Council of Student Personnel Associations (COSPA). (1975). Student development services in post-secondary education. *Journal of College Student Personnel,* 16 (6), 524-528.

National Association of Student Personnel Administrators (NASPA). (1987). *A perspective on student affairs: A statement issued on the 50th anniversary of the student personnel point of view.* Washington, DC: Author.

Whitt, E. J., Carnaghi, J. E., Matkin, J., Scalese-Love, P., & Nestor, D. (1990). Believing is seeing: Alternative perspectives on a statement of professional philosophy for student affairs. *NASPA Journal,* 27 (3), 178-184.

American College Personnel Association [ACPA]. Commission XII, Professional Preparation. ACPA National Office, One Dupont Circle, N.W., Suite 300. Washington, DC 20036-1110. (202) 835-2272; Fax (202) 296-3286. http//www.acpa.nche.edu

# MASTERS LEVEL STUDENT AFFAIRS ADMINISTRATION PREPARATION PROGRAMS
## CAS STANDARDS and GUIDELINES

## Part 1. MISSION and OBJECTIVES

The mission of professional preparation programs shall be to prepare persons for professional positions in student affairs in postsecondary education through graduate education.

The mission should also include providing in-service education, professional development, research, and consultation for student affairs professional staff members.

Each program of professional preparation must publish a clear statement of mission and objectives prepared by the program faculty in consultation with collaborating student affairs professionals and relevant advisory committees. The statement must be readily available to current and prospective students and to cooperating faculty and agencies. It must be written to allow accurate assessment of student learning and program effectiveness. The statement must be reviewed periodically.

The faculty should consider recommendations of local, state, regional, and national legislative bodies and professional groups concerned with student affairs prior to developing and publishing the mission and objectives. The mission and objectives should reflect a consideration of the current issues and needs of society, of higher education, and of the student populations served. The mission and objectives should be developed and periodically reviewed with the assistance of current students, graduates of the program, and personnel in cooperating agencies. Personnel in cooperating agencies and faculty members with primary assignments in other disciplines should be fully informed of the program's mission and stated objectives and actively involved in their achievement.

The mission and objectives should specify both mandatory and optional areas of study and should include a plan for assessing student progress throughout the program of study. The mission and objectives may address recruitment, selection, retention, employment recommendations, curriculum, instructional methods, research activities, administrative policies, governance, and program evaluation.

## Part 2. RECRUITMENT and ADMISSION

Accurate descriptions of the preparation program including the qualifications of its faculty and records of its students' persistence, graduation, and subsequent study or employment must be made readily available for review by both current and prospective students.

Students selected for admission to the program must meet the institution's criteria for admission to graduate study. Admission decisions must be made by faculty using written criteria that are disseminated to all program faculty members and to prospective students.

Students admitted to the program should have ample intellectual capacities, strong interpersonal skills, serious interest in the program, commitment to pursuing a career in student affairs, the potential to serve a wide range of students of varying developmental levels and backgrounds, and the capacity to be open to self-assessment and growth. Criteria known to predict success in the program for students of various backgrounds and characteristics should be used. Students from diverse cultural and ethnic backgrounds should be encouraged to apply and should be given equal opportunity for entry into the program.

## Part 3. CURRICULUM POLICIES

The preparation program must specify in writing and distribute to prospective students its curriculum and graduation requirements. The program must conform to institutional policies and relevant legal mandates and must be fully approved by the Institution's administrative unit responsible for graduate programs. Instruction must be performed only by faculty with credentials that clearly reflect professional knowledge, ability, and skill.

Any revisions to the program of studies should be published and distributed to students in a timely fashion. Course syllabi should be available that reflect purposes, methods, and outcome objectives. All prerequisite studies and experiences should be identified clearly in the syllabi.

The equivalent of two academic years of full-time study must be required for the masters degree.

Full-time enrollment should be encouraged, and part-time options should be provided. Part-time enrollment will result in a program of more than two academic years of study. Appropriate consideration and provisions should be made for students with extensive student affairs experience.

A sequence of basic and advanced studies and other associated learning experiences must be included in the required program of studies. Opportunity for students to develop understandings and skills beyond minimum program requirements must be provided through elective course options, supervised individual study, and/or enrichment opportunities.

The program should provide special enrichment opportunities beyond the formal curriculum for students and encourage participation in informal learning activities such as student affairs organizations, professional associations and conferences, and campus student affairs outreach projects and programs.

An essential feature of the preparation program must be the spirit and practice of inquiry and the production and use of research, evaluation, and assessment information by faculty and students alike.

Instruction and supervision of practical experience should make frequent use of and reference to research, evaluation, and assessment findings.

# Part 4. THE CURRICULUM

All programs of study must include the three components of (1) Foundational Studies, (2) Professional Studies, and (3) Supervised Practice. Foundational Studies must include the study of the foundations of higher education and student affairs. Professional Studies must include the five related areas of (a) Student Development Theory, (b) Student Characteristics and Effects of College on Students, (c) Individual and Group Interventions, (d) Organization and Administration of Student Affairs, and (e) Assessment, Evaluation, and Research. Supervised Practice must include practica and/or internships consisting of supervised work involving at least two distinct experiences. Demonstration of minimum knowledge in each area is required of all program graduates.

The curriculum described represents areas of study and should not be interpreted as specific course titles. The precise nature of courses should be determined by a variety of factors, including institutional policies and practices, faculty judgment, current issues, and student needs. It is essential that appropriate courses be available within the institution, but it is not necessary that all be provided directly within the department or college in which the program is located administratively. Although all areas of study must be incorporated into the academic program, the precise nature of study may vary by institution and student preference and the requirements for demonstration of competence and minimum knowledge in each area should be established by the faculty and regularly reviewed to assure that students are learning the essentials that underlie successful student affairs practice. A formal comprehensive examination designed to provide students the opportunity to exhibit their knowledge and competence toward the end of their programs of study is encouraged.

Programs of study may be designed to emphasize one or more distinctive perspectives on student affairs such as educational program design, implementation, and evaluation; individual and group counseling and advising; student and human development; and/or administration of student affairs in higher education. Such program designs should include the most essential forms of knowledge and groupings of skills and competencies needed by practicing professionals and should be fashioned consistent with basic curriculum requirements. The wide range of expertise and interest of program faculty members and other involved and qualified contributors to curriculum content should be taken into account when designing individual programs of study.

# Part 4A. FOUNDATIONAL STUDIES

This area must include study in the historical, philosophical, psychological, cultural, sociological, and research foundations of higher education that inform student affairs practice. The study of the history and philosophy of student affairs are essential components of this standard.

This standard encompasses studies in other disciplines that inform student affairs practice, such as leadership; management; organization theory and development; human development; social and cultural contexts of higher education; law, governance, and finance of higher education; international education and global understanding; research; ethics; and history and philosophy of student affairs. Studies in this area should emphasize the diverse character of higher education environments. The foundational studies curriculum component should be designed to enhance students' understanding of higher education systems and exhibit how student affairs programs are infused into the larger educational picture.

# Part 4B. PROFESSIONAL STUDIES

This area must include studies of basic knowledge for practice and all programs must encompass five related areas of study comprised of (a) student development theory; (b) student characteristics and effects of college on students; (c) individual, group, and organizational interventions; (d) organization and administration of student affairs; and (e) assessment, evaluation, and research.

## Subpart 4Ba. STUDENT DEVELOPMENT THEORY

This component must include studies of student development theories and related research relevant to student learning and personal development. There must be extensive examination of theoretical perspectives that describe students' growth in the areas of intellectual, moral, ego, psychosocial, career, and spiritual development; racial, cultural, and ethnic identity; sexual identity, and learning styles. Study of collegiate environments and how they interact with students to affect their development also is required.

This component should include studies of and research about human development throughout the life span and models and processes for translating theory and research into practice. Studies should include theories of intellectual, moral, ego, psychosocial, career, and spiritual development; racial, ethnic, and cultural identity development; sexual identity development; learning styles; and person-environment interaction and campus ecology. Studies should stress differential strengths and applications of student development theories relative to student age, gender, ethnicity, race, culture, sexual orientation, disability, religion, and resident/commuter status. Studies should also include specialized theories of development particular to certain populations or groups.

## Subpart 4Bb. STUDENT CHARACTERISTICS and EFFECTS of COLLEGE on STUDENTS

**This component must include studies of student characteristics, how such attributes influence student educational and developmental needs, and effects of the college experience on student learning and development.**

This component should include, but is not limited to, student characteristics such as age, gender, ethnicity, race, religion, sexual orientation, academic ability and preparation, socioeconomic status, disability, developmental status, cultural background and orientation, and family situation. Also included should be the study of specific student populations such as resident and commuter, part-time and full-time students, student athletes, members of Greek organizations, nontraditional students, adult students, and international students. This area also should include studies of the effects of college on students, satisfaction with the college experience, and factors that correlate with student persistence and attrition.

## Subpart 4Bc. INDIVIDUAL, GROUP, and ORGANIZATIONAL INTERVENTIONS

**This component must include studies of techniques and methods of assessing, designing, and implementing interventions with individuals, groups, and organizations.**

This component should include opportunities for studies of advising, counseling, instructing, mediating, leading, and managing strategies and techniques and how they can be used to assist individuals, groups, and organizations. In addition to exposure to intervention theory, programs of study should include instruction in individual and group techniques and practices for addressing personal crises and developmental issues as well as problem solving, self-examination, and instructional needs. Further, studies should include organizational problem analyses, evaluations, and intervention designs as well as the assessment and understanding of organizational cultures. Studies should emphasize theory, skills, and practice in communication and individual, group, and organizational interventions that are appropriate for and applicable to diverse populations. The program of study should include substantial instruction in counseling, group dynamics, and organization development. Students should be exposed to a variety of theoretical perspectives, provided opportunities to practice individual, group, and organizational interventions, and receive extensive supervision and feedback. Intervention skills are complex and require periods of time to practice under supervised conditions.

## Subpart 4Bd. ORGANIZATION and ADMINISTRATION of STUDENT AFFAIRS

**This component must include studies of organization, management, and leadership theory; student affairs functions; and professional issues, ethics, and standards of practice.**

This component should include opportunities for the study of student affairs functions such as admissions, financial aid, orientation, counseling, academic advising, residence life, judicial services, student activities, commuter student programs, recreational sports, career planning and placement, and health services among others. Studies of professional ethics; professional issues; applicable standards of practice; organization, management, and leadership theory; and organizational and administrative issues (e.g., budgeting and finance, planning, legal issues, computer technology applied to organizations; and the selection, supervision, development, and evaluation of personnel) should be included as well.

## Subpart 4Be. ASSESSMENT, EVALUATION, and RESEARCH

**This component must include studies of student and environmental assessment and program evaluation. Studies of research methodologies and critiques of published studies are essential.**

This component should include studies of the assessment of student needs and developmental attributes, the assessment of educational environments that influence student learning, and the assessment of student outcomes of the educational experience. Also, this area should include studies of program evaluation models and processes suitable for use in making judgments about the value of a wide range of programs and services. Students should be introduced to methods and techniques of quantitative and qualitative research and to research models and methodology in student affairs. Students should develop the ability to critique research, especially that in student affairs, and should obtain practical experience in designing, implementing, and reporting research.

# Part 5. SUPERVISED PRACTICE CURRICULUM

**A minimum total of 300 hours of supervised practice, consisting of at least two distinct experiences, is required.**

Supervised practice includes practica and internships consisting of supervised work completed for academic credit in a student affairs functional area. One of the major purposes of supervised practice is to add both breadth and depth to the student's professional experience. Practical experiences should include developmental work with individual students; program planning, implementation, and evaluation; staff training and supervision; and administrative functions and processes. The value of students being exposed to diverse settings and working with diverse clientele or populations should be encouraged. Because direct supervision of students in practica and internships is a highly individualized and labor intensive instructional responsibility, faculty members assigned direct supervision responsibilities should limit enrollment to a maximum of six students per section.

A graduate assistantship in a student affairs functional area, which provides both substantive experience and professional supervision, may be used as one of the two distinct experiences. For this to be effective, faculty members responsible for assuring quality learning outcomes should work closely with graduate assistantship supervisors in students' assignment and evaluation processes. Appropriate consideration and provisions should be made for students with extensive experience in student affairs.

**Supervision must be provided on-site by competent professionals working in cooperation with qualified program faculty members. On-site supervisors must provide direct supervision and regular evaluation of students' experiences and comply with all ethical principles and standards of the American College Personnel Association, the National Association of Student Personnel Administrators, and other relevant professional associations.**

Well qualified student affairs professionals possessing appropriate student affairs education and experience should be invited to sponsor and supervise students for practicum and internship experiences. Typical qualifications include at least a masters degree in student affairs administration or a related area of professional study and several years of successful professional experience. Student affairs professionals serving as on-site supervisors and evaluators of students in training should be acceptable to the responsible faculty member as being competent to accomplish this task. Supervisors should be approved in advance by program faculty. When determining practicum and internship course loads, faculty members should receive instructional credit for the equivalent of one academic course for every six students provided direct practicum or internship supervision during any academic term [e.g., a faculty member who provides direct individualized supervision for 12 practicum students should be recognized as teaching the equivalent of two academic courses during that term].

**Preparation of students for practica and internships is required. Students must comply with all ethical principles and standards of the American College Personnel Association and the National Association of Student Personnel Administrators.**

Practica and internship experiences should be reserved for students who have successfully completed a sequence of courses pertaining to the most basic knowledge of professional practice. Preparation of students for supervised practice may be accomplished through special prepractica seminars, laboratory experiences, and faculty tutorials. Student membership in professional associations should be strongly encouraged.

# Part 6. EQUAL OPPORTUNITY, ACCESS, and AFFIRMATIVE ACTION

**An academic preparation unit must adhere to the spirit and intent of equal opportunity laws in all activities. The unit must ensure that its services and facilities are accessible to and provide hours of operation that respond to the needs of special student populations including traditionally under-represented, evening, part-time, and commuter students. Personnel policies must not discriminate on the basis of race, gender, color, religion, age, sexual orientation, national origin, or disability. In hiring and promotion policies, faculty and administrators must take affirmative action that strives**

**to remedy significant staffing imbalance, particularly when resulting from past discriminatory practices; and must seek to identify, prevent and remedy existing discriminatory practices.**

The program should recognize the importance of diversity among its students and faculty and encourage recognition of and adherence to the spirit of multiculturalism by all who are allied with the program's educational enterprise. Likewise, the program should encourage establishment of an ethical community by its constituents including the identification of shared values and beliefs that enhance quality practice. Further, program leaders should strive to promote student retention in the program.

# Part 7. ACADEMIC and STUDENT SUPPORT

## Subpart 7A. FACULTY and STAFF

**The institution must provide adequate faculty and support staff members for all aspects of the student affairs preparation program.**

**The institution must provide an academic program coordinator who is qualified by preparation and experience to manage the program and to supervise research, curriculum development, and field placements.**

The program coordinator or administrative director should have responsibility for managing the program's day to day operations, convene the program faculty as required, and generally administer the preparation program within the context of the academic unit to which it is assigned. This individual should be the person responsible for guiding faculty teaching assignments, establishing and maintaining connections with student affairs staff members and practicum/internship venues, guiding general program activities, and representing the program to external constituencies.

**A minimum of the equivalent of two full-time core faculty members with primary teaching responsibilities in the student affairs preparation program is required. At least one faculty member must be devoted full time to the program.**

Faculty members should be available according to a reasonable faculty-student ratio that permits quality teaching, advising, supervision, research, and professional service. Most desirably this faculty-student ration would be approximately 1:8. A "core" faculty member is one who identifies principally with the preparation program, "primary teaching responsibility" in the program is recognized when a core faculty member's instructional responsibilities are dedicated half-time or greater to teaching the program's curriculum, and "devoted full time to the program" is defined as a faculty member whose institutional responsibilities are fully dedicated to the program. Teaching loads should be established on the basis of institutional policy and faculty assignments for service, research, and supervision. A system within the program and the institution should exist for involving professional practitioners who are qualified to assist with faculty responsibilities. Collaboration between full-time faculty members and student affairs practitioners is recommended for the instruction, advisement, and practicum and internship supervision of students in the preparation program. Student affairs practitioners should be consulted in the design, implementation, and evaluation of the preparation program, particularly regarding practicum and internship requirements.

**The institution must provide opportunity and resources for the continuing professional development of program faculty members. To ensure that faculty members can devote adequate time to professional duties, the academic program must have sufficient clerical and technical support staff. Such support must be of sufficient quantity and quality to accomplish activities such as typing, filing, bookkeeping, corresponding, telephoning, receiving students, making appointments, maintaining records, organizing materials, scheduling classes, and monitoring examinations.**

## Subpart 7B. RESOURCE MATERIALS

**Adequate resource materials must be provided to support the curriculum.**

Academic support resources may include career and educational information; standardized tests and technical manuals; and materials for simulations, structured group experiences, human relations training, and data-based interventions for human and organization development. Resources also may include information on human and organizational development theory, research, and practice; instruments and assessment tools that measure development and leadership from various theoretical points of view; and materials that facilitate leadership, organizational design, management style, conflict management, and time management development.

**Library resources must be provided for the program including current and historical books, periodicals, and other media for the teaching and research aspects of the program. The library resources must be selected carefully, reviewed and updated periodically by the program faculty, and accessible to students.**

The library resources should be available days, evenings, and weekends and should include adequate interlibrary loan services, ERIC and similar data sources, computerized search capabilities, and photocopy services.

**Research support must be adequate for both program faculty and students.**

Computing services, data collection and storage services, research design consultation services, and adequate equipment should be available in support of research activities of both students and faculty members. The program should provide students with individualized research project development and implementation supervision and guidance.

## Subpart 7C. ADVISING

**Faculty members must provide high quality academic advising.**

Academic advising should be viewed as a continuous process of clarification and evaluation. High quality academic advising should include, but is not limited to, development of suitable educational plans; selection of appropriate courses and other educational experiences; clarification of professional and career goals; knowledge and interpretation of institutional and program policies, procedures, and requirements; knowledge of course contents, sequences, and support resources; evaluation of student progress; referrals to and use of institutional and community support services; and knowledge and interpretation of professional ethics and standards. Advisors should be readily available to students and should possess abilities to facilitate a student's career exploration, self-assessment, decision making, and development of responsible behavior in interactions with others. Advisors should be able to interpret the scores of the Graduate Record Examination and other relevant academic assessment tools.

## Subpart 7D. CAREER PLANNING and PLACEMENT

**The institution must provide professional career assistance, either by an institutional career planning and placement service or by the program faculty.**

Students should be assisted in clarifying objectives and establishing goals; exploring the full range of career possibilities; preparing for the job search; presenting oneself effectively as a candidate for employment; and making the transition from graduate student to professional practitioner. Services should include assistance in the preparation of placement credentials such as applications, correspondence, and resumes; development of employment interview skills; identification of appropriate job search networks including professional associations; selection of suitable positions; and comprehension of ethical obligations of those involved in the employment process. Faculty members should collaborate with campus career service providers to develop an active program of assistance including job listings, credential services, notification of position openings, and registration of candidates. Ideally, these services should be available to graduates throughout their professional careers.

## Subpart 7E. STUDENT FINANCIAL SUPPORT

**Information must be provided to students about the availability of graduate assistantship, fellowships, work study opportunities, research funding, travel support, and other financial aid opportunities.**

Graduate assistantships should be made available to provide both financial assistance to student and opportunities for supervised work experience.

## Subpart 7F. FACILITIES and OTHER RESOURCES

**The institution must provide facilities accessible to all students and a budget that ensures continuous operation of all aspects of the program.**

A program office should be located in reasonable proximity to faculty offices, classrooms, and laboratory facilities. Adequate and appropriate space, equipment, and supplies should be provided for faculty, staff members, and graduate assistants. There should be facilities for advising, counseling, and student development activities that are private, adequate in size, and properly equipped. Special facilities and equipment may include audio and video recording devices, one-way observation rooms, small group rooms, and access to computing. Adequate classroom, seminar, and laboratory facilities to meet program needs also should be available. Adequate office and technical equipment should be provided including access to the internet resources such as e-mail, gophers, and the world wide web.

## Part 8. PROFESSIONAL ETHICS

**Faculty members must comply with all ethical principles and standards of the American College Personnel Association, the National Association of Student Personnel Administrators, and the CAS Functional Area Standards. Faculty members must demonstrate the highest standards of ethical behavior and academic integrity in all forms of teaching, research, publications, and professional service and must instruct students in ethical practice and in the principles and standards of conduct of the profession. Ethical expectations of graduate students must be disseminated in writing on a regular basis to all students. Faculty members must be skilled as teachers and knowledgeable about current theory, research, and practice in areas appropriate to their teaching or supervision assignments.**

Ethical principles and standards of all relevant professional organizations should be consulted and used as appropriate. An ethical climate should prevail throughout the preparation program wherein faculty members model appropriate ethical behavior at all times for students to experience, observe, and emulate. Faculty members should present various theoretical positions and encourage students to make comparisons and to develop personally meaningful theoretical positions. Faculty members are expected to ensure that educational experiences focusing on self-understanding and personal growth are voluntary or, if such experiences are program requirements, that reasonable effort be made to inform prospective students of them prior to admission to the program. Students should be held accountable for appropriate ethical behavior at all times with special attention paid to the ethics' components of the various CAS functional area standards when students participate in related practicum and internship assignments.

**Preparation program faculty members must evaluate annually all students' progress and suitability for entry into the student affairs profession. Evaluation of students' ethical behaviors must be included. Faculty members must keep students informed about their progress toward successful program completion.**

Appropriate responses leading to remediation of the behaviors related to students' academic progress or professional suitability should be identified, monitored, evaluated, and shared with individual students as needed. After appropriate remediation has been proposed and evaluated, students who continue to be evaluated as being unsuitable for the profes-

sion, making poor academic progress, or having ethically problematic behaviors should be dismissed from the preparation program following appropriate due process procedures.

Through continual evaluation and appraisal of students, faculty are expected to be aware of ethically problematic student behaviors, inadequate academic progress, and other behaviors or characteristics that may make a student unsuitable for the profession. Faculty are expected in cases of significant problematic behaviors to communicate to the student the problems identified and the remediation required to avoid being terminated from the preparation program. If termination is enforced, faculty members are expected to explain to the student the grounds for the decision.

**Faculty must respond to requests for employment-related recommendations by students. When endorsement cannot be provided for a particular position, the student must be informed of the reason for non-endorsement.**

Faculty members should base endorsements on personal knowledge and address only the particular knowledge of the competencies, skills, and personal characteristics of the student. Each candidate should be informed of procedures of endorsement and for obtaining certification and licensure, if applicable.

**Faculty must inform all students of the institutional and program policies regarding graduate student liability when working with others under supervision.**

Program policy should be established to assure that all students are periodically informed of their liabilities and options for protection. Programs may wish to establish policies requiring students to hold membership in particular professional associations and to purchase liability insurance prior to entering into practica or internships.

## Part 9. PROGRAM EVALUATION

**Planned procedures for continuing evaluation of the program must be established and implemented.**

Criteria for program evaluation should include knowledge and competencies learned by students, professional contributions to the field made by graduates, and quality of faculty teaching, advising, and research. Evaluation of program effectiveness should reflect evidence obtained from former students; supervisors from institutions and agencies employing graduates of the program; personnel in state, regional, and national accrediting agencies during formal reviews; and clientele served by graduates.

Review policies and procedures relating to recruitment, selection, retention, and career services should be included in program evaluations. The timing and regularity of evaluations should be determined in accordance with institutional policy. Generally, the length of time between comprehensive program evaluations by the program faculty should not exceed five years.

# Appendix A
## CAS Member Associations†

| Associations | Member Since |
|---|---|
| American Association For Employment In Education (AAEE) | 1979 |
| American Association Of College Registrars & Admission Officers (AACRAO) | 1991 |
| American College Counseling Association (ACCA) | 1993 |
| American College Health Association (ACHA) | 1995 |
| American College Personnel Association (ACPA) | 1979 |
| American Counseling Association (ACA) | 1983 |
| Association Of College & University Housing Officers-International (ACUHO-I) | 1979 |
| Association Of College Unions International (ACUI) | 1979 |
| Association For Counselor Education And Supervision (ACES) | 1983 |
| Association Of Fraternity Advisors (AFA) | 1981 |
| Association For Student Judicial Affairs (ASJA) | 1990 |
| Association Of University & College Counseling Center Directors (AUCCCD) | 1982-1987 |
| Association On Higher Education & Disability (AHEAD) | 1981 |
| Canadian Association Of College & University Student Services (CACUSS) | 1994 |
| College Reading & Learning Association (CRLA) | 1993 |
| International Association Of Counseling Services (IACS) | 1982-1987 |
| National Academic Advising Association (NACADA) | 1981 |
| National Association Of Campus Activities (NACA) | 1979 |
| National Association Of College Admission Counselors (NACAC) | 1979 |
| National Association Of Colleges & Employers [NACE] | 1979 |
| National Association Of Developmental Educators (NADE) | 1992 |
| NAFSA: Association Of International Educators (NAFSA: AIE) | 1989 |
| National Association Of Student Financial Aid Administrators (NASFAA) | 1991 |
| National Association Of Student Personnel Administrators (NASPA) | 1979 |
| National Association For Women In Education (NAWE) | 1979 |
| National Clearinghouse For Commuter Programs (NCCP) | 1980 |
| National Council Of Educational Opportunity Associations (NCEOA) | 1994 |
| National Council On Student Development (NCSD: AACJC Council) | 1979 |
| National Intramural Recreational Sports Association (NIRSA) | 1981 |
| National Orientation Directors Association (NODA | 1979 |
| National University Continuing Education Association (NUCEA) | 1981-1982 |
| Southern Association For College Student Affairs (SACSA) | 1982 |

† Current and Former CAS Member Associations as of June 1997

# Appendix B
## CAS Functional Area Standards and Guidelines†

1. Academic Advising [1986 & 1997]

2. Admission Programs & Services [1987 & 1997]

3. Alcohol & Other Drug Programs [1990 & 1997]

4. Campus Activities [1986 & 1997]

5. Career Planning & Placement [1986 & 1997]

6. College Unions [1986 & 1997]

7. Commuter Student Programs [1986 & 1997]

8. Counseling Services [1986 & 1997]

9. Disability Support Services [1986 & 1997]

10. Financial Aid [1996]

11. Fraternity & Sorority Advising [1986 & 1996]

12. Housing & Residential Life Programs [1986 & 1996]

13. International Student Programs & Services [1995]

14. Judicial Programs & Services [1986 & 1997]

15. Learning Assistance Programs [1986 & 1997]

16. Minority Student Programs & Services [1986 & 1997]

17. Outcome Assessment and Program Evaluation [1986 & 1997]

18. Recreational Sports [1986 & 1997]

19. Registrar Programs and Services [1995]

20. Religious Programs [1986 & 1997]

21. Student Leadership Programs [1996]

22. Student Orientation Programs [1986 & 1997]

23. Women Student Programs & Services [1990 & 1997]

24. Masters Student Affairs Preparation Programs [1979, 1985, & 1997]

† Dates of Origin and Revision

# Appendix C
## CAS Member Association and Representatives on
## CAS Board of Directors
## November 1986 to May 1997

**DIRECTOR**                                                    **ALTERNATE DIRECTOR**

American Association For Employment In Education (AAEE) Formerly ASCUS
    Charles A. Marshall, AAEE                Androniki Fallis, Longwood College
    Ray Lewis, No. Texas State U. [1986-87]      Anna Tackett, U. MD-College Park [1986-95]

American Counseling Association (ACA)
    Camille Clay, ACA                     Phyllis Mable, Longwood College
    Phyllis Mable, Longwood College [1986-93   Nancy Pinson-Millburn, ACA [1988-91]

American Association of College Registrars And Admission Officers (AACRAO)
    Wayne E. Becraft, AACRAO           Roger M. Swanson, AACRAO
    Laurie Robinson, AACRAO [1992-94]
    Doris Johnson, AACRAO [1991-92]

American College Counseling Association (ACCA)
    Laura Dean, Pfeiffer University
    Phyllis Mable, Longwood College [1993-97]

American College Health Association (ACHE)
    Charles H. Hartman, ACHE

American College Personnel Association (ACPA)
    Ted K. Miller, University of Georgia        Don G. Creamer, Virginia Tech
                                    Robert F. Rodgers, Ohio State U. [1986-88]

Association For Counselor Education & Supervision (ACES)
    Barbara Griffin, Clemson University       Ted Remley, Mississippi State U. [1987-89]
    Sue Spooner, U. of Northern Colorado [1986-93]  Barbara Griffin, Clemson U. [1991-93]

Association of College & University Housing Officers - International (ACUHO-I)
    Rita Moser, Florida State University       Gary Kimble, Univ. of Southern Mississippi
    Michael E. Eyster, University of Oregon [1986-97]  David Stephen, Arizona State U. [1992-94]
                                    Virginia Arthur, Iowa State U. [1988-91]
                                    Gary North, U. of Illinois [1986-88]

Association of College Unions International (ACUI)
    Jim Carruthers, U. Cal.-San Diego       Marsha Herman-Betzen, ACUI
    Marsha Herman-Betzen, ACUI [1994-96]   Nancy Davis Metz, ACUI [1996-97]
    Scott Rickart, ACUI [1992-94]          George Preisinger, U. MD. Baltimore Co. [1987-96]
    Richard D. Blackburn, ACUI [1986-91]    Boris Bell, George Washington U. [1986-87]

Association of Fraternity Advisors (AFA)
    Douglas K. Lange, S.D. School of Mines & Tech.  Jo Rumsey, U. of Michigan [1986-92]
                                    Rick Barnes, Texas Christian U. [1995-96]

Association for Student Judicial Affairs (ASJA)
    Donald D. Gehring, Bowling Green State Univ.  Timothy F. Brooks, U. of Delaware

| **DIRECTOR** | **ALTERNATE DIRECTOR** |
|---|---|

**Association on Higher Education & Disability (AHEAD)**
William R. Scales, U of Maryland-College Park   Linda Donnels, George Washington U. [1986-93]
Patricia Pierce, Vanderbilt U. [1990-92]

**Canadian Association of College & University Student Services [CACUSS]**
Garth Wannan, U. of Manitoba   Peggy Patterson, U. of Calgary
Peggy Patterson, U. of Guelf [1994-96]

**College Reading & Learning Association (CRLA)**
Martha Maxwell   Georgine Materniak, U. of Pittsburg

**National Academic Advising Association (NACADA)**
Eric White, Penn State University   Linda C. Higginson, Penn State University
Sara Looney, George Mason U. [1986-88]   Eric White, Penn State U. [1987-88]

**National Association for Campus Activities (NACA)**
Jan Arminio, Shippensburg University   Nancy Coyle Walborn, NACA
Peter Simonds, College of Holy Cross [1986-88]

**National Association for College Admission Counseling (NACAC)**
Joyce E. Smith, NACAC
Helen J. Pape, NACAC [1988-90]   Frank E. Burtnett, NACAC [1987-92]
Marilyn J. Dearning, NACAC [1987-88]   Pamela Bloomquist, NACAC [1986-88]
Joyce Suber, Drew U. [1986-87]

**National Association for Developmental Education (NADE)**
Susan Clark Thayer, Suffolk University   Georgine Materniak, U. of Pittsburg

**National Association of Colleges & Employers (NACE)**
Marvin J. Roth, Lafayette College   Rochelle Kaplan, NACE
Jean Yerian, VA Commonwealth U. [1989-94]   William M. Carson, Morgan State U. [1989-92]
Alva Cooper [1987-88]   Jean Yerian, VA Commonwealth U. [1987-88]
   Alva Cooper [1986-87

**NAFSA - Association of International Educators (NAFSA-AIE)**
Bill Carroll, NAFSA-AIE   Juliette Gregory, NAFSA-AIE [1991-92]
Richard Reiff, U. of Georgia [1989-95]   Bill Carroll, NAFSA-AIE {1993-95]

**National Association of Student Financial Aid Administrators (NASFAA)**
A. Dallas Martin, Jr., NASFAA   Joan Holland Crissman, NASFAA

**National Association of Student Personnel Administrators (NASPA)**
William L. Thomas, Jr., U. MD-College Park   Donald D. Gehring, Bowling Green State U.
   E.T. "Joe" Buchanan, Tidewater Com. Col. [1986-91]

**National Association for Women in Education [NAWE]**
Linda Donnels, George Washington U.   Carmen G. Neuberger, ACPA
Marylu McEwen, U. MD-College Park, [1989-96]   Patricia Rueckel, NAWDAC [1986-87]
Carmen Neuberger, Dickinson Coll. [1987-89]   Marylu McEwen, U. MD-College Park [1987-89

**National Council Educational Opportunity Associations [NCEOA]**
Andrea Reeve, U. of Wyoming   Dan Connell, Morehead State U.

| DIRECTOR | ALTERNATE DIRECTOR |
|---|---|

**National Clearinghouse for Commuter Programs (NCCP)**
Barbara Jacoby, U. of Maryland-College Park — Martha Baer Wilmes, U. of Maryland-College Park

**National Council On Student Development (NCSD)**
Gail Quick, Tech. College of the Low Country — Charles R. Dassance, Central Florida Community College
Don J. Slowinski, Essex Com. College [1987-93] — Walter G. Bumphus, Howard Community Col. [1986-87]
Charles Dassance, Florida Jr. College [1986-87]

**National Intramural-Recreational Sports Association (NIRSA)**
Will M. Holsberry, NIRSA — Dixie Bennett, Loyola University of Chicago
Bruce D. Anderson, U. of Minnesota, [1990-94] — Betty Montgomery, Southern Illinois U. [1995-96]
Richard F. Mull, Indiana U. [1986-89] — Will M. Holsberry, NIRSA [1986-89]

**National Orientation Directors Association (NODA)**
Gerry B. Strumpf, U. of Maryland-College Park — Donald Perigo, U. of Michigan [1986-94]

**Southern Association for College Student Affairs (SACSA)**
Tony W. Cawthon, Clemson University — Ted K. Miller, University of Georgia
Fred Badders, Appalachian State U. [1996-97]
Ted K. Miller, U. of Georgia, [1993-96]
Linda Mahan, U. of Montevallo [1992-93]
Annette Gibbs, U. of Virginia [1990-92]
Barbara Mann, Florida State U. [1989-90]
Roger Winston, U. of Georgia [1986-88]

**Public Directors:**
Sara C. Looney, George Mason University
Marianne R. Phelps, US Department of Education
Charles L. Lewis, Executive V.P. Emeritus, APGA [1990-95]
Herbert R. Kells, Rutgers U. [1986-88]
Kathleen M. Downey [1986-87]

**1996-1998 CAS Officers and Executive Committee Members**
President — Phyllis Mable, Longwood College [ACA]
Secretary — William L. Thomas, University of Maryland [NASPA]
Treasurer — Carmen G. Neuberger, ACPA, Washington, DC [NAWE]
Past-President — Ted K. Miller, The University of Georgia [ACPA]

**CAS Mail Address:**
CAS c/o ACPA
One Dupont Circle, NW
Suite 300
Washington, DC 20036-1110
(202) 835-2272

The Council for the Advancement of Standards in Higher Education [CAS] is a not-for-profit consortium of 29 International, national, and regional professional associations established to develop, disseminate, and promote professional standards and guidelines for the practice and preparation of student services and student development program professionals in higher education settings.

# Appendix D
## CAS Functional Area Standards
## Contextual Statement Authors and Reviewers

| | | |
|---|---|---|
| Academic Advising | Eric R. White [NACADA] | Pennsylvania State University |
| Admission Programs | Joyce Smith [NACAC] | NACAC National Office |
| Alcohol & Other Drug Programs | William Bryan | U. North Carolina-Wilmington |
| Campus Activities | Jan Arminio [NACA] | Shippensburg University |
| Career Planning & Placement | Marvin Roth [NACE] | Lafayette College |
| College Unions | Nancy Davis Metz [ACUI] | ACUI National Office |
| Commuter Student Programs | Barbara Jacoby [NCCP] | U. Maryland at College Park |
| | Martha Baer Wilmes [NCCP] | U. Maryland at College Park |
| Counseling | Laura Dean [ACCA] | Pfeiffer University |
| Disability Support Services | Bill Scales [AHEAD] | U. Maryland at College Park |
| Financial Aid Programs | Joan H. Crissman [NASFAA] | NASFAA National Office |
| | A. Dallas Martin, Jr. | NASFAA National Office |
| | Timothy A. Cristensen | NASFAA National Office |
| Fraternity & Sorority Advising | Doug Lange [AFA] | South Dakota School of |
| | AFA Executive Committee | Mines & Technology |
| Housing and Residential Life | Mike Eyster [ACUHO-I] | University Of Oregon |
| International Students | Bill Carroll [NAFSA-AIE] | NAFSA-AIE National Office |
| Judicial Programs | John Wesley Lowery [ASJA] | Bowling Green State Univ. |
| Learning Assistance Programs | Georgine Materniak [CRLA/NADE] | University of Pittsburg |
| | Martha Maxwell [CRLA] | Retired |
| | Susan Thayer [NADE] | Suffolk University |
| Minority Student Programs | Andrea Reeve [NCEOA] | University of Wyoming |
| | Christopher Davis | NCEOA National Office |
| Recreational Sports | Dixie Bennett [NIRSA] | Loyola University Chicago |
| | Christina Nardacc | NIRSA National Office |
| Registrar | Wayne Becraft [AACRAO] | AACRAO National Office |
| Religious Programs | Diane L. Cooper | The University of Georgia |
| Outcome Assessment & Program Evaluation | Roger B. Winston, Jr. | The University of Georgia |
| Student Leadership Programs | Susan Komives | U. Maryland at College Park |
| | N. Lucas, T. Tyree, A. Breeze | U. Maryland at College Park |
| | Dennis Roberts | Miami University |
| Student Orientation | Gerry Strumpf [NODA] | U. Maryland at College Park |
| | Chris Boyer [NODA] | U. Maryland at College Park |
| Women Student Programs | Kathryn Brooks [NAWE] | University of Utah |
| | Carmen Neuberger [NAWE] | ACPA National Office |
| Masters Level Preparation | Ted K. Miller [ACPA, SACSA] | The University of Georgia |

# Appendix E
## PROTOCOL for REVIEW and REVISION of EXISTING CAS STANDARDS and GUIDELINES

1. The CAS Board of Directors will systematically review CAS Functional Area Standards and Guidelines on a four year staggered review of approximately five standards per year to determine need for revision. Member associations with interests in the functional area(s) under review may be called upon to assess the need for revision as well.

2. When the CAS periodic review identifies a CAS Functional Area Standard that requires revision, a Review Team of three to five CAS Directors will be formed to guide the revision process.

3. The Review Team will initially identify all CAS member associations [and other non-CAS professional organizations] that have a significant interest in the functional area under consideration. Copies of the current functional area standards [incorporating the recently adopted CAS General Standards] will be sent to leaders of the identified organizations with a request for review and recommendations for revision. A minimum of two months return time will be allowed for response.

4. The Review Team will also identify a minimum of five recognized expert practitioners in the functional area under consideration and request critical comment and suggested revisions. Among these experts, the diversity of the national student population should be represented. A minimum of two months return time will be allowed for response.

5. The Review Team will evaluate all recommendations for revision and provide its own well considered ideas to the revision process.

6. The Review Team will prepare an initial draft of the revised functional area standards and guidelines for review and comment from CAS Directors, CAS member association leaders, and identified experts. This draft should be prepared within six months of initiation of the process.

7. Following a minimum of two months critique and comment review time, the Review Team will revise the draft as appropriate based upon critiques received.

8. The Review Team will submit its final draft proposal to the CAS Executive Committee.

9. The CAS Executive Committee reviews the draft and formulates the penultimate revision draft for consideration by the CAS Board of Directors.

10. The CAS Board of Directors takes required action to adopt the standards and guidelines

11. The revised standards, upon adoption by the Board, is then put into the *CAS Self Assessment Guide* format for distribution to the profession at large

Protocol adopted by the CAS Board of Directors May 1995.

# Appendix E (continued)
# PROTOCOL for DEVELOPING NEW
# CAS STANDARDS and GUIDELINES

1. The CAS Board of Directors identifies and defines the functional area for which a CAS standard is to be written. Functional areas for which standards are developed may be proposed by any professional entity or group of concerned professional practitioners. If a standard currently exists, CAS will identify its source and seek its sponsoring agency's cooperation on developing CAS standards and guidelines for that functional area. The CAS Board of Directors must agree by majority vote to sponsor development of a new professional standard.

2. When the CAS Board determines that a new CAS Functional Area Standard needs to be developed, a Development Team of three to five CAS Directors will be formed to guide the development process.

3. The Development Team will initially identify all CAS member associations [and other non-CAS professional organizations] that have a significant interest in the functional area for which standards are to be developed. The CAS General Standards will be used as the foundation for any newly developed functional area standard. A request will be sent to leaders of the identified organizations for substantive recommendations for the new standards and, if they wish, rough draft copies of proposed standards. A minimum of four months return time should be allowed for response.

4. Non-CAS member organizations with interest in the functional area under consideration will be invited to join the CAS enterprise. Failure of such an association to join CAS will not deter CAS from moving forward on developing the new standards.

5. The Development Team will evaluate all substantive recommendations and provide its own well considered ideas to the standards development process.

6. The Development Team will prepare an initial draft of the functional area standards and guidelines, using the CAS standards and guideline format, for review and comment by CAS Directors, CAS member association leaders, and a minimum of five recognized expert practitioners who reflect the diversity of the national student population. If several proposed standards were developed by the associations involved, the Team will unify them into one draft. This draft should be prepared within 10 months after initiation of the process.

7. Following a minimum of two months critique and comment review time, the Development Team will revise the draft as appropriate based upon critiques received.

8. The Development Team will submit its final draft proposal to the CAS Executive Committee.

9. The CAS Executive Committee reviews the draft and formulates a penultimate draft for consideration by the CAS Board of Directors.

10. The CAS Board of Directors takes required action to adopt the standards and guidelines.

11. The newly developed standards, upon adoption by the Board, are then framed in the *CAS Self Assessment Guide* format for distribution to the profession at large.

Protocol adopted by the CAS Board of Directors May 1995.

# Appendix F
# GLOSSARY OF TERMS

**accreditation.** A voluntary process conducted by peers through nongovernmental agencies for purposes of improving educational quality and assuring the public that programs and services meet established standards. In higher education, accreditation is divided into two types—institutional and specialized. Although both are designed to assure minimum levels of quality, the former focuses on the institution as a whole while the latter focuses on specialty professional or preprofessional programs (such as law, business, psychology, or education) or services such as counseling centers within the institution.

**affirmative action.** Policies and/or programs designed to redress historic injustices committed against racial minorities and other specified groups by making special efforts to provide members of these groups with access to educational and employment opportunities. This may apply to students as well as to faculty and staff members.

**best practice.** A level of professional conduct or practice identified as being necessary for college and university personnel to exhibit in their daily work with students and institutional programs, if the programs or services are to be judged satisfactory or sufficient and above minimal quality.

**CAS.** The Council for the Advancement of Standards in Higher Education. A consortium of 29 professional associations concerned with the development and promulgation of professional standards and guidelines for student support programs and services in institutions of higher learning. The Council's Board of Directors is composed of representatives from member associations and meets semi-annually in the spring and fall in or near Washington, DC. Prior to 1992, the consortium's name was the Council for the Advancement of Standards for Student Services/Development Programs.

**CAS Blue Book.** The name by which the CAS Standards and Guidelines for Student Services/Developmental Programs 1986 is most commonly called. This book was the first iteration of CAS Standards and Guidelines and was published by the American College Testing (ACT) program in support of the CAS standards development initiative.

**CAS Board of Directors.** A body of representatives from each of the currently 29 professional higher education associations in the United States and Canada who are CAS dues-paying members. Each member association may designate two official representatives [a Director and an Alternate Director] to CAS Board of Directors' meetings; each association has one vote on the Council.

**CAS consortium.** An alliance of currently 29 professional higher education associations who have established a partnership of professionals to develop, promulgate, and educate higher education personnel about professional standards and guidelines designed to enhance the quality of student life and students' educational experiences through programs and services.

**CAS Executive Committee.** A body of elected CAS officers, including the president, secretary, treasurer, and past-president. Other individuals may be elected to the body at the discretion of the Board of Directors.

**CAS general standards.** Statements that present criteria representative of the minimal essential expectations established and agreed upon by the profession at large for all higher education student support programs and services. As with all CAS Standards, these "boilerplate" standards are presented in **bold** type and use the auxiliary verbs "must" and "shall."

**CAS member association.** One of the currently 29 professional higher education associations who have joined the CAS consortium and are committed to the development and promulgation of professional standards and guidelines for college student support services.

**CAS functional area standard.** A statement that presents a criterion that describes minimal essential expectations of practice established and agreed upon by the profession at large for a given function. Each standard is presented in bold type and uses the auxiliary verbs "must" and "shall." Currently there are 23 sets of CAS functional area standards (see Appendix B).

**CAS Preparation Program Standards.** A set of professional standards developed and promulgated for purposes of providing student affairs administration master's level programs with criteria to guide the professional education and preparation of entry-level practitioners in student affairs.

**CAS Public Director.** An individual appointed to the CAS Board of Directors who represents the public at large. CAS By-laws authorize the appointment of two public directors who may or may not be employed in higher education but do not represent a specific functional area or professional association.

**CAS Self-Assessment Guide (SAG).** An operational version of the CAS Standards and Guidelines designed to provide users with an assessment tool that can be used for self-study or self-assessment purposes. A SAG is available for the assessment of each functional area for which a standard exists.

**CAS Standards and Guidelines.** Published criteria and related statements designed to provide college and university student support service providers with established measures against which they can assess or evaluate their programs and services.

**certification.** Official recognition by a governmental or professional body attesting that an individual practitioner meets established standards or criteria. Criteria usually includes formal academic preparation in prescribed content areas and a period of supervised practice, and may also include a systematic evaluation (that is, standardized test) of the practitioner's knowledge.

**compliance.** Adherence to a standard of practice or preparation. Compliance with the CAS Standards implies that an institution or program meets or exceeds the minimal essential criteria established for a given functional area program and service or for master's level student affairs administration preparation.

**guideline.** A statement that clarifies and amplifies professional standards. Although not required for minimally acceptable practice, a guideline is designed to provide institutions with suggestions and illustrations that may assist them in establishing programs and services that more fully address the needs of students than those mandated by a standard. Guidelines may be thought of as providing guidance in ways to exceed minimal requirements, to approach excellence, or to function at a more optimal level.

**inservice education.** Educational skill building activities provided staff members within the context of their work responsibilities. A form of staff development and professional development designed to strengthen the ability of professional and other practitioners to carry out their duties more effectively.

**licensure.** Official recognition, by a governmental agency (usually a state), that authorizes practice in the public arena. A license is usually granted only upon the presentation of compelling evidence that the individual is well qualified to practice in a given profession. Granting of a professional license typically authorizes holders to announce their qualifications to provide selected services to the public and attach professional titles to their names. Insurance companies often require licensure of individuals to be qualified to receive third-party payments.

**paraprofessional.** An individual who has received an adequate level of training and supervision to work in support of professional staff members and the offices and programs they represent. Such individuals may be students or staff members who have not undertaken professional preparation or earned credentials to function as a professional staff member.

**preprofessional.** An individual who is in the process of obtaining professional education designed to prepare them for professional practice (e.g., a graduate student).

**program.** Often used in reference to one of two types—organizational, which refers to a departmental level administrative unit or a sub-unit thereof, and activity, which refers to a student support service activity such as an invited lecture, a workshop, a social event, or a series of organized activities presented over time (e.g., a "lunch and learn" program.

**quality assurance.** The raison d`être for the CAS Standards and virtually all other types of credentialing activities devised to assure the public that educational programs and services and the institutions and agencies providing them exhibit excellence, and that those who take advantage of available programs and services will benefit accordingly.

**registry.** An official record or list of the names, and possibly qualifications, of individuals who meet some preestablished criteria to function within the context of a profession. The names of professionally licensed and/or certified practitioners are typically listed in a registry. In some instances a professional "register" may be maintained for purposes of providing individuals, institutions, or organizations with the names of individuals who are not licensed or certified but who meet an established level of competence for employment or other activity such as consulting or speaking. A registry may also be used to identify persons who have been judged to meet certain standards of knowledge and skill outside the context of licensure.

**self-study.** An internal process by which institutions and programs evaluate and assess their quality and effectiveness in reference to established criteria such as the CAS Standards. This process, typically used for institutional and specialty accreditation purposes, results in a formal report that represents the results of the internal evaluation accomplished by those employed by the institution. For accreditation purposes, this report is then validated externally by a visiting committee of peers from comparable institutions or programs.

**self-regulation.** The recommended process by which the CAS Standards and Guidelines can best be used to evaluate and assess student support programs and services. This approach implies that institutions and programs establish, maintain, and enhance the quality of their offerings and environments by using the criteria provided by the standards to evaluate themselves. From the CAS perspective, individual institutions and programs can and should seek to regulate their own best practices rather than rely on outside agencies of higher education to do so.

**staff development.** Participation of professional and other staff members in programs, activities, and conferences designed to increase their capacity to effectively meet work responsibilities.

**standard.** A statement framed within the context of a professional arena designed to provide practitioners with criteria against which to measure the quality of the programs and services they offer. A standard reflects an essential level of practice that, when met, represents quality performance.

**student development.** Those learning outcomes that occur as a result of students being exposed to higher education environments designed to enhance academic, intellectual, psychosocial, psychomotor, moral, and faith/spiritual (for some institutions) development. This concept is based on application of human development theories within the unique context of higher education. The term has also been applied to college and university administrative units (e.g., director, division, or office of student development).

# CAS BOOK PURCHASE INFORMATION

Additional copies of this book may be purchased using the following order information.

Domestic Orders:   1 to 9 copies, priced at $22.00 plus $3.00 postage and handling [$25.00 per book]. 10 or more copies, priced at $20.00 each, postage paid by CAS.

International Orders:   1 to 9 copies, priced at $22.00 plus $8.00 postage and handling [$30.00 per book]. 10 or more copies, priced at $25.00 each, surface postage paid by CAS.

Payment by check or money order in US dollars only made payable to CAS or the Council for the Advancement of Standards in Higher Education. Federal ID #: 52-122-8597 Institutional or other Purchase Orders cannot be honored.

Credit card orders accepted:   MasterCard or Visa only. Include type of charge card, account number, full name of card holder, expiration date of card, and cardmember's signature.

Shipping Address:   Include with order the name, street/building mailing address [no P.O. Boxes please], city, state, zip code, and country if other than US of recipient.
For follow-up purposes please include phone number and e-mail address

Send orders to:   CAS, c/o ACPA
One Dupont Circle, NW
Suite 300
Washington, DC 20036-1110